D1034693

ROBERT W. BERTRAM, Editor

THEOLOGY
IN THE
LIFE
OF THE
CHURCH

Fortress Press   PHILADELPHIA

Library of Congress Catalogue Card Number 63-7905

Printed in U.S.A.   UB929

ACKNOWLEDGMENTS

Acknowledgment is made to the following publishers for permission to use copyrighted material: Abingdon Press; Association Press; The Bethany Press; University of Chicago; Christian Theological Seminary, Indianapolis, Indiana; Harper & Brothers and Harper's Magazine; The Macmillan Company; Meridian Books, Inc.; Charles Scribner's Sons; The Society for Promoting Christian Knowledge; Student Christian Movement Press; and The Westminster Press.

PREFACE

The hope of theology lives in this balance: Quod vitam theologiae, id Ecclesiae animat, et Ecclesia, quae ad vitam pertinet, eadem ad theologiam.

> What is life for theology
> Is life for the Church,
> And the Church for life
> Is the Church for theology.

Accordingly, the Conference of Lutheran Professors of Theology, hopeful alike for the theological life of the Church and the churchly life of theology, has conceived in lively hope the present symposium.

For hope there is when theology is animated by that Life who Himself is *Christus Vivificator*. He it is who at the very sources of theology, in Bible and tradition and history, marks the difference between the Bible as Law and as Gospel, between the dead and the living tradition of the confessors, between the history unto death and the history unto resurrection. And the Church whose theology is alive with him can be alive herself, in her worship around preaching and sacraments, in her cure of souls, in her world mission. Likewise the Church whose own life is Christ can be pertinent, as he is, to all of life, as men must live it in society and family and education. Finally, to complete the circle, it is the pertinent Church which comes alive again in theology, in the doctrine *de Ecclesia:* the ministering Church, ordered to no other end but the Gospel's, a Church of the churches. Luther's word for Jesus Christ is still, in the midst of her mortal conflict, a word for the Church and her theology: *Vivit*.

Moreover, we hope that this symposium, though consciously Lutheran, may contribute to the vitality of the Church far beyond the churches called Lutheran. Less than that we dare not hope and still be Lutheran. Already fifteen years ago this book's predecessor, *What Lutherans Are Thinking,* was offered "in the spirit of ecumenical Lutheranism"— all the more wondrous in view of the synodical differences which at that time still awaited resolution. If in the meantime the Lord has prospered our confessional unity, we should be nothing but ungrateful were we to shirk that larger symposium in which all Christians confess with and to one another. Where differences persist, also within Lutheranism, this book does not conceal them. For, as we all have learned, our differences too are better confessed than denied, again for the sake of the whole Church.

This book owes much, as I do, to a wise and patient editorial committee: E. Clifford Nelson (chairman), Theodore S. Liefeld, Alvin D. Mattson, Martin H. Scharlemann, and Theodore G. Tappert. A generous grant, without which the book would have died unborn, was provided by Lutheran Brotherhood. Special thanks for the thankless tasks go to my secretary, Miss Marlo J. Tellschow.

Valparaiso, Indiana
Sexagesima, 1962

ROBERT W. BERTRAM

CONTENTS

PART ONE

WHAT IS LIFE FOR THEOLOGY . . .

Chapter 1

THE FUNCTIONS OF THEOLOGY

By *Jaroslav J. Pelikan*

There is no biblical term for "theologian." The nearest equivalent in the New Testament—"scribes and Pharisees"— does not help to make the work of the theologian any more appealing to the Christian Church. And Kierkegaard's lampoon about "becoming a professor of the fact that Another has suffered" [1] invests with even deeper ambiguity the work of one who must study Scripture and tradition in order to discover that not study, but the obedience of faith, is what God requires. Yet the Church as we know it would be unthinkable without the work of the theologian. This is true not only of the present stage in the history of the Church, in which specialization and the division of labor have shaped the task of theology, but of most of the Church's past as well. Perhaps the histories of the Church have overemphasized the role of theology in its life, and have meanwhile ignored the "silent in the land," whose everyday faith was often more profound although sometimes more pagan than the learned theology of the bishops, monks, and professors. Nevertheless, even the discovery that the church histories have fallen short has come through the work of theology. If for no other rea-

---

[1] Søren Kierkegaard, *Journals,* ed. and trans. Alexander Dru (Oxford: Oxford Univ., 1938), No. 1362; cf. Jaroslav J. Pelikan, *Fools for Christ* (Philadelphia: Muhlenberg, 1955), pp. 1-27.

son, the Church would need formal theology in order to be rescued from bad theology.

The Church needs theology for other reasons as well, and theology has a function beyond that of patrolling itself. Whatever that function or those functions may be, this much is clear: the proper locus of theology is the Church, as contemporary theologians of the most varied hue have agreed.[2] One way to arrive at a "job description" of theology in the life of the Church is to analyze the needs of the Church past and present and to determine which of these needs (if any) are the special responsibility of theology. By "theology" here I mean not systematic or dogmatic theology alone, but the entire range of research and dialogue about the meaning of the Christian faith being carried on by the theological faculties of the Church—although, thank God, not only by them. Sometimes from biblical or historical studies, sometimes from renewed attention to worship or preaching or pastoral care, sometimes from its conversation with "the world," theology has helped to bring new life into the life of the Church, even while theology has continued to draw its life not indeed *from* the Church, but *through* the Church from the Source of the Church's life and of life itself.

THE CONFESSIONAL FUNCTION OF THEOLOGY

The Church in whose life theology must find its function is a church that is empirically divided, however "one in hope and doctrine" it may or may not be. A theology

---

[2] Thus the first sentence of Paul Tillich's *Systematic Theology* (Chicago: Univ. of Chicago, 1951), I, 3: "Theology, as a function of the Christian church, must serve the needs of the church." See also H. Richard Niebuhr, *The Meaning of Revelation* (New York: Macmillan, 1941), pp. 49-52; Emil Brunner, *Dogmatik* (Zurich: Zwingli-Verlag, 1946), I, 3-6; and, above all, Friedrich Schleiermacher, *Der christliche Glaube nach den Grundsätzen der evangelischen Kirche dargestellt*, ed. Martin Redeker (Berlin: Walter de Gruyter & Co., 1960), I, 10-14, 41-47, 119-125.

that stands in the service of the Church must serve a concrete church or denomination: this is one of the facts of life. What such a church or denomination has a right to expect of its theologians is usually less than what it does expect of them in actual practice. Usually it expects of them that they parrot, or provide learned footnotes to support, the current party line of the denomination—more of this later on. The denomination does have a right to ask of the theologian as teacher and scholar that he deepen his own response to its confessional heritage, and that he help the denomination to respond more profoundly to its tradition. The basis of this right is not merely the economic reality that the denomination is paying for his groceries, but the psychological and theological reality that no one can jump out of his own skin or pretend that he belongs to the whole Church in general while he ignores his responsibilities to one church in particular.

In the history of the confessions that have arisen since the Reformation, this insistence upon the confessional function of theology has not always taken the same form or been enforced with the same seriousness.[3] Where it has been ignored, however, there not merely denominational loyalty but true ecumenical responsibility has suffered. For, as later essays in this volume will point out, we have access to the Tradition only through the traditions; and while it is only the Tradition itself, i.e., the revelation given in Christ and communicated to and through the apostles, that we are to take with utmost earnestness, we take the Tradition with such earnestness when we listen gratefully to the specific traditions out of which we have come. Here, at least, the philosophical

---

[3] See the outdated but still useful survey of A. G. Rudelbach, *Historisch-kritische Einleitung in die Augsburgische Confession* (Dresden: Verlag von Justus Naumann, 1841), pp. 169-252. See also Otto Ritschl, *Dogmenge-schichte des Protestantismus* (Leipzig: J. C. Hinrichs, 1908), I, 212-267.

axiom holds true, that we know the universal in the particular. When a denomination asks its theologians to be loyal to its traditions, therefore, it asks in the name of the one Tradition by which both denomination and theologians want to be judged. The term "confessional" has both a descriptive and a normative meaning here. Theology is confessional when it uses the particular confessions of its tradition to describe itself and to give an account of the way it has heard the Word of God through these confessions. But "confessional" is also normative, because the theologian is asked to make this confession his own confession—not in addition to, nor yet in competition with, but as an interpretation of the Word of God in the Bible.

When the confessions of the Reformation say, "We believe, teach, and confess," however, they are bearing witness for something (*pro-testantes*) and against something. In an age of flabby interconfessional toleration it needs to be pointed out that confessional theology is by definition polemical. What must separate the confessional polemics of our day from its earlier forms is a greater willingness to listen before we speak and to understand before we criticize. This willingness to listen, born of historical study and Christian charity, acknowledges that from Christian sources all over the ecclesiastical map we can learn much about the meaning of our common faith. It acknowledges, too, that our sins and shortcomings as individuals and as a church have often prevented us from listening and learning. Nevertheless, amid such acknowledgment a confessional theology is still obliged to confess. "To confess," in both its Greek and its Latin form, means two things: to acknowledge one's sin before God and the Church; and to bear witness to one's faith, likewise before God and the

Church, as well as before the world.[4] Because previous generations often appeared to speak the truth without love, it is
understandable that many theologians are reluctant to engage
in polemics. The very word "polemics," like the words "pious"
and "sermon" and "preaching," has almost lost its usefulness
because of past abuses. The restoration of fraternal polemics
to its rightful role in theological discourse is one of the assign-
ments facing confessional theology today.

Another assignment facing confessional theology as it
attempts to define itself today is the realization that confessional theology is not, and should not be, merely biblical
theology. So long have Protestant theologians been content
to say, in the famous motto of William Chillingworth, "the
Bible, and the Bible only, is the religion of Protestants," [5] that
they have claimed to find in the formal acceptance of this
motto the guarantee that their theology is indeed biblical, and
neither more nor less than biblical. To the charge that the
confessional principle did introduce an additional criterion
into theology they indignantly replied that since their confessions merely summarized the teachings of the Bible, the single
principle of "Scripture alone" still prevailed. Theology is confessional in its function because it is more sensitive than is
much "biblical theology" to the forms and traditions of interpretation through which we both hear and speak the biblical
message. Instead of ignoring these forms and traditions as
though they did not exist, a confessional theology includes
them in its purview, not idolatrously nor yet superciliously,
but with critical reverence. The Church has the right to

---

[4] Cf. Otto Michel, s.v. "homologeo" in Theologisches Wörterbuch zum
Neuen Testament, ed. Gerhard Kittel (Stuttgart: W. Kohlhammer Verlag,
1933 ——), V, 119-220, especially 209-213 and 215.

[5] William Chillingworth, The Religion of Protestants, A Safe Way to
Salvation ("The Works of William Chillingworth," Vol. I [Oxford: Oxford
Univ., 1838]), pp. 157-280.

expect of her theologians that they hearken to her voice as she speaks to them through the historic confessions.

THE CONSERVING FUNCTION OF THEOLOGY

Yet there is almost no historic confession that claims to stand alone. Almost all of them refer at least to the ancient creeds, and most of them mention one or another church father or church tradition. Theology has not discharged its confessional responsibility, therefore, when it has described the polemical stance of its particular confession, for beyond and beneath this confession is the wealth of Christian history. Conserving this wealth is also a function of theology in the life of the Church. The Church needs a theology that will remind it of the hidden treasures in Christian history and thus deliver it from the tyranny of the here and now. And the Church needs a theology that will do this even when—indeed, especially when—the Church does not want such a theology.

Theology performs its conserving function when it reminds the Church of neglected issues in its message and thought. For example, considerable evidence supports the generalization that "in theology since the beginning of the nineteenth century the doctrine of creation has taken second place to the doctrine of redemption." [6] When theology permitted this to happen, it was neglecting its conserving function and simply taking its cue from the Church. For in the life of the Church since the beginning of the nineteenth century the importance of creation has truly taken second place—or last place— behind the doctrine of redemption. For a variety of reasons too complex to sketch here, ranging from the impact of modern science to the "Jesus-centered" piety of the evangelical

[6] Wilhelm Lütgert, *Schöpfung und Offenbarung: Eine Theologie des ersten Artikels* (Gütersloh: C. Bertelsmann, 1934), p. 27.

movements in the Protestantism of the past century, the life and message of the Church have lost the dynamic awareness of the meaning of creation. The recovery of that meaning, which appears to be a feature of contemporary Christian life, is due at least in part to the new emphasis upon creation in Christian theology. And this new emphasis, in turn, is due at least in part to the historical discovery that at one time creation occupied a more central place in Christian thought than it occupied in evangelical Protestantism.[7] When it assumed once more its responsibility for conserving the treasures of the Church's past, contemporary theology helped to enrich the thought and life of the Church by reviving one of the most vital and most neglected issues in the Christian faith.

Sometimes the life of the Church tends to neglect not so much the issues of the faith as some of its resources. Theology meets this neglect by dusting off those shelves in the ecclesiastical library to which the Church has forgotten to turn. If I may draw another illustration from the theological trends of our own time, contemporary Protestant theology seems to be paying more attention to the theological implications of liturgy than it has for centuries. Many Protestants, including many Protestant theologians, have looked upon liturgy as "trappings," the multiplication of unnecessary ceremonies, "merely symbols," and the last place in the Church to look for theological resources. If this view of the liturgy were valid, theology would have to control liturgy and to demand that the gestures, postures, actions, and formulas of worship correspond to the rules of clarity and meaning that dogmatic theology has established. Today theologians are beginning to realize that the relation between theology and liturgy is a

---

[7] J. N. D. Kelly, *Early Christian Doctrines* (New York: Harper, 1958), pp. 83-87.

reciprocal one, and the principle *lex orandi, lex credendi* has achieved currency in many sections of Christendom.[8] Students of the Scriptures have discovered the elements of cult and ritual in both the Old and the New Testament; students of the history of theology have seen, for example, that worship of Christ as divine preceded the elaboration of precise theological formulas about the divinity of Christ.[9] When the Church neglects such a resource as the liturgy, it is the task of a conserving theology to call that resource to the Church's remembrance.

A related neglect is the preoccupation of a denomination with its own parochial history at the expense of the rest of the Church's history. Theology performs its conserving function when it demands that the Church of today listen not only to the Church of yesterday, but to the Church of last week and last month, even though that Church may speak in a strange accent. It has been said somewhat waggishly that the difference between tradition and traditionalism is the difference between the living faith of the dead and the dead faith of the living. Deliverance from traditionalism can come through the broadening and liberating power of tradition. Perhaps the best illustration of such deliverance is the study of the church fathers. That study has fallen upon evil days in much of Protestantism, even as a new and exciting era of patristic study has begun in Roman Catholicism. It seems clear that Protestantism neglects this aspect of church history at its peril. Now that the focus of attention in patristic study has shifted from the dependence of the fathers upon Greek

[8] On this motto see the comment of Hermann Sasse, *This Is My Body* (Minneapolis: Augsburg, 1959), p. 13, n. 1.

[9] As G. L. Prestige puts it, "the doctrine of the Trinity sprang from the inherent necessity to account for the religious data of Christianity, not from the importation of pagan metaphysical presuppositions," *God in Patristic Thought* (London: SPCK, 1956), p. xxii.

and Roman thought to their exegesis of the Scriptures,[10] Protestant theology should be able to discover its affinities with and its derivation from the church fathers. In doing so, it can discover also the vitality of faith and confession that each generation of the Church has had to rediscover in the fathers. From their vitality can come new life in the Church of today, as it is delivered from the tyranny of the recent past and reintroduced to the great conversation with the fathers and saints of the Christian centuries. A genuinely "conservative" theology is one which recognizes this as its assignment: to make the Church of this generation sensitive to the great conversation.

THE CATHOLIC FUNCTION OF THEOLOGY

The great conversation is still going on in the Christian Church, and theology is one of its principal subjects. In the life of the Church, theology has the catholic function of reflecting and carrying on the continuing conversation. The institutional Church can often be the victim of its own successes, being tempted by them to forget its needs and responsibilities beyond its own organizational boundaries. When it succumbs to this temptation, it confines theology to its own boundaries; or if it does go beyond them, it is only with the purpose of demonstrating the correctness of its own theological position. To such a limitation of its scope theology must object, not alone for its own sake, but for the sake of the life of the Church. If "catholicity" means "identity plus universality," [11] theology has the twofold catholic function of direct-

---

[10] Cf. Robert M. Grant, *The Letter and the Spirit* (New York: Macmillan, 1957); R. P. C. Hanson, *Allegory and Event* (London: SCM, 1959); Henri de Lubac, *Histoire et esprit* (Paris: Aubier, 1950).

[11] Jaroslav J. Pelikan, *The Riddle of Roman Catholicism* (New York: Abingdon, 1959), pp. 21-22.

ing the life of the Church to its specific identity and of pointing the vision of the Church to its inclusive universality.

The theology of the Church is living proof that our need for our fellow Christians always crosses denominational lines. It is simply impossible for a theologian today to carry on his work without the support of men and movements that do not belong to his own tradition. To study the church fathers one needs the great edition of their writings by the French Benedictines, the critical studies of their thought by the German Lutherans of the Ritschlian school, and the standard translation by the Reformed divines of Britain and America. From all indications the theological thought and research of the next generation will give even more evidence of such dependence upon the entire community of Christian scholarship. Already the results of scholarly co-operation are evident in the area of biblical study, where Roman Catholics and various kinds of Protestants have been working and conversing long enough to have achieved a degree of consensus, however limited and tentative that consensus may be.[12] The day of a theology written of a denomination, by a denomination, and for a denomination is happily past. Theologians have no alternative but to learn from one another and to bear one another's burdens.

Theologians are obliged to point out that the Church has no alternative either. As the theology of past generations simultaneously echoed and commanded the limited loyalties of its denomination, so the theology of this generation must

---

[12] It is instructive to compare the discussion between Oscar Cullmann, *Peter: Disciple—Apostle—Martyr*, trans. Floyd V. Filson (Philadelphia: Westminster, 1953), and Charles Journet, *The Primacy of Peter from the Protestant and from the Catholic Point of View*, trans. John Chapin (Westminster, Md.: Newman, 1954), with the Reformation debates on the primacy of Peter and the exegesis of Matt. 16:18; cf. Jaroslav J. Pelikan, *Luther the Expositor* (St. Louis: Concordia, 1959), pp. 113-118.

in its own work display its catholic character and by its insights remind the Church of her catholic obligations. Too often, the case for Christian unity is put on the pragmatic grounds of efficiency, on the relativistic grounds of doctrinal indifference, or on the sociological grounds of greater corporate consciousness. Each of these certainly has its role to play, and we do need a theological interpretation of "nontheological factors." But we also need a theological interpretation of the catholic responsibility of the Church. Those denominations which have gone into ecumenical alliances or mergers without attention to basic theology need to hear from their theologians that catholicity means identity as well as universality. Those denominations which refuse to enter any alliance or merger which they cannot dominate must learn that identity without universality is a sectarianism that corrodes identity itself. Theologians, then, need to invest their theological definitions of genuine catholicity with such clarity and urgency that the churches will hear them and heed them.

The place for the theologians to begin this is their own work. Although a theologian must depend upon the whole community of Christian scholarship as well as upon scholars outside the Christian community, theology still has a long way to go before it outgrows its own parochialism. The writings of John Wesley seem to be the private hunting ground of Methodist scholars; very few Lutherans have written so much as an article about John Calvin; and the Anabaptist reformers, once the victims of right-wing persecution, are now the victims of left-wing patriotism. Theology cannot summon the churches to a deeper catholicity unless the range of its own concerns and sources is broadened. We may contemplate with amusement the prospect of Luther research amplified by the unique contributions of Roman Catholic scholars or of Thomıstic studies carried on by Protestants, but just such mutual concern is what theology will have to discover. When theology takes up this catholic responsibility, it uncovers implications in the several Christian traditions that reach directly into the contemporary life of the Church. No doctrine of the Lord's Supper, be it Roman Catholic or Reformed or Lutheran, can afford to ignore the radical consequences of the biblical and historical research of the past fifty years.[13] That research makes some fundamental discussion of the Sacrament within and among the traditions both possible and necessary. Thus theology is performing its catholic function of working within the context of the entire Church and of calling upon the entire Church to recognize that this is likewise the context of its own life and work.

THE CRITICAL FUNCTION OF THEOLOGY
The churches are not always ready to hear this reminder from their theologians, just as the theologians are not always ready to issue the reminder. When the confessional function of theology is distorted into partisan loyalty, not only theology, but the denomination, is the loser. Because a denomination defines itself in relation to a larger and longer Tradition than its own family history, it must erect within its own life the agencies that will keep it conscious of that larger Tradition. To be confessional rather than merely denominational in its service to the Church, theology must exercise a critical function. The measure of true churchmanship is the willingness

[13] Cf. Ernst Käsemann, *Leib und Leib Christi* (Tübingen: J. C. B. Mohr, 1933); Joachim Jeremias, *The Eucharistic Words of Jesus,* trans. Arnold Ehrhardt (New York: Macmillan, 1955); Henri de Lubac, *Corpus mysticum: L'eucharistie et l'église au moyen age* (Paris: Aubier, 1949). Even Sasse, for all his zeal to restore the confessionally Lutheran doctrine of the Lord's Supper, must concede that there have been significant changes in the interpretation of the New Testament since the Reformation: *op. cit.,* pp. 351-359.

of ecclesiastical administrators to encourage and support this critical function of theology, even when the theology is critical of the current party line of the denomination.

The obligation of the theologian to exercise this critical function provided the Protestant reformers with justification for their work. Discussing his attacks upon Rome, Luther said: "I have never wanted to do it and do not want to do it now. I was forced and driven into this position in the first place when I had to become Doctor of Holy Scripture against my will. Then, as a doctor in a general free university, I began, at the command of pope and emperor, to do what such a doctor is sworn to do, expounding the Scriptures for all the world and teaching everybody. Once in this position, I have had to stay in it, and I cannot give it up or leave it yet with a good conscience." [14] During the four centuries since the Reformation, Continental Protestantism has entrusted a large part of the responsibility for theological teaching and research to the theological faculties of universities over which ecclesiastical authorities have had little or no control. Those faculties have often lost any sense of loyalty to the empirical Church, to the distress of all concerned,[15] but they also have provided the churches with a constant critical voice that has troubled the easy conscience of church leaders. In this way the university faculties of theology perform a function somewhat analogous to that of the teaching orders within Roman Catholicism. At their best, these faculties are close enough to the churches to speak to them, yet far enough away to be more than an echo. The founders of the American denominations having often experienced the estrangement of such theo-

[14] Martin Luther, "Commentary on Psalm 82," *Luther's Works*, XIII, ed. Jaroslav J. Pelikan (St. Louis: Concordia, 1956), 66.
[15] See Agnes von Zahn-Harnack, *Adolf von Harnack* (Berlin: Walter de Gruyter & Co., 1951), pp. 115-127.

logical faculties from the churches or even from the Gospel, much, though not all, theological education in the United States has been more closely tied to the organizational life of the churches.[16] Nevertheless, it has not altogether lost its sensitivity to the critical function without which theology is not truly loyal either to the Church or to the churches.

Like the catholic function of theology, the critical function must be applied first of all to theology itself. For this reason, among other reasons, theology dare not become the exclusive prerogative of the theological professors; its place in the life of the Church requires that the academic theologians be summoned to relevance and responsibility by the theologians whose ministry expresses itself chiefly through preaching, counseling, and administering the sacraments. St. Augustine, after all, was not a theological professor, but a bishop! Indeed, it is often the critical function of theology that is most deserving of criticism. When it becomes the carping of the academician or the snobbishness of the pedant, critical theology must hear a critical word from the "men of action" whom it claims to despise. On the other hand, the situation receives little help from those men of action in the Church who insist upon perpetuating the dubious distinction between "men of ideas" and "men of action" and whose only weapon in combating the academic theologians is a homely illustration or pious epigram drawn from last week's instruction of the catechumens. The history of the Church is littered with the corpses of such churchmen and of the theologians whom they opposed; neither group comprehended the critical function of theology in the life of the Church.

Because "the Church interprets Scripture, and Scripture

---

[16] H. Richard Niebuhr, Daniel Day Williams, and James M. Gustafson, *The Advancement of Theological Education* (New York: Harper, 1957), pp. 42-53.

judges the Church," as one Roman Catholic theologian has put it,[17] theology exercises its critical function within the bipolarity of Church and Scripture. The interpretation of Scripture is certainly the duty of the entire Church, not only of its theologians; yet much of that duty falls upon the theologians, and it should. After subordinating itself to the Word of God in Scripture, the Church asks its theologians to do the same; then it asks them to interpret the Word to the Church, so that Scripture may judge the Church, including the theologians. It would be too neat a formulation to speak in this connection about a "balance of powers," for the history of the Church manifests many cases of imbalance. As often as not, moreover, this imbalance has been more characteristic of the theologians than of the Church in general. Overemphasis upon one favorite theological point is an occupational disease of theology. When a theology afflicted with this disease summons the Church to share its affliction, the health of the Church requires that she refuse. Therefore the theological faculty must not be permitted to become the corporate pope of the church body. Having said that, however, one must go on to say that often the Church has been most defensive and deaf on the very issues where she needed the critical function of theology most.

Then theology has the duty to speak out critically, even though it knows that it may possibly be mistaken. Few documents in the history of theology are more moving than the personal statements of theologians whose conscience forced them to oppose the public teaching of the Church they loved.[18]

[17] Edmond Ortigues, "Écritures et traditions apostoliques au Concile de Trente," *Recherches de science religieuse,* XXXVI (1949), 296.

[18] On Archbishop Peter Richard Kenrick at the Vatican Council, see the documents cited in John Rothensteiner, *History of the Archdiocese of St. Louis* (St. Louis: Blackwell Wielandy, 1928), II, 303-318. See also Karl Adam, *The Spirit of Catholicism,* trans. Justin McCann (New York: Doubleday, 1954), pp. 230 ff.

Like Jeremiah, they have known the loneliness and doubt of being misunderstood. Yet the burden of their duty to the Church as God intended it forced them to denounce the Church as men had deformed it. The Reformation doctrine *simul justus et peccator,* when applied to the empirical Church,[19] means that in the name of the Church as Church it is sometimes necessary to attack the Church as Christendom. When this distinction is taken to mean that there is a permanent dichotomy between Church and Christendom, the result is sectarianism. But when the distinction is forgotten, as it sometimes has been in both Roman Catholicism and Protestantism, the result is idolatry. For the Church to be the Church and for Christendom to become the Church, theology must both hear and speak a critical word.

THE CORRELATING FUNCTION OF THEOLOGY

Probably the most telling critical words being spoken to the Church and about the Church today are coming not from theologians, but from "the world." Church leaders may permit the external successes and internal enthusiasms of the Church to beguile them into ignoring these words, or they may simply dismiss them on the grounds that the Cross has always been foolishness to the Greeks. Theologians may make the same mistake, but when they do, they neglect a function that theology has claimed at least since the days of the apologists: the function of correlating Christian and "secular" thought.

Theology assumes this function both for its own sake and for the sake of the Church, because both the Church and its theology need the enrichment and the criticism that can come only from life and thought beyond the walls of the Church. The basis of this need is not only that theologians must study

---

[19] Cf. Luther's "Commentary on Psalm 90," *op. cit.,* pp. 88-90.

non-Christian thought in order to refute its errors, but also that they must learn from non-Christian thought what only it can teach them about man and his situation. Where but from the novels and drama of the past two generations can theologians and churchmen learn to be sensitive to the new seriousness about death and fate that characterizes our age? From whom can theology hear about present images of the cosmos if it refuses to listen to modern physics? Surely the preaching of the Church has a stake in what men today believe about death or about man's place in a cooling universe. Indeed, it seems necessary to say that the preaching of the Church must take its start from what men today know about death or about the cosmos—which is not always identical with what they believe—and must attach its message to these known quantities. If the preaching of the Church has any such assignment, it would seem impossible for the theology of the Church to evade the assignment of correlating the thought of the Church with current trends in the interpretation of man and the universe.

Sometimes this will mean that theology has to side with "the world" against the empirical Church. Sometimes it will mean that theology has to interpret "the world" sympathetically to a Church whose traditional ears are unaccustomed to modern accents. And sometimes it will mean that, in the name of the Church, theology has to raise fundamental questions about the secular thought it is trying to correlate with its message. Into the vacuum created by the secularization of thought during the past several centuries have crept false theologies of various sorts. Usually their dogmas are implicit and therefore seem obvious to everyone. Such a dogma was the doctrine of progress so widespread during the nineteenth century. Ironically, the Church succumbed to this dogma almost as uncritically as did "the world," and it is still an unsolved question whether the force that destroyed the doctrine of progress in the Church was the biblical message or the realities of the twentieth century.[20] The function of theology in the presence of such secular dogmas is, first of all, to point out that they are indeed dogmas, and that the Christian faith has no monopoly on unexamined presuppositions. Then theology has the responsibility of raising basic questions about these dogmas and of asking whether these dogmas really do make better sense of life and reality than the dogmas and faith of the Christian Church. Beyond this, no theology— and, for that matter, no evangelism—can go. It can show that Christian faith is a possibility. The rest is the business of the Holy Spirit.

Today, more than ever before in its history, the Church needs this correlating function of theology. It faces a culture in which its traditional answers are meaningless because its traditional questions are irrelevant. If theology insists upon these questions simply because they are the questions to which the Church has become accustomed, the task of the Church will shrivel still more into the cultivation of private inner piety among those who find the modern world too much to stand.[21] That would be the abdication of theology, as the Church has understood theology from the beginning. The problem of correlation is, to a considerable degree, a problem of logistics. Can the Church sustain a theological enterprise comprehensive enough to exercise this function of correlation? Can it afford it? To this the only answer a theologian can make is: Can the Church afford anything less?

[20] See the wry comments of Karl Barth, *Church Dogmatics,* ed. G. W. Bromiley and T. F. Torrance (Edinburgh: T. & T. Clark, 1960), III/2, 115.
[21] In Reinhold Niebuhr's epigram, "Nothing is so incredible as an answer to an unasked question," *The Nature and Destiny of Man* (New York: Scribner's, 1943), II, 6.

For theology has a function in the life of the Church more profound than any of those outlined above, the function of carrying on the love of God with the mind. As H. Richard Niebuhr has noted, "Though intellectual love of God and neighbor is not the supreme exercise of love, yet it is required and possible since man is also mind and does not wholly love his loves if his mind does not move toward them. . . . When the whole man is active the mind is also active; when the whole Church is at work it thinks and considers no less than it worships, proclaims, suffers, rejoices and fights." [22] To carry on this function, theology needs to be confessional, conserving, catholic, critical, and correlating—all of these, and no one of them without all the others. Only thus can it assume its share of the Church's fragmentary yet faithful obedience to the greatest of all commandments: "Thou shalt love the Lord thy God with all thy heart, and with all thy soul, and with all thy mind."

SUGGESTIONS FOR FURTHER READING

NIEBUHR, H. RICHARD. *The Purpose of the Church and Its Ministry.* New York: Harper, 1956.

OUTLER, ALBERT C. *The Christian Tradition and the Unity We Seek.* New York: Oxford Univ., 1957.

WILLIAMS, DANIEL D. *What Present-Day Theologians Are Thinking.* New York: Harper, 1959.

[22] H. Richard Niebuhr, *The Purpose of the Church and Its Ministry* (New York: Harper, 1956), p. 111.

Chapter 2

THE BIBLE

By Warren A. Quanbeck

The development of historical and scientific studies in the nineteenth century brought on a crisis in theology. For centuries theologians had been fighting on the front between Rome and the evangelical churches. They had grown familiar with their opponents, had developed skills in the use of their weapons, and possessed time-proven strategic and tactical methods. Now they discovered new enemies in the field, were compelled to occupy new positions, and found themselves without proper weapons or methods of warfare. In the confusion some tried to pretend that the situation was not really changed, some took flight, and others fought bravely and desperately.

Chief among the Protestant weapons developed in the warfare with Rome was the doctrine of inspiration. The sole authority of the Bible was the evangelical counter to Roman Catholic arguments supported by Scripture and tradition. The work of the Holy Spirit was seen as guarantee of the authority, clarity, and efficacy of the biblical writings. The doctrine of inspiration was formulated on the basis of an intellectualist epistemology which assumed both the accessibility of truth to human investigation and the possibility of giving this truth adequate expression in propositional language. Because Aristotelian categories were regarded as the universal categories of human thought, no one dreamed of suggesting that the biblical writers might have moved in a different atmosphere or used different categories of expression. Theologians read the Bible as a collection of revealed propositions unfolding the truth about God, the world, and man. Because the Holy Spirit was the real author of Scripture, every proposition in it was guaranteed infallible and inerrant, not only in spiritual, but in secular matters.

Because of this insistence on the Bible's inerrancy in historical and scientific matters, the blows struck by studies in historical and natural science were crushing in their force. When men approached the Bible as a collection of historical books they saw plainly the human character of its writers and their obvious dependence upon the sources of information available in their day. They recognized also that the scientific outlook of the writers was that of their time, and could not be a substitute for present-day scientific investigation and experiment. When theologians insisted that the religious message of the Bible stood or fell with its scientific and historical information they assumed an impossible apologetic task. For those influenced by scientific developments this could only mean the end of biblical authority in religious as well as scientific affairs.

The Church seemed to be confronted by a dilemma: it could either maintain its theology and give up hope of preaching the Gospel effectively in the modern world, or accommodate its teachings to scientific standards and thus lose the uniqueness of its message. The first is the path of fundamentalism: to cling to the old ways even at the cost of a double standard of truth or isolation in an ecclesiastical ghetto. Those who followed the second path frequently found themselves parroting the spirit of the age under the supposed

auspices of the divine Spirit. Fortunately the two paths do
not exhaust the possibilities, and the Church has been able
to find a more promising alternative. The impact of scientific
and historical studies has been very great, at times indeed
apparently disastrous, but through the shaking of venerable
traditions and much anguish of spirit has come a thorough
re-examination of theology and of the Bible itself, a process
which has produced a renewed and revitalized theology. With
it has come a new willingness to ask fundamental questions
about theological axioms and methodology, as well as a new
and deepened understanding of the message of the Bible.
Theologians have learned that Jesus Christ remains the same,
nor does the Gospel change, but the forms of theological
expression may well be re-examined from time to time.

The historical study of the Bible seemed at first a dangerous and menacing development. It has turned out to be one
of the most fruitful theological movements of modern times.
It has shattered the easy complacency of theologians in their
approach to the Bible; it has challenged traditional viewpoints
as to authorship, provenance, date, and purpose of the biblical books. The fuller understanding of the historical circumstances from which the biblical writings have emerged has not
taken away the power of their message, as many have feared,
but rather made it clearer and more meaningful.

A RE-EXAMINATION
OF THEOLOGICAL PRESUPPOSITIONS

The new and deepened understanding of the biblical message has led to a re-examination of theological axioms. Where
the scholastic theologians assumed that truth is accessible to
human investigation, it has become clear that the biblical
writers make no such assumption. They believe that truth is

God's, and that it lies beyond man's experience or perception, except as God makes it known to man through revelation. Knowledge of God's truth is possible only in response to the God who speaks; it depends upon faith, as the relationship by which the believer knows God and lives in him.

A second axiom is also challenged: the assumption that truth can be expressed adequately in propositional form. Since human language is always relative, being conditioned by its historical development and usage, there can be no absolute expression of the truth even in the language of theology. Truth is made known in Jesus Christ, who is God's Word, his address to mankind. Christ is the only absolute. Theological statements, which have an instrumental function, find their meaning in relation to him; they do not contain the truth nor give adequate expression to it. At best they point to Jesus Christ as the one in whom one may know the truth. Truth is not a matter of intellection only, but of obedient discipleship. Only by "abiding in Christ" can one know the truth.

THE HISTORICAL CHARACTER OF REVELATION

The historical study of the Bible has led also to a new realization of the historical character of God's revelation. Revelation is not the imparting of information about God, or the unveiling of true ideas. Revelation is the activity of God, by which he makes himself known to men through his intervention in history. Under the old covenant God made himself known to Israel in the events of the Exodus, the Exile, and the restoration, and through the institutions of the covenant—the torah, the Sabbath, and the temple. The climax of God's revelatory activity is his drawing near to men in the man Jesus, the Messiah of Israel.

The recovery of the historical understanding of revelation

brings with it a recovery of the biblical and Reformation understanding of faith. In the modern world, faith most commonly means belief, the acceptance of a teaching as true. In the biblical world, faith involves the entire personality of man, not only his intellectual qualities. It is the response of the total person to God's confrontation of man in Christ. Faith and revelation are correlative terms: faith is response to revelation, submission to the sovereign God who addresses man. In revelation God does not only give knowledge of true ideas; he gives himself in fellowship with man in faith.

THE BIBLICAL UNDERSTANDING OF THE CONCEPT "WORD OF GOD"

With the new understanding of the historical character of revelation has come a new willingness to listen to the teaching of the Scriptures. The Bible does not simply confirm us in traditional theological opinions, but addresses a strange message to us, one that we do not always find easy to receive. After reading traditional theological assertions concerning "the Word of God," it is a fresh experience to read what the Bible has to say on this topic.

The concept of the Word of God is prominent in the Old Testament. A large number of different words are used but the basic teaching can be summarized under two aspects, the creative Word of God and the prophetic Word of God.

The creative Word of God. The strangeness of the biblical point of view is clearly apparent at this point. Whereas we think of origins in scientific language of cause and effect, the biblical writers think rather in terms of God's creative address. His speech, his Word, is the instrument of his power and the medium of his creative purpose. He speaks and it is done, he commands and it stands fast (Ps. 33:9). He says, "Let

there be light," and there is light. The creation story repeats
the formula "and God said" seven times, emphasizing that
every aspect of creation is the result of God's speech. The
proliferation of words in the modern world makes us think
of them as mere chatter, but the Old Testament has a high
estimate of speech, and regards the address of God as the
creative force in the world. His Word is event. When he
speaks something happens.

The prophetic Word of God. The same Word of God that
called the world into being is addressed to men in the words
of the prophets. What the prophet says is not his own, but
the message given him by the Lord. Through the prophet
God speaks with power, to address his Word of invitation, to
make known his will and purpose, and to pronounce judgment
upon those who defy him and disobey his commandments. By
his Word God created for himself a people, calling a band of
wandering Arameans (Deut. 26:5) to be his servants. He
promised abundant blessings to them and their descendants,
not because they were deserving but because he was gracious
and merciful. To a proud and complacent Israel the Word
of God came as judgment and doom. To a scattered and
demoralized nation in captivity his Word brought the promise
of restoration and salvation. But through all Israel's prosperity and disaster the prophets reminded the people that it
is God who accomplishes all things.

The creative and the prophetic Word are not two different
words of God, but two aspects of God's relationship to man
and the world. God relates himself to his creation by his creative Word, and he addresses man, his creature, with the same
Word of power.

The Old Testament tradition of the creative and prophetic
Word of God is the starting point of New Testament usage.

There was no uniform understanding of the divine Word in the time of Jesus. The Sadducees maintained that God's address to man was enshrined in the Pentateuch and that no further revelation of the divine will could be expected. The Pharisees looked for new manifestations of the prophetic Word, for they believed that God had not said his last word to his people.

The renewal of the prophetic Word in John the Baptist. The hope of the Pharisees found realization in the preaching of John. The voice of prophecy was now heard again in the land and excitement rose with the prospect of new manifestations of divine activity. The event-character of the prophetic Word is underlined by John's proclamation of a baptism of repentance. Here God's act accompanies his Word. The divine address not only promises but accomplishes the cleansing of the sinner in preparation for Messiah's coming.

The Word of Jesus. At the outset of his ministry Jesus startled his contemporaries by the note of authority in his proclamation. In commenting on Scripture in the services in the synagogue he did not defer to the tradition of the elders, or even to the torah itself, but spoke as the authoritative interpreter. Even the best-trained rabbis expressed their submission to the torah by deferring to the interpretative tradition, but a housebuilder untrained in theology ignored it and assumed magisterial authority over the divine torah. He assumed a similar authority over Israel's other institutions, declaring himself Lord of the Sabbath, asserting that in his mission "something greater than the temple is here," and giving substance to his claim by cleansing the temple courts of money-changers and livestock.

The renewal of the prophetic Word in Jesus was accompanied by demonstrations of power in the exorcism of demons and in restoration of sight to the blind, hearing to the deaf, and life to the dead. He cleansed lepers and healed the sick with a word. He commended the Roman centurion for perceiving that the Word of Jesus is a Word of power. Here again the Word of God is both prophetic and creative. When God addresses man, his Word is not without results but accomplishes his purpose.

The apostolic proclamation as the Word of God. After Pentecost the apostles proclaimed Jesus as Messiah. Their proclamation possessed the same authority and power as the Word of Jesus. Through preaching in the name of Jesus, the sick were healed, the dead were raised, and the poor heard good tidings. The presence of the Spirit in the apostolic community gave power to the apostolic preaching.

Jesus as the Word of God. In the Fourth Gospel, the Epistle to the Hebrews, and Revelation, the climactic stage in the understanding of the Word of God is attained. The divine Word of power spoken through men is now visible in the person of Jesus of Nazareth. He is the divine address to mankind; his coming is the culmination of the revelatory process. The event-character of the Word of God comes to its fullest expression in the Incarnation, where God confronts man in a person, Jesus the Messiah.

This understanding of the Word of God is not marginal in the New Testament, as some assert, but represents a profound grasp of Jesus' interpretation of the Scriptures and of his own mission. The collision between Jesus and the Jewish religious authorities came about because of differing interpretations of the Hebrew Scriptures. The interpretation dominant in the time of Jesus saw the torah as the eternally valid revelation of God's will; the covenant as the enduring arrangement for God's people; and the Sabbath, the temple, and the sacrificial cultus as institutions which would endure to the end. Jesus shocked them and earned their enmity by interpreting his own life and mission as the goal of God's purpose, and the Scriptures as pointing to and preparing for himself. He saw the law not as an end in itself, but as a preparation for his coming. The covenant was to be superseded by a better one, sealed by his own sacrificial death. Sabbath, temple, and sacrificial cultus were all prophetic institutions looking forward to the coming of God's servant, the Messiah. The religious authorities interpreted these assertions as blasphemy and found in them their ground for his condemnation and for their sense of doing God's will in executing him.

The reaction of the Jewish authorities was reinforced by other elements in Jesus' interpretation of the Scriptures. He interpreted his miracles as fulfilment of the prophetic vision of the messianic age (Matt. 11:4-6). Although he shared the Jewish conviction that only God could forgive sins, he claimed authority to do so. He rejected the tradition of the elders, asserting by implication that he knew better than Israel's wise and holy men what the Scriptures really meant. He ignored the "hedge about the law" and its requirements of strict observance, and consorted openly with sinners and tax collectors. When rebuked for his conduct he countered with the claim that his way of life was the true expression of God's will (Matt. 9:12-13). When questioned about his disciples' failure to observe the rules of fasting, he defended the disciples on the ground that they were attendants at a wedding, where fasting would be out of place—an implied claim to be the Bridegroom of Israel (Mark 2:19).

Jesus agreed with the Jewish authorities that the Scriptures reveal the will of God, but differed from them in interpretation. The Jewish authorities understood the will of God as law, the revelation of God's standard for life within the covenant. Their religion at its best was a religion of grace, of man's response to God's promise in the covenant. But response to law, however graciously understood, meant obedience, and this led to the understanding of religion as achievement. This was the flaw that separated Jesus from the Pharisees, with whom he had otherwise so much in common. For Jesus understood God's will as Gospel, God's gracious purpose as having fellowship with sinners. The essence of religion in Jesus' understanding is not man's achievement, but God's gift, and his own life and ministry as the embodiment of that gift. On man's side religion is acceptance of the gift, a life in fellowship with God. Life in God's fellowship is obedient response to God's purposes, but the obedience is never the ground for a claim on God. Life in the new covenant is life in Christ. He is the manifestation of God's purpose, the content of the Gospel.

To understand that Jesus Christ is the Word of God is to have the proper perspective for comprehending the assertion that the Bible is the Word of God. Too often this is understood to mean that the Bible is a stenographic transcription of a communication from heaven. This leads to an absolutizing of the words of the Bible and an insistence on atomistic and literalist interpretation. To take seriously the historical character of God's self-disclosure and of the books of the Bible is to recognize that the words of the Bible must not be absolutized. They must always be read against the background of the historical context in which they were written.

THE BIBLE AS THE WORD OF GOD

God's revelation has taken place in events, the culminating event being the Incarnation of the Word in Jesus the Messiah.

Through these events God gives himself to those who respond in faith. The place of the Bible in this process of divine self-giving is threefold.

The Bible as record of revelatory evènts. The problem of historical events is that they are contemporary with only one generation. If a historical event is to have decisive significance for other generations it must be preserved in some way for human memory. The collection of books we call the Bible is itself an event in the history of salvation, for it is through these books that the events disclosing God to man are remembered.

The Bible as interpretation of revelatory events. The Exodus could be interpreted as a series of natural and historical coincidences, but the Bible testifies that these events are the work of God who wills the redemption of his people. The Exile could be understood as the result of blunders of Jewish political leadership: the prophets insist that it is God's judgment upon a proud and disobedient people. Jesus of Nazareth could be interpreted in purely human terms as a religious genius, a great prophet, or an ethical teacher: the books of the New Testament assert that in Jesus the God of the covenant confronts man with his offer of life. Thus the Bible is not merely a monument. It not only records important events of the past, but furnishes an inspired interpretation of these events as the manifestation of God's redemptive purpose.

The Bible as instrument of the Spirit. The Bible is the instrument by which the Holy Spirit makes the saving events contemporary with sinners of all times. Through the activity of the Holy Spirit, the Word spoken once for all in Jesus Christ is spoken again in the witness of the Christian community, confronting men with God's offer of life. The Bible as record and interpretation of the redeeming event becomes the means of the re-presentation of God's saving act in the proclamation of the Church. The revelation which has taken place in the past becomes a living reality in the present. Confrontation occurs not through some power inherent in the Bible, but through the working of God who wills man's salvation, has acted in Christ to save man, and continues to act in the redeemed community to draw men to himself. Where the Church acts in obedience to the divine purpose, there God continues his saving action. The Scripture is the bearer of Christ and is itself an event in the history of salvation, the source and norm of all proclamation.

The authority of the Bible is the authority of the *deus loquens,* the God who speaks in the Bible. He who made the world, and called Israel to be his servant, and raised Jesus from the dead speaks his Word of power in the Scriptures. He not only gives us an impressive source of theological knowledge, he gives us himself: in the Bible we are confronted with the Word of the living God. This is not to be understood as an authority intrinsic in the Bible itself, based upon claims that the Bible makes for itself. The biblical books say surprisingly little about such matters. The Book of Mormon or the Koran, on the other hand, make strong claims of this kind, although Christian theologians do not usually find them persuasive. The tendency to regard the Bible as intrinsically authoritative is in danger of centering authority in the book rather than in the God who speaks in the book. This can easily degenerate into a form of idolatry, which is the more perilous because an authoritative book can be manipulated by the theologian. The God who speaks in Scripture cannot, however, be manipulated. He remains sovereign Lord of his creation and of his Church.

There is no way in which the inspiration and authority of

the Bible can be demonstrated a priori. The arguments based on the Bible's realism, the beauty of its language, the inner consistency of its teachings, and its numerous other excellences speak persuasively to one who has already experienced its power, but have little force for those outside the household of faith. The Christian conviction of the authority of the Bible is rooted in the fact that God the Holy Spirit has spoken authoritatively from its pages. It is the inner witness of the Spirit, the *testimonium spiritus sancti internum,* that leads men to acknowledge the authority of the Bible.

THE BIBLE AS LAW AND GOSPEL

The recognition of the historical character of the Bible has led to a new appreciation of Luther as an interpreter. The modern exegete discovers that Luther has already wrestled with some of the problems that perplex us, and that his theological formulations can be of assistance to us. His distinction of a threefold form of the word of God shows his realism and insight. The primary manifestation of the Word of God is Jesus Christ, but the Word comes to man also in the Scriptures and in the Church's proclamation. To see Christ as the content of God's address is to find the perspective for interpreting the entire Bible. This perspective is not to be arbitrarily imposed upon the Bible in a capricious application of allegorical methods. It is rather the recognition that the Old Testament, for example, contains a number of theologies, but that from these theologies our Lord selects one and gives it his sanction. It is entirely possible to derive from the Old Testament a theology of achievement which understands religion as character development. It is also possible to insist that the Servant passages of Isaiah refer to the nation and not to any individual. But Jesus interprets the Old Testament as a mes-

sage of God's gift of life, and the Servant songs as finding
their fulfilment in his own person and career. Nothing in the
Old Testament itself compels a scholar to come to christological interpretations of these passages, as the flourishing of
Jewish biblical interpretation today shows. He who accepts
Jesus as Messiah, however, accedes to the tremendous claims
that Jesus made for himself, and these involve a comprehensive christological interpretation of the Old Testament.

The Bible presents formidable problems of interpretation.
Because it is composed of many books, written over a period
of several centuries and out of different cultural situations, it
requires the services of many specialists in order to yield its
meaning. Apart from establishing the text which is in itself
a major undertaking, biblical interpretation requires specialists
in language, literary forms and style, processes of transmission, and cultural influences. It demands knowledge of the
history, customs, and habits of thought of the people who
produced and read the books, an understanding of the total
historical situation in which a book was written, and an insight into the purpose of the author. Interpretation of the
Bible can never be an easy task; it requires trained literary
skills, trained historical skills, and sensitive qualities of
appreciation.

There are those, of course, who have no patience with this
exacting process of critical interpretation and prefer to deal
with the Bible as a book with no relationship to its time—a
timeless book, one fallen from heaven. Their motives are not
always questionable or vicious; they frequently react to what
they consider a relativizing of the biblical message. They
fear that once the critical process is under way, it will be
impossible to point to a sure message from God. It is important to recognize that the historical character of the Bible

makes the critical process not only permissible but necessary. It is the only proper approach to the biblical message.

It should also be noted that the Gospel is not present in the Bible as precious metal in unprocessed ore, gold surrounded by dross. We cannot print certain passages in red letters as the divine message and dismiss all others as merely human verbiage. The entire Bible is the Word of God. Because God manifests himself in history, every part of the Bible has its proper place in the unfolding of the divine purpose, though not every passage has the same function. The theological insights of the Book of Joshua are not on the same level as those of the Fourth Gospel, but Joshua has nevertheless its proper place in relation to the coming of the Christ. The message of the Bible comes to its focus in the person of him who is the Word of God. The relationship of each part of the Bible to its total message can be determined by its relationship to Christ; that is, by what it contributes to our understanding of God's purpose in him.

Biblical interpretation requires therefore not only literary and historical principles but a theological principle as well. God's message to us varies with our relationship to him. He whose relationship to God is rebellion or evasion will hear God's address to him as the demand for responsibility. Until he listens to this message and comes to know himself as God's creature required to live responsibly before God, he will make no sense of anything else God says to him in the Bible. When he has discovered the meaning of his humanity as responsibility to God, and is aware of the "infinite qualitative difference" between God and himself, he can listen comprehendingly to the message of the Gospel which invites him to life in Christ. At its deepest level, biblical interpretation demands not only a sound critical sense, but also an existential relationship to the God who speaks in Scripture. This is to distinguish Law from Gospel, to discern the difference between the things that prepare the way for the Messiah and the presence of Jesus Christ himself. That is Law which prepares for the coming of Christ—historically in Israel, existentially in the life of the individual. The Gospel is Christ—historically in the man crucified under Pontius Pilate, existentially in the coming of the risen and glorified Lord to sinful men through the Word in proclamation and Sacrament. The preparation is not to be scorned; without it there would be no Messiah. Neither is it to be made an end in itself; that is to prefer the shadow to the substance. Luther called the distinction between Law and Gospel the most difficult theological art, taught only by the Holy Spirit.

It is wrong to make Law into Gospel: to interpret the message of the Bible as a demand for character development. But it is also wrong to turn Gospel into Law: to assume that the authority of the Bible has a legal character. The Bible does not confront man externally, with each passage exercising exactly the same force. It makes its impact through its message, the Gospel, as the reader encounters God's judgment or forgiveness. The Lordship of Christ is perceived only in the experience of repentance and faith. It is made known most commonly not to an individual reading his Bible in isolation from the Christian tradition, but in the setting of the Church's worship and proclamation. The interpretative context for Bible study is provided by the testimony of the Christian Church given in sermon, song, Sunday-school lesson, visitation of the sick and needy, and Christian fellowship. Wherever the Church shows forth the love of Christ in word and work, the living context for understanding the Bible is created, and the Spirit acts anew to declare the saving Word.

THE WORD AND THE SACRAMENTS

Just as the Bible is not to be understood apart from the worshiping and serving community, so it should not be seen in isolation from the administration of the sacraments. The co-ordination of Word and Sacrament stresses the Word as event in the life of the Church. Word and sacraments stand together, interpret one another, and safeguard each other from misunderstanding. Without the sacraments, the Word readily degenerates into literalist biblicism, or sterile rationalism, or at worst mere prattle. Seen with the sacraments, its character as event becomes manifest. God has spoken in the past. He speaks also today, and his speech is an event, an act: he confronts man with his Word of judgment and grace, and offers a change in the conditions of human life. The God who makes a child his own in baptism and who meets the repentant believer with his mercy at the Lord's Table is the same God whose love is manifest in the Cross and whose power is demonstrated in the Resurrection. As the congregation lives out its function as the body of Christ, the God who acted in Israel and in Christ continues to act, drawing men into his purpose for the redemption of the world. The proclamation in Word and Sacrament of what God did in Christ is the means through which he continues to act in the present.

SUGGESTIONS FOR FURTHER READING

BARTH, KARL. *Church Dogmatics,* ed. G. W. BROMILEY and T. F. TORRANCE, I/1–II/3. Edinburgh: T. & T. Clark, 1960.

BLACKMAN, E. C. *Biblical Interpretation.* Philadelphia: Westminster, 1957.

BULTMANN, RUDOLF. *Der Begriff der Offenbarung im Neuen Testament.* Tübingen: J. C. B. Mohr, 1929.

DODD, C. H. *The Bible Today.* New York: Macmillan, 1947.

DUGMORE, C. W. (ed.). *The Interpretation of the Bible.* London: SPCK, 1944.

ELERT, WERNER. *Der christliche Glaube.* Hamburg: Furche Verlag, 1956.

HAHN, HERBERT F. *Old Testament in Modern Research.* Philadelphia: Muhlenberg, 1954.

RICHARDSON, ALAN. *Preface to Bible Study.* Philadelphia: Westminster, 1944.

WRIGHT, G. ERNEST. *God Who Acts: Biblical Theology as Recital.* London: SCM, 1952.

Chapter 3

TRADITION

By Willard D. Allbeck

As Protestants see it, part of the task of the Reformation was to free the Church from two tyrants: tradition and the papacy. "For Protestants the word 'tradition' has always been tainted." [1] For many years it was assumed that tradition had been completely exiled from Protestant church life. It was also assumed that adherence to the principle of "Scripture only" is so complete, consistent, and adequate that nothing of tradition is involved. Thus it appeared that the problems raised by tradition could safely be ignored.

THE NEW LOOK AT TRADITION

Now the situation has changed. Three circumstances make it necessary to restudy the question of tradition. One of them has arisen in the realm of biblical and historical scholarship, where the meaning of tradition in the New Testament and the Early Church is being investigated with considerable importance for biblical criticism. The second lies within the ecumenical movement, where churches whose doctrinal systems differ, although based on the same Scriptures, find it necessary to explain that discrepancy. "One of the most familiar experiences in ecumenical conversation," says Outler, "is the impasse

---

[1] Einar Skydsgaard, "Scripture and Tradition," *Scottish Journal of Theology,* IX (1956), 345.

created when the same Scripture is interpreted in sharply differing ways because of the different traditions of the interpreters." [2] To study this problem the World Council of Churches has set up a Commission on Tradition and Traditions. The chairman of the North American section of this commission reports, "We are firmly convinced, after three years of fumbling labor, that we are at grips with a basic, unavoidable issue, a real ecumenical problem which, though vast and probably unmanageable, is nonetheless relevant and urgent." [3] The Eastern Orthodox position concerning tradition has made this problem focal. Third is the fact that Roman Catholics, among whom there is a vigorous upsurge of biblical scholarship, have been restudying their doctrine of tradition and its relation to Scripture.

The bridges of conversation which have been thrown across the chasms of isolation have impelled the churches face to face with each other to become conscious of their individual heritages. "The fact is that Protestantism, no less than Orthodoxy and Roman Catholicism, has a substantial body of tradition, even though it is not often acknowledged as such." [4] Insofar as the Reformation was a purified continuation of historic Christianity, and not a complete and radical rejection of it, tradition must be assigned its proper sphere. If there is in any sense a denominational tradition, even though existing under some other designation such as "confessionalism," it is entitled to analysis and evaluation. "The notion of a non-traditionary church is a fiction." [5] This statement of Outler's

[2] Albert C. Outler, *The Christian Tradition and the Unity We Seek* (New York: Oxford Univ., 1957), p. 106.

[3] Paul S. Minear (ed.), *The Nature of the Unity We Seek* (St. Louis: Bethany, 1958), p. 88.

[4] J. Robert Nelson, "Tradition and Traditions as an Ecumenical Problem," *Theology Today*, XIII (1956), 164.

[5] Outler, *op. cit.*, p. 109.

is echoed by Jenkins: "Protestantism needs to see with a new clarity that the Church lives always in the dimension of tradition." [6]

APOSTOLIC, ECCLESIASTICAL, MAGISTERIAL

It quickly becomes apparent that there are several kinds of tradition. They are not always clearly distinguished. Sometimes efforts are made to combine them into a single comprehensive definition.

First of all, there is apostolic tradition, the sum-total of Gospel teaching. This is the basic Christian message. It is the deposit of faith handed on by the apostles to those appointed to proclaim the message. Christians have always accepted the New Testament as the authentic primitive tradition committed to writing. To Paul, tradition was Christian doctrine (II Thess. 2:15) or ordinances (I Cor. 11:2). It came from the Lord (I Cor. 11:23) and not from men (Col. 2:8).[7]

The church fathers did not uniformly distinguish between tradition and teaching (*paradosis* and *didaskalia*), yet they considered the message basically apostolic. Irenaeus in *Against Heresies* (III, ii, 2) speaks of ". . . that tradition which originates from the apostles [and] which is preserved by means of the successions of presbyters in the Churches." He declares (III, iii, 4) that Polycarp "departed this life having always taught the things which he had learned from the apostles, and which the Church has handed down, and which alone are true." In this sense he writes (III, iv, 1-2):

---

[6] Daniel Jenkins, *Tradition, Freedom, and the Spirit* (Philadelphia, 1951), p. 10. Cf. George F. Thomas (ed.), *The Vitality of the Christian Tradition* (New York: Harper, 1944), chap. 8, "The Christian Tradition in American Culture," by Amos Wilder, and Bibliography.

[7] Cf. Friedrich Büchsel, *s.v. "paradosis"* in *Theologisches Wörterbuch zum Neuen Testament*, ed. Gerhard Kittel (Stuttgart: W. Kohlhammer Verlag, 1933——), II, 174-175.

"For how should it be if the apostles themselves had not left us writings? Would it not be necessary [in that case] to follow the course of the tradition which they handed down to those to whom they did commit the churches? To which course many nations of those barbarians who believe in Christ do assent, having salvation written in their hearts by the Spirit without paper or ink, and carefully preserving the ancient tradition . . ." For Irenaeus, oral tradition thus formed an "unwritten New Testament," equivalent to the written New Testament.[8]

The written tradition soon took precedence over the apostolic oral tradition. For Origen, as Hanson reports, "the primary and only indispensable source of tradition is the Scriptures." This position was reinforced by the establishing of the New Testament canon. Cullmann insists, "By establishing the *principle* of a Canon the Church recognized in this very act that *from that moment* the tradition was no longer a criterion of truth." [9] The primacy of Scripture is asserted even by John of Damascus, in his *Concerning the Orthodox Faith* (I, 1): "All things, therefore, that have been delivered to us by Law and Prophets and Apostles and Evangelists we receive, and know, and honour, seeking for nothing beyond these."

Yet it was not asserted in ancient times that the New Testament is an exhaustive embodiment of apostolic tradition. It is clear that the Four Gospels do not include all that our Lord did (John 21:25) or said, for there were other statements of his which the apostles knew and quoted (Acts 20:35). This extra-canonical tradition has been used by

[8] John Lawson, *The Biblical Theology of Saint Irenaeus* (London, 1948), p. 87.
[9] Oscar Cullmann, *Christ and Time* (Philadelphia: Westminster, 1950), p. 171. See also his "Scripture and Tradition," *Scottish Journal of Theology,* VI (1953), 113 ff.

Roman Catholicism to justify the principle of a tradition supplementary to Scripture.

Thus, in the second place, there is ecclesiastical tradition. Gradually it came about that virtually the whole complex of the Church's teaching was included in tradition without any distinction between what was apostolic and what was ecclesiastical. In part, ecclesiastical tradition was interpretive of Scripture, summarizing the basic elements in "rules of faith." In part it consisted of the dogmas defined by councils in times of controversy. In part it was developmental, taking what was seminal in Scripture and bringing it to fuller systematic expression, as in the doctrine of the Trinity. In part it was supplementary to Scripture, as in the case of the doctrines of the Virgin Mary.

Since the prestige of the Church was enhanced by the rise and enforcing of ecclesiastical tradition, there arose a third tradition, namely, that of the *magisterium,* the teaching and dogmatic authority of the hierarchy. The claim was that the apostolic "deposit" required depositories responsible for its preservation and transmission. First these were appointees of the apostles; later they were bishops. Thus the episcopacy was a *magisterium* possessing the power of proclaiming, preserving, and enlarging ecclesiastical tradition.

Supporting the magisterial tradition is the doctrine of apostolic succession. It claims that the power transmitted unbrokenly from the apostles includes that of discerning truth, of distinguishing truth from error in case of controversy, and, by the function of teaching, of clarifying and amplifying ecclesiastical tradition.

A further development was the idea of infallibility. Since it was the *magisterium* which responsibly defined doctrine, it was affirmed that the councils did not err. When papalist views prevailed it was simply logical to decree the infallibility of the pope.

By the time of the Reformation, Christendom was accustomed to the three traditions: apostolic, ecclesiastical, and magisterial. We shall speak of these hereafter as Scripture, tradition, and *magisterium*.

Though the three were supposedly harmonious, the Reformation made it clear that Scripture had in fact been dominated by tradition and that both Scripture and tradition had been dominated by the *magisterium*. Luther, challenging in part Tetzel's interpretation of tradition and in part tradition itself, quickly found himself accused of attacking the authority of the papacy. His discussion of the three walls of the papacy in *The Babylonian Captivity* indicates how clearly he had uncovered the Roman Catholic supremacy of the *magisterium* over both tradition and Scripture. This supremacy is revealed in the remark of Pope Pius IX, "I am tradition."

The fact that all was not harmonious in the relation of Scripture and tradition, or even within tradition itself, was pointed out long before the reformers broke into print. Abelard's *Sic et non* made theologians unhappily aware that their predecessors had not been in complete agreement. The feeling of the Brethren of the Common Life that they were on safer ground when they relied on Scripture furnished a mood out of which could arise the polemics of the reformers. Scripture alone was to be decisive. Concerning the Scriptures, Luther said, "Alongside this sun no lantern is to be held."

The question remained, What to do with tradition? To reject its authority as superior to Scripture was one thing. To discard all of it as utterly useless was quite another thing. The Reformation did provide a new freedom for critically examining all tradition, not excluding the canon of Scripture.

Luther's judgments on canonicity and his rearrangement of the position of Hebrews and James are well known. Yet he accepted much of tradition in these matters. It was the Anabaptists who wanted to make a clean sweep of tradition. They blithely assumed that it is possible and desirable to shave the Church clean of all tradition, unaware that like a beard it keeps growing. In both instances the conservative and the radical wings of the Reformation were actually beginning new traditions.

THE LIVING TRADITION

There is, therefore, a modern effort to define tradition anew. The Second World Conference on Faith and Order said in 1937 at Edinburgh: "By tradition is meant the living stream of the Church's life." [10] In this sense, tradition is a heritage currently being utilized. It corresponds to the psychological concept of apperceptive mass. As James Moffatt has described it, tradition is not a wearisome "same old thing" but "the pulse of the timeless in time. " [11] It is that which makes a confessional church also a confessing church. It is a deposit of good news with dramatic, transforming consequences today. This is understood, though with somewhat different connotations, in Eastern Orthodoxy: "Authentic tradition is existential, it is the spiritual life. An established and hide-bound tradition is, however, spiritual death." [12] Even within Roman Catholicism, with all its archaic formalism and its legalistic use of tradition, it is possible to say, "This deposit is not an inanimate thing passed from hand to hand . . . it must be represented as a current of life and truth coming from God

---

[10] Leonard Hodgson (ed.), *The Second World Conference on Faith and Order* (New York: Macmillan, 1938), p. 229.

[11] James Moffatt, *The Thrill of Tradition* (New York: Macmillan, 1944), p. 3.

[12] Nicolas Berdyaev, *Spirit and Reality* (London, 1939), p. 188. Quoted in Jenkins, *op. cit.,* p. 15.

through Christ and the Apostles to the last of the faithful who repeats his creed and learns his catechism." [13] Of course, for Roman Catholics there must be the guidance of the living *magisterium;* yet tradition is a force leading to action. For them "tradition, which—as the word of the church outside the Scriptures—in a special sense represents and manifests the seething life of the church," is a vital reality.[14]

A THREE-PHASE CONTINUUM

A living tradition recognizes that Christianity is a communicated continuum. It is naive to assume that the communication is made devoid of tradition simply by asserting, "The Bible says . . . ," for a concatenation of Bible texts can be a travesty on the Scriptures. The effort to avoid tradition by declaring, "Where the Bible speaks we speak, where the Bible is silent we are silent," establishes a tradition which is anti-theological, and therefore inadequate.

From a theological point of view, the living tradition is to be found especially in three phases: the use of Scripture, the guidance of creeds and confessions, and the fruits in worship and life.

An explicit or implied doctrine of the Scriptures is characteristic of Christianity. It has been typical of Calvinism rather than of Lutheranism to begin systematic theology with that doctrine. In both instances, it is customary to insist that all evangelical doctrines are based on Scripture. Roman Catholics, in rejecting the Protestant position, have demanded

---

[13] Jean Bainvel, "Tradition," *Catholic Encyclopedia,* XV, 9. This article presents the Roman Catholic position with a sensitivity to Protestant criticisms.

[14] Gerrit C. Berkouwer, *The Conflict with Rome* (Philadelphia: Presby. & Reformed, 1958), p. 31. Skydsgaard, however, interprets the idea of "living tradition" in Roman Catholicism as an effort to relieve the tension between renewed biblical studies and an infallible *magisterium: op. cit.,* p. 343.

biblical proof that the Scriptures assert their own supremacy over tradition, and in that demand implied that such proof cannot be found.

On the evangelical side, the defense of the supremacy of Scripture has been variously presented. The Buxtorfs among the Calvinists have asserted the verbal inerrancy of the biblical text. Others have felt that the strongest point of defense was the inspiration of Scripture. Against the Roman Catholic demand for an authoritative *magisterium* to certify the meaning of the Bible, there has been the evangelical claim that Scripture is self interpreting. In yet other instances the main evangelical defense has been based on the message of the Bible, the Gospel as the living voice of God. Since the preceding chapter dealt with the doctrine of the Scriptures, it is enough here simply to point out that some kind of defense of the supremacy of Scripture is characteristic of Protestant tradition.[15]

Christians also have a tradition concerning the authority of creeds and confessions. To the degree that these documents are the guides for responsible teaching in the Church they are tradition. They furnish both substance and phraseology. The clean simplicity of the Apostles' Creed or the considered complexity of the Nicene Creed affirm Christian positions in words difficult to improve. The confessional churches treasure their historic statements as a rich heritage by no means to be discarded.

Continued acceptance and use of creeds and confessions is based on the conviction that they properly speak the authentic Gospel message. They state briefly what the Bible

---

[15] It must not be assumed that Scripture is neglected in Roman Catholicism. Bainvel wrote: "We admit that God speaks to us in the Bible more directly than in oral teaching . . . When a controversy arises recourse is had first to the Bible." *Loc. cit.*

says in full. They affirm with coherence what the apostles said with some variety. They say theologically what the Bible presents, often, dramatically. They represent correct exegesis and proper deductions.

When we subscribe to the creeds and confessions, we are assuming that they, and we, come to the Scriptures in the proper mood, with an appropriate framework of ideas, and with adequate methods. It obviously makes a difference whether we come to Scripture in a critical or a credulous mood; with Hebraic, Platonic, or modern thought patterns; with analogy, logic, or paradox. It may be affirmed that the creeds and the confessions largely surmount these difficulties, although they do not surmount them completely.

Worship and life—discussed in another chapter—need be discussed here only as they share in tradition. Since we recognize that Christianity has a distinguishing cultus and ethic, we need simply note that the forms they take, though strongly influenced by history, have an apostolic core.

The living Church exists visibly wherever the Word is properly preached and the sacraments are properly administered. This is the affirmation of the Augsburg Confession and of several other confessional documents. Typically, Christian worship in history has had two foci: the preaching of the Word, and the Eucharist. Both embody God's gracious bestowal, which is the basic motif—a "morphology," as Joseph Sittler pictures it, in "an inverted parabola." [16]

Typically and traditionally, Christian worship is strongly biblical, both in Protestantism and in Catholicism. Variations in theology have influenced the selection of scriptural passages used in worship so that varying effects are produced. It cannot be said that all Protestant services quote more of Scripture

[16] Minear, *op. cit.*, p. 110.

than do either the Roman Catholic mass or the Eastern Orthodox holy liturgy. Indeed, in some Protestant areas the tradition of biblical simplicity turns out to be impoverishment rather than richness.

The expression of the practical activity of the Church forms its own aspect of tradition. Especially in America, increase in membership results either from revivals or from other types of evangelism. The patterns are strongly established. In the field of Christian education the parochial or the Sunday school is firmly fixed as typical strategy. The work of mercy finds expression in institutions and charitable organizations of many kinds—work which "activist" Americans could not possibly discontinue. And morals, however much they tend to become codified in prohibitions and censorships, express the sensitivity of the Christian conscience even in circles of quite liberal theology.

TRADITION AND FOUR RELATED DOCTRINES

If tradition is to be examined as to its relation to theological principles, it may be suggested tentatively that at least four doctrines are involved: God, Christ, Holy Spirit, and Scriptures.

The words of the Apostles' Creed, "I believe in God the Father Almighty," express faith in the God who not only possesses all power but also is continually using it. Tradition as a process in time must recognize God in history. It is much more than human invention and decision. It cannot accept a deist absentee God. Thus George Florovsky speaks of "the sacred character of the historic process of the church." [17] In the report of the Oberlin Conference, Robert L. Calhoun remarks that "both our unity and our diversity . . . . arise

[17] Quoted in Skydsgaard, *op. cit.*, p. 339.

out of God's working with men in history." [18] Oscar Cullmann
italicizes his statement that *"All Christian theology in its inner-
most essence is Biblical history."* [19] The ongoing of tradition,
involved as it is with human choices, is paradoxically the
activity of God.

A living tradition has the living Christ at its center. The
famous statement of Ignatius in *Letter to the Smyrneans*
(viii), "Wherever Jesus Christ is, there is the catholic church,"
expresses both catholicity and life. In *Letter to the Philadelphians* (iii), Ignatius wrote, "Jesus Christ is the sum of all
the official records"—the heart of Scripture. The Second
World Conference on Faith and Order spoke for our century,
"There has been in the Church through the centuries, and
still is, a divinely sustained consciousness of the presence of
the living Christ." [20] Tradition, whether expressed in doctrine
or in liturgy, needs careful scrutiny as to whether it exalts or
obscures the Lord. It is a keen and valid judgment which
says, "The problem of tradition is fundamentally the problem
of the apprehension of the truth of God as revealed in Jesus
Christ." [21] For in Word and Sacrament the Church meets
her Lord.

The Holy Spirit, "the Lord and Giver of life" as the Nicene
Creed says, provides guidance and vitality for the living tradition of the Church. Skydsgaard observes that "the connection
between tradition and the Spirit is one of the special characteristics of early Christian tradition." [22] The very handing-on
process, says Outler, "this *actus tradendi* . . . is the act and
office of the Holy Spirit." [23] We need to be warned, as Hök

[18] Minear, *op. cit.,* p. 52.
[19] Cullmann, *Christ and Time,* p. 23.
[20] Hodgson, *op. cit.,* p. 254.
[21] Nelson, *op. cit.,* p. 152.
[22] Skydsgaard, *op. cit.,* p. 354.
[23] Minear, *op. cit.,* p. 84.

has warned us, that nineteenth-century romanticism and belief in progress gave overtones to the doctrine so that "the Holy Spirit was conceived of as the author of history, and especially the history of the Church in which tradition, interpreted as a work of the Holy Spirit, is developed and transformed." [24] Yet whatever our theory of the pattern of history—rising curve, or pulsations, or decline—it is typically Christian to believe that the guiding force is personal. The renewed interest in the doctrine of the Holy Spirit should give valuable insights into the course of tradition.

The Scriptures are the means whereby the Holy Spirit guides and judges tradition. They are both impulse and correction. As Hök wisely observes, "All that is called tradition is not necessarily of God." It is true that in general "tradition is of God, but it should not be accepted unless it harmonizes with the biblical witness." [25] Berkouwer reminds us that the principle of "Scripture only" results in a hearing church (*ecclesia audiens*) as well as a teaching church (*ecclesia docens*).[26] This perspective on the Bible is much different from using the Bible as a code of morals or a volume of proof-texts for doctrine. It is a sense of dwelling where the living voice of the Word is heard—and dwelling there a long time. "Great is the moral and mental authority of the church of the Gospel, tempered and natured by an agelong experience of human life in contact with the last, the Eternal, Reality." [27] Thus the place of Scripture in the living tradition of the Church needs careful study.

[24] Gösta Hök, "Holy Spirit and Tradition," *Scottish Journal of Theology,* X (1957), 393.
[25] *Ibid.,* p. 395.
[26] Berkouwer, *op. cit.,* p. 33.
[27] P. T. Forsyth, *The Principle of Authority* (New York, 1912), p. 369.

SOME DIFFICULTIES

Lest all this appear to be illusively easy it may be well to spot quickly a few difficulties. One of these is the need for freedom in exegetical studies. The boundary between faithfulness to research and loyalty to the Church can be hard to draw. Tradition can so dull our ears that we hear in Scripture only the old customary sounds, only the typical denominational tones.

A related difficulty is the tension between conformity and individualism. The one can be firm and stable, but may also be hard and dead; the other can be pliable and alive, but also indecisive and vacillating. Lutherans usually accept the confessions "because" (*quia*), rather than "in as far as" (*quatenus*), they accord with Scripture. Though *quia* by all odds is the preferred term, it says too much, while *quatenus* says too little. *Quia* may carry with it an air of finality, almost of infallibility, which no confessional tradition dare claim. It tends to absolutize statements which are human and never absolute. The strength of *quia* lies in the fact that the Church needs to declare her faith with conviction. *Quia* is the declaration that the Gospel is true, that on the basis of the best exegesis its meaning is clear, and that the expression of it is appropriate and valid, though limited by human factors.

Quatenus, for all its humility, its openness to scholarship, and its sense of human fallibility, tends to be indecisive. It opens the way to the dominance of individual opinion, whereby the voice of the Church is not heard. At its best it keeps confessional tradition pliable and productive. At its worst it can substitute the opinion of today for the seasoned wisdom of the centuries.

The problem of tradition's place is partly the problem of the strain between Church doctrine and private judgment.

The Augsburg Confession begins, "Our churches with common consent do teach . . ." (Confessional statements, of course, all say or imply this. The French Confession of 1559 was "made in one accord by the French people who desire to live according to the purity of the Gospel." The Scotch Confession of 1560 stated the "Faith and Doctrine believed and professed by the Protestants of Scotland." The Thirty-nine Articles of the Church of England were agreed upon by "the Archbishops and Bishops of both provinces and the whole clergy.") This *magno consensu* was both territorial and historical. When Lutherans were asked, "Where was your doctrine before Luther?" they quoted extensively from the patristic literature. Quotations from the church fathers were collated as evidence of a consensus. The doctrine of the Church must represent a unity, free of the vagaries of personal opinion, yet without killing scholarship and investigation. A way must always be found whereby personal opinion under the law of love melts into the fellowship.

A further problem is how to keep confessional tradition alive rather than static. Lutherans in America accept the Lutheran Confessions; the conflict over that is dead. A mature confessional Lutheranism must be prepared to move out from its isolated concern with the issues of the past and use these victories as bases for new contests. We must stand on the past to face the future.

SUMMARY

From a Lutheran perspective the foregoing points may be summarized as follows:

1. Tradition exists. It is a complex of doctrines, work, and worship. Despite its unhappy historical connotations, Lutheran theology may well study it critically and assess it

objectively. The modern word for dynamic tradition is "ideology." Jenkins remarks that formalism ". . . prevents even modern Catholic theologians from understanding how an ideology can be formed in the theological realm." [28] Perhaps a similar charge can be made against Lutherans.[29]

2. Tradition carries and accumulates weight. This, too, must come under criticism. There must be no silencing of inquiring scholarship by invoking the blessed word "confessional." We must resist the pressure to turn us into what Jenkins calls stuffed "dummies who will make the expected and calculable noises if squeezed in the right places." [30]

3. Tradition has values. It offers roots for an uprooted, migrant generation. It is a direction-finder at a time when ideological compass points have shifted. It guards against the eccentricities of individualism. It recognizes the importance of history and the Church.

4. Tradition must be maintained as a living thing. To do so involves the paradox of identity and growth. Especially is this difficult as we face the problems of our secularized age—an age which in conflict with anti-Christian Communism wants to be pro-Christian without being Christian. Lutherans need to be active on this front.

5. Our tradition must always be closely related to Christ through the Word and the sacraments. Within this living tradition the voice of the living Lord is heard.

SUGGESTIONS FOR FURTHER READING

HANSON, R. P. C. *Origen's Doctrine of Tradition.* London: SPCK, 1954.

[28] *Op. cit.*, p. 15.
[29] Cf. Jaroslav J. Pelikan, "Tradition in Confessional Lutheranism," *Lutheran World*, III (1956), 214-222.
[30] Jenkins, *op. cit.*, p. 145.

HODGSON, LEONARD (ed.). *The Second World Conference on Faith and Order.* New York: Macmillan, 1938.

JENKINS, D. T. *Tradition, Freedom, and the Spirit.* Philadelphia: Westminster, 1951.

MINEAR, PAUL S. (ed). *The Nature of the Unity We Seek.* St. Louis: Bethany, 1958.

MOFFATT, JAMES. *The Thrill of Tradition.* New York: Macmillan, 1944.

OUTLER, ALBERT C. *The Christian Tradition and the Unity We Seek.* New York: Oxford Univ., 1957.

THOMAS, GEORGE F. (ed.). *The Vitality of the Christian Tradition.* New York: Harper, 1944.

Chapter 4

HISTORY AND ESCHATOLOGY

By Gilbert A. Thiele

ESCHATOLOGY TODAY

During the discussions in Europe which preceded the publication of the 1954 Evanston Study Document, *Christ the Hope of the World,* one of the Advisory Commission members repeatedly emphasized that this theme was primarily eschatological. An American member of the group, after trying to digest the far-reaching implications of this conviction, said: "For me this has no meaning."

Before the opening of the Evanston Assembly in August, 1954, *The Christian Century* referred to the "theological fogbank" rolling toward the shores of Lake Michigan from Europe—a threat to any really meaningful accomplishment by the Assembly as it unfolded and applied the theme "Christ the Hope of the World." The reference was to the eschatological emphasis, and implied opposition to letting it become dominant or even important during the Assembly.

At the Assembly itself, considerable disparity was evident between the essays on the theme by Robert Calhoun of Yale and Edmund Schlink of Heidelberg. The Evanston "Message," however, strongly emphasized not only the propriety but the inescapable necessity of the eschatological note at that moment in the history of Christendom and of the World Council of Churches. The "Message" closes with these words:

57

We do not know what is coming to us. But we know Who is coming. It is He who meets us every day and who will meet us at the end—Jesus Christ our Lord.

Therefore we say to you: Rejoice in hope.[1]

It was generally agreed during the Evanston Assembly that Calhoun's address was more "historical" and less "eschatological" than Schlink's. Thus the entire thrust of the Assembly "Message" is evidence that even some Americans present, including Calhoun, were persuaded that eschatology, both as a teaching of the Church and as a reality in the Church's life, is inescapable.

Three years after Evanston, an American ecumenical meeting was held in Oberlin, Ohio: The North American Conference on Faith and Order. As evidence of the increased American appreciation of eschatology as inseparable from the Church's historical existence, Dr. Calhoun's statements at Oberlin may be cited:

It is the grace of God, not the goodness of man, that keeps the Church, more than any other historical, institutional community, open toward heaven. This is another way of saying that the existence of the Church is eschatologically as well as historically determined. The Church of the Lord's purpose and of our hope, to be "presented before him in splendor, without spot or wrinkle," is most naturally to be understood as the Church fulfilled beyond the end of earthly history. To this issue we must return in due course.

Finally, the Church is an *eschatologically oriented* [italics Calhoun's] community. On earth it is a pilgrim people, a *diaspora,* a vast company of faithful "strangers and exiles on the earth . . . seeking a homeland," that is not here. On earth it is a rock-based fortress, from which the gates of hell are being stormed. But in final truth it is "the new Jerusalem." Its members have "the Jerusalem above" as their mother, and they can endure suffering joyfully with a view to "the glory that is to be revealed." The writer to the Hebrews by a superb *tour de force* of anticipation can write: "But you have come

---

[1] W. A. Visser 't Hooft (ed.), *The Evanston Report* (New York: Harper, 1955), p. 3.

to Mount Zion and to the city of the living God, the heavenly Jerusalem, and to innumerable angels, in festal gatherings, and to the assembly (ekklesia) of the first born who are enrolled in heaven, and to a judge who is God of all, and to the spirits of just men made perfect, and to Jesus, the mediator of the new covenant." Thus present and future and "a kingdom that cannot be shaken" blend in ecstatic vision.

. . . where God is—in bush or stable or "the place of a skull"— there is holy ground, but not holiness unclouded, even in the Church. And even at the end, we shall not become God and so achieve perfection. Our hope is, rather, that in the Church transformed and purged, we may see and rejoice in God's holiness, and in our ways reflect it and be lighted by it.[2]

To some the eschatological emphasis in theology, particularly in recent European and American thought, appears to be a form of apocalypticism, having its origin in the acute and critical experiences of World War II. If this is true, then the experiences in countries other than Germany must not have been as critical or acute as those of the German citizenry— which is difficult if not impossible to believe. At any rate, the theologians in such countries as Great Britain, France, The Netherlands, Norway, and Denmark were not persuaded by the apocalyptic catastrophes of their war years—which were certainly equal to those endured by the Germans—to emphasize eschatological theology.

The man some Americans and even more continental Europeans look upon as theologically very important at the moment, the German professor emeritus of the University of Marburg, Rudolf Bultmann, devoted his *Gifford Lectures* in 1955 to this very matter, eschatology. He says:

. . . in early Christianity history is swallowed up in eschatology.
. . . now we can say: the meaning of history lies always in the

[2] Robert Calhoun, in *The Nature of the Unity We Seek*, ed. Paul S. Minear (St. Louis: Bethany, 1958), pp. 65, 68-69, and 77. Used by permission.

present, and when the present is conceived as the eschatological present by Christian faith the meaning of history is realized. In every moment slumbers the possibility of being the eschatological moment.[3] One rarely finds such a dismissal of eschatology in favor of history among non-German theologians today. Consequently we can say that emphasis on eschatology, or for that matter de-emphasis of it, need not be linked with apocalypticism of whatever degree.

The wheel has then come full turn for Bultmann and for others like him who—since Albert Schweitzer's famous *Quest for the Historical Jesus*—base their dismissal of eschatology, or at least their existentialist relativization of it, on an insistence upon history. In early Christianity, according to these views, history was swallowed up in eschatology. Today in the twentieth century's presumably more advanced Christianity, or at least in a Christianity that exists in the more advanced twentieth century of history, history swallows up eschatology. Jesus, we are asked to believe, held and offered to his followers an eschatological hope which in history was and apparently still is unrealized. His followers must, therefore, conclude that there is no such thing as an eschatological hope connected with an end of the world, with a return of Christ as judge, with a resurrection of the dead, and with an everlasting life. Christ's followers are to believe, in this view, that the unfulfilled hope of Jesus and of the primitive or early Church must always remain unfulfilled. More important, the twentieth-century Christian and the twentieth-century Church should hold to a realized eschatology, realized in history, in the *now*. There will be no end. The theology that rejects eschatology of the future in favor of history goes to this extreme: because

---

[3] Rudolf Bultmann. *The Presence of Eternity: History and Eschatology* (New York: Harper, 1957), pp. 37 and 155.

something has not yet happened we must believe that it never will happen.

BOTH MAN AND GOD

That eschatology is important especially in relation to history is suggested by the fact that this present symposium by theological writers who belong to the Lutheran community of Christendom in the United States includes a statement on these matters.

In general, the view that has dominated Christian thought when it concerns itself with history, of whatever kind and period, has been: History is lived, made, and recorded by man, but it is guided by God.

Only man lives the story that has come down to us over the years—only man, not an animal, not the apparently lifeless nor the living world of chemical and plant life, not angels nor devils. Man has made, is making, and, so it seems, will continue to make history. History is his story. Furthermore, all historical records which we possess or ever will possess are provided for man by man. In a loose sense, everything preceding generations of men have left to our generation is part of the history of man, but more specifically those records which tell his story in writing—those products of man's own effort to leave a record on stone or on leather or on paper of what he has been, thought, dreamed, and hoped for—these tell us his history.

The Christian view never has been coupled with a belief in the autonomy of man, certainly not in his absolute autonomy. The Christian certainty of God, which grows out of the earlier Hebrew certainty of God, undergirds and overarches history. That is why we can say: "History, man's history, is guided by God."

To ward off any misunderstanding that the statement

"History is lived, made, and recorded by man" might in some way militate against the belief widely held in the Church, particularly in the Lutheran Church, that the Scriptures are the Word of God, we need be reminded only that the written record of God's words and actions in man's history was, after all, set down by men. This does not change the fact of the divine and revelatory character of the Scripture, for here we have a convincing example of God's guidance in the living and making as well as in the recording of man's history: in this case, the history of man's relationship to God, initiated by God.

TIME

Part of the guidance of God in man-made history is reflected in the fact of time. When one accepts God as the Creator who stands behind the existence of man from first to last, and without whose preservation no man can continue to exist for even an instant, then God's creation must include the creation of time and of the means whereby man has learned, in his own way, to measure it. When time was given to man, it appeared—for all too brief a period—that he would not need to die. Even without the subsequent intervention of the Fall, his continued existence would still have had to be measured by time.

Certainly since man's fall, throughout his development and world-wide dispersion he has been making use of the creation of God in the form of celestial bodies and of the day-night alternation to measure his life and to organize, in retrospect, his memories and recollections. This is true whether he uses such sophisticated measuring tools as electronic chronometric devices, or relies on a simple clock (or watch), a sun dial, or a calendar. Man measures his history in units of time. That is to say, his categories of recent or long-ago, of ancient or modern, and of present, past, or future, are a reflection of his use, as a historical being, of this basic built-in feature of the world into which he has been planted and on which, until very recently, he has been content to live, make, and record his history.

HISTORICAL SCIENCE

Within this framework of time, man has lived and will continue to live his history, his record of inhabiting the earth and of exploring and conquering its immediate surroundings and, conceivably, its more distant ones.

Now man has been on the earth, and more recently a little distance away from it, for a sufficiently long time to have lived, made, and recorded a great deal of history. Historians of our own generation and century have combed the record to produce compendiums and interpretations and philosophies of history more comprehensive than those that were possible or at least were produced in previous generations. Important and impressive as they were in their own day and right, the *Magdeburg Centuries* of Flacius Illyricus or their counterpart, the *Annales* of Cesare Baronius, cannot be compared for comprehensiveness, interpretative adroitness, or depth with such twentieth-century polyhistories as Spengler's *Decline of the West,* distorted as it may be,[4] or the even vaster *A Study of History* by Toynbee.[5] Reporting combined with careful interpretation—from a particular viewpoint, of course—has characterized historical writing to a far greater degree since

[4] R. G. Collingwood does not hesitate to call this work "radically unsound," chiefly because it is both "positivistic" and "naturalistic"; i.e., Spengler, though credited with "a mass of historical learning," distorts his facts to fit his thesis, which is that there is really no historical significance or relationship, but only a sequence of natural and inevitable facts, in history. *The Idea of History* (Oxford: Oxford Univ., 1949), pp. 182 ff.

[5] Collingwood is kinder to Toynbee, but still classifies him as a positivistic naturalist, to whom perhaps affiliation between historical events and societies is possible, but never interrelationship. *Op. cit.,* pp. 159 ff.

the works of Leopold von Ranke and Jacob Burckhardt, in particular, have become part of our common historical literature. We are, in short, in possession today of a volume of historical information that is rich, almost embarrassing in its opulence and, more often than not, impressive in its accuracy and skillful interpretation. Be it remarked, not merely marginally, that such productions as the completed *History of the Expansion of Christianity* and the about-to-be-completed *Christianity in a Revolutionary Age,*[6] both by Kenneth Scott Latourette, are in their own way and for their own particular purpose as encyclopedic, serviceable and weighty as the two secular histories of our century by Spengler and Toynbee or the nineteenth century productions of von Ranke and Burckhardt.

Yet, when he reflects on these monumental works stating the thought of the past for our own and succeeding generations, the Christian still asks himself in what sense they indicate that man's history is guided by God. What do we mean when we use the expression "God and history," [7] "the Kingdom of God in history," or similar locutions?

It should be observed with utter candor that talk about God's guiding of human history involves a clear presupposition or, as some would say, assumption, or even number of assumptions: First, that there is a God, and second that he

---

[6] Latourette's work still awaits authoritative historiographical and theological evaluation, perhaps because it is comparatively recent. Its sweep appears to be generally acknowledged and appreciated. Its depth has yet to be plumbed.

[7] Such titles come to mind as *Christianity and History* (New York: Scribner's, 1950) and *Christianity in European History* (New York: Macmillan, 1953), by Herbert Butterfield, or *The Belief in Progress* (New York: Scribner's, 1951), by John Baillie and *The Beginning and the End* (London: Geoffrey Bles, 1952), by Nicolas Berdyaev. The former two studies elaborate on the significance to the Christian of history in general and European history in particular. Baillie's book sees meaning in history as it is guided by God toward Him, Berdyaev sees history as meaningful *only* as one is enlightened by the grace and Spirit of God.

is aware of, even concerned with man, his history, and his end. For this the Christian, more particularly the historian who is a Christian, makes no apology. We do not here propose to enter into a refutation of the canard that while history may be somewhat scientific when it tries to be objective, reasoned, and non-doctrinaire, history viewed from a Christian perspective cannot hope to be scientific. The practitioners of the so-called exact sciences, the physical, biological, and mathematical disciplines, have been known to look with jaundiced eye on what they like to call the subjectivity of the historian. Historians have been known to question the right of the historian who takes the Christian view—that God guides history—to the name of scientific historian. It is sufficient to say over against these objections that the scientist in the so-called exact sciences and the historian who questions or denies the validity of the principle that "God guides history" do not operate without presuppositions or assumptions. These may be mathematical postulates, they may be formulas, they may be biological or physical axioms based on experiment and observation, they may even be philosophical or logical assumptions. Assumptions they remain, and they are the indispensable presuppositions with which the various persons operate and without which they cannot work. Does anyone then have the right cavalierly to dismiss historical research and historical writing when it is done and produced by a believer in God, or more specifically, by a committed Christian?

THE HISTORY-MAKING JESUS CHRIST

It would perhaps be going too far to say that only eschatology—that branch of theology concerned with the belief in and study of ultimates, ends, and goals of man as determined and revealed by God in the Scriptures—gives meaning to history and historical studies. But there are events in the history of man which the Christian views as of such importance that without them nothing makes any real sense. And, as we shall see, these events have eschatological significance.

Without committing ourselves unreservedly to everything that has been subsumed under the terms *Heilsgeschichte* and *heilsgeschichtlich,* we can freely admit that when we say "God guides history" we mean that the Christian herewith states his faith. There is a God; he has revealed himself and his concerns and works in behalf of mankind, particularly in his son Jesus Christ; he desires that all men everywhere and always be directed to this Son, their Savior; and he will in the end achieve in man's history what he intends to achieve.

This already indicates how the fact that history is lived and made by man in no way militates against belief, but is rather reinforced by the events of the life of Jesus Christ. The incarnation of the eternal God in the man Jesus was history-making, if anything ever was. It was certainly the greatest single act of divine revelation up to the time of its occurrence since creation. Even as creation included the creation of man, who fell, so in the mid-course of the history of fallen man God entered that history in the form of a man, who made history. In Christ God entered history. Christ lived his life in history. This life, the New Testament testifies, redeemed the world to God. It included the death of Christ, which was swiftly followed by his return from death in his bodily resurrection. Without question, the Scriptures boldly present the post-resurrection forty days of Jesus and his ascension as facts in history, not only as the history of Jesus but also as facts in the history of man. Thus the historical Jesus, understood as a man who actually lived at a given time and in certain given places, made history as he lived it. The Christian is convinced from the records available to him that nothing has ever been quite the same since. Before we continue to expand on this, we must make something else clear.

The Scriptures of the New Testament never indicate, nor has the Church of Christ ever believed, that God was not using men to make history *before* the Incarnation. The entire weight of the Old Testament and the story it tells of man, particularly of man since the time of Abraham and most particularly since the time of Moses, is this: The men of the Old Testament were addressed by the words and actions of God. In a response which God granted them to that divine addressing, and also in their rebellion from time to time against that divine addressing, men lived and made history. Those who were allowed to set down in story, poetry, and prophecy the record of that history were themselves aware of this divine guidance toward a goal. And we certainly have the right to believe that their awareness reflected a similar awareness current in greater and lesser clarity and intensity among their contemporaries. There is a "people of God"— God calls it "my people" repeatedly throughout the Old Testament. In the fraternity of Old Testament scholars, there is a varying degree of certainty about the chronology, the acceptance, the extent of circulation, and the definiteness of messianism in Israel and in the book of its life. But the overpowering continuum, God's initiation and repeated reinforcement of Israel's hopes for salvation, is admittedly incontestable. It is convincingly pointed toward a goal.

The New Testament writings and the Church in the midst of which they came into existence accept this continuum as reaching fulfilment in the arrival, person, life, work, and eventual return of Jesus Christ.

Jesus himself identified his arrival on the scene of man's

history with the coming of the kingdom. Sometimes he called it the kingdom of God, sometimes the kingdom of the heavens. Under the more frequently used *basileia tou theou,* he understood not only an organizational and institutional congeries of people who would in faith accept the grace and rule of God through him, but more. Under the term in any of its variations he understood the reign, the very act of ruling, of the God of the heavens.[8] Jesus established—indeed brought, revealed, and promised to continue to sustain to the end—the divine rule, the *basileia.* The ascription to him by the New Testament of such titles as the Anointed, the King, and, above all, the *Kyrios*—the Lord—supplies us with the certainty of God's rule, through him the Savior, by grace.

THE FUTURE HOPE

Now for Christians living many centuries after the events of the life of Jesus but, as they believe, in the enjoyment of the blessings of salvation and divine rule established by Jesus and the salvation he wrought, immense importance attaches to the prophetic words of Jesus and others in the New Testament. These prophetic words clearly indicate that something is coming which is prefigured in what we have, know, and believe, but is still to be accomplished in future events. This involves hope and, for us, the obligation to speak of the Christian hope. The parables of Jesus about the kingdom, the various versions and variations on the theme unfolded in

---

[8] Vast and convincing evidence on the term *"basileia"* and related Old and New Testament words is gathered in Gerhard Kittel (ed.), *Theologisches Wörterbuch zum Neuen Testament* (Stuttgart: W. Kohlhammer Verlag, 1933——), I, 562 ff. Particularly, the contribution by K. L. Schmidt, pp. 573-595, clarifies New Testament and Early Church use of this important term. For elaborate information on the use of "kingdom" throughout the ages of the Church's life, see the major work by Ernst Staehelin, in which six volumes are projected, cited at the end of this chapter.

Mark, chapter 13, reflected in the eschatological portions of the Epistles and Revelation—all this rich material speaks of the manner in which the history of the rule of God will develop as time goes on and culminates in the second coming of Christ.

It is of course clear that Christians of the first century expected this coming to take place soon. Yet the obvious fact that the second coming of the Son of Man on clouds of glory has not yet taken place has never prevented Christians from clinging firmly to the faith that it will indeed occur, and could come at any moment. It should not prevent them from holding such a faith today. If the redemption which Christ wrought in his coming almost two millennia ago has any meaning and value at all, it certainly includes the clear promise that after the life of man ends in death and after the world comes to an end in the transformation of the last day there is a future reality awaiting all men. The future which awaits those who have been given the response of faith and the life of faith is the inheritance of the saints in light. The Scripture is equally emphatic that those who have rejected the gift of faith and of the life of faith, and have thus in effect and in fact said "No" to the King, the Kingdom, and the Lordship of the King, will have no part in this inheritance.

"The Christian hope," "Christ the Hope of the World"—these and similar phrases which have been used as titles of books and documents express what is customarily understood when such terms as eschatological, eschatological hope, the last things, second coming, are employed. Eschatology is thus a subdivision in the study of theology and as such receives considerable attention in seminary and parish courses of study. For our purpose, however, in line with the role which the great events of our salvation play in the history of man, we have to think of eschatology as the direction as well as the goal of history. The big difference, as we would see it, is that while history is the living, making, and, in a sense, the recording of man's life under God, eschatology is the fulfilment of God's eternal purposes for man. We return now to an earlier reference to the restriction of eschatology to the moment in which at any given time a man finds himself confronted with Christ.

Now it certainly is undeniable that when a man has become and is a Christian God is fulfilling an eternal purpose already in the present, the *now* of that man's life. This, however, does not and should not preclude the hope for the future. For the fully completed work of Jesus Christ includes his second coming, the resurrection of the dead, and the eternal assignment of the risen to the right and the left, to heaven and hell. Therefore the eschatological element in the Christian's ongoing life in Christ is and must be linked with the hope which will crown his faith with sight when it is fulfilled. Any and all forms of so-called secular progress can never replace or lessen the Christian's or the Christian Church's assurance that everything in this earthly life is incomparable with the glory that shall be revealed in us. The New Testament, the fathers of East and West, the Lutheran confessions, the post-Reformation and the present-day Lutheran dogmaticians and exegetes all agree: We live by faith *and* hope.

IMMORTALITY AND RESURRECTION

On the somewhat vexed questions which surround the words "immortality," "intermediate state," and "resurrection of the body, the dead, or the flesh," a notable effort appears to be under way in present-day theological writing, Lutheran and otherwise, to try to grasp once more so far as possible the biblical evidence on all these matters. To be "biblical" in this sense invariably means to try to get at the Hebrew conceptions, as they prevail in both Old and New Testament writings, unaffected by Hellenism, pagan and Jewish, and to try to point out that both Eastern and Western Christian thought was, if not badly distorted, then severely modified by the theological and philosophical climate in which the Church developed over the centuries.[9] Only a complete survey of the handling of the problem would give any idea of the seriousness with which biblical theology is working today on eschatological questions. It will best serve our present and concluding purpose to make use of summaries:

The position can be set forth somewhat as follows:

1. Man, body and soul, is a unity, a creature, a mortal being.
2. The whole man is mortal; there is in him no soul substance or ideal element that is eternal.
3. Christ died and rose (God raised Him) from the dead. He was really dead and is alive for evermore.
4. Those who are "In Christ" die with Him and rise with Him
   a. by baptism in this life and
   b. with a spiritual body in a future resurrection.
5. The resurrection is God's act and by His power; it is not a survival of some divine or deathless element in man's personality.

But to maintain the faith of the primitive church poses very difficult questions for theology today. I list the most obvious here; there doubtless are others:

1. How far and by what principle are we to demythologize the New Testament? We may reject Bultmann's existentialist answer but the question still remains.
2. There is the problem of the historicity of Christ's resurrection.
3. There is the general problem of time and eternity.
4. There is the problem of the "pneumatic" body.
5. There is the problem of those who died without knowing Christ.

[9] Cf. Oscar Cullmann, *Immortality of the Soul or Resurrection of the Dead? The Witness of the New Testament* (New York: Macmillan, 1958).

6. There is the problem of those "not in Christ" either through lack of faith or because they have never heard of him.[10]

Of all the points under the first summary, which White calls "historically almost obvious," it appears necessary to mention only the second. While no one can well dispute the mortality of man—there has always been sufficient evidence of that to preclude denial—there is perhaps not universal agreement on the fact that the "whole" man is mortal. The eternity of soul substance or of an ideal element in man is certainly a common element in most if not all non-Christian, or for that matter, non-Hebraic, non-biblical, religions. It is a truism to point out that classic Greek thought and all its varying descendent systems of thought hold to the presence in man of an immortal soul and to either a complete denial or a bland disregard of any sort of resurrection.[11] As men living in New Testament times, Christians should be aware that speculation from non-biblical sources on vexed questions may be of *assistance* in clarifying matters supposedly unresolved by the Scriptures but can scarcely *determine* answers purporting to be biblically based. The admittedly sparse Old and New Testament evi-

[10] Hugh Vernon White, "Immortality and Resurrection in Recent Theology," *Encounter*, XXII, No. 1 (Winter, 1961), 55-56. This issue includes material on Death, Immortality in Old and New Testament, and Death in contemporary non-Christian writing.

[11] A recent eschatological research study in patristics has this comment: "Christianity has no doctrine of the soul; or, more precisely, it has several. If Christian theology is to make sense of the references to the 'soul' in the Bible, it needs a doctrine of the soul from some other source. This need prompts Christian thought to borrow from the speculation of several centuries of Greek thinkers regarding the distinction between body and soul. During the first half of the twentieth century it has become a ritual for Protestant theologians of varying positions to lament this borrowing from Greece, and often with good reason, but the lamentation becomes irresponsible when it gratuitously assumes that instead of borrowing from the Greeks Christian theology should simply have stayed with the 'clear teachings' of the Bible about the soul. Either, the Christians are not to speak about the soul in any consistent or reasoned manner at all, or they must be willing to learn about the soul from other places, in addition to their Scriptures." Jaroslav J. Pelikan, *The Shape of Death* (Nashville: Abingdon, 1961), pp. 33-34.

dence of continued human existence after death in a disembodied state is more than balanced by the overwhelming emphasis in the New Testament on the essential character of man's hope determined by Christ's resurrection. We can also add that when a writer completely negative as to the immortality of the soul has, to his own satisfaction, presented what he considers a documented refutation of that belief, he assumes that he has demolished one of the chief pillars supporting the edifice of Christian faith and thought.[12] In order to demolish not just a supposed pillar beneath but all of faith and life for Christians it would, rather, be necessary to destroy something entirely different.

ALL OR NOTHING

The center and core, the heart of hearts of Christian hope is found in the historic event of the resurrection of Jesus Christ from the dead and, based on that resurrection, in the promises throughout the New Testament of the resurrection of the dead. The alarm with which on many sides the modern renewal of the denial of the resurrection of Jesus, with the inevitable corollary denial of the resurrection of the dead, is being attacked makes it clear that Christian theology is aware that this is a situation of "all or nothing." [13] Thus we have a reflection of the absolute, the drastic alternatives rehearsed in I Corinthians, chapter 15.[14] Give up Easter, the empty tomb,

[12] Cf. Corliss Lamont, *The Illusion of Immortality*, with an Introduction by John Dewey (3d ed.; New York: Philosophical Lib., 1959).

[13] Aside from Bultmann's all-too-well-known demythologization of the Resurrection, "There is no empty grave," reference should be made here to a devastating product by one of his followers: Hans Grass, *Ostergeschehen und Osterberichte* (Göttingen: Vandenhoeck und Ruprecht, 1956).

[14] The section by Cullmann on resurrection is particularly strong: *op. cit.,* pp. 40-41 and *passim.* Cf. also Karl Barth's commentary on First Corinthians, in which the entire exegesis of the Epistle is linked to the exegesis of the fifteenth chapter: H. J. Stenning (trans.), *The Resurrection of the Dead* (London: Revell, 1933 [1924]).

and the reality of the post-Easter appearances as historic occasions—and all is lost. This is theology at the crossroads.

What can be said or done? That which has always been done—believe and proclaim. It took a great deal to convince even some of the apostles that Easter had occurred. No appearance of the risen Christ to any but "his own" is recorded in the New Testament. His ascension precludes further appearances except the one referred to as having occurred on the road to Damascus before Saul. Since Pentecost, under orders from their Lord, the apostles together with their associates and all successive generations of Christians have believed and proclaimed the resurrection of Jesus Christ from the dead. The centrality of the climax of Christ's earthly life, the Resurrection from the dead, to the faith prefigures also the centrality in all eschatological thought of his return for the purpose of raising the dead, all of them. Only in that he lives is he the hope of the world. The Cross is an offense only if it is the cross of one who lives and reigns to all eternity; otherwise, it is a symbol of failure, of heroic frustration.

Herein then lies whatever solution one can offer to the questions listed earlier which, we fully agree, add up to this, that to maintain the faith of the Primitive Church poses very difficult questions for theology today. On demythologization of the New Testament one can say with utmost seriousness that denial of the reality of the resurrection of Jesus, the empty tomb, and of the ultimate resurrection of the dead can only lead to denial of the historic reality of Christmas and Good Friday, and all that lies between. It should not be undertaken or supported. If a question remains it need not be answered for the believer. For the gainsayer—well, repetitions of the conversion of Saul in numberless variety are not impossible today. Why should the Resurrection be a greater historical problem than anything else recorded of the life of Christ? The historical reality of the Resurrection is probably no more rationally or scientifically demonstrable than the saving reality of the Cross, but both realities are incontestable.

Even with the remarkable richness of the material in II Corinthians, chapter 5, and I Corinthians, chapter 15, on the resurrection body, which Paul calls "pneumatic," we will scarcely know all that it signifies till we are in the resurrection body ourselves. But this much is certain, the bodies of the risen, all of them, will not be wraiths but bodies, real bodies, as they were before death, with this great difference: they will be like the body of Christ—incorruptible, and they will never die again. Some of them and their owners will be consigned— it can hardly be doubted on the basis of the cumulative New Testament evidence—to the fate of eternal rejection by a God and Lord whom they have purposely rejected during their lifetime on earth. The "second chance" or *apokatastasis* doctrine is scarcely in accord with the New Testament. As to those who die without knowing Christ because they have never heard of him, the missionary imperative to the Church by the Lord is our greatest incentive to keep that number as low as possible, and one can only commend to the mercy of God those who through death have gone beyond our power to reach them. The Church is bound gratefully by God to a revelation and to its dissemination and perpetuation by all means which Christ gives into her hands. That is our eschatological task in view of the last judgment, the return of Christ, the resurrection of the dead, and the life eternal. To what God has bound himself aside from that revelation, he alone knows.

Without falling into apocalyptic particularism, the Church of today, including the Lutheran community in the North American continent out of whose life these pages have come, clings to her eschatological proclamation while she continues to hold to her own historical convictions. Nothing else will do. Echoing words which we quoted at the very outset, for Christians this has meaning, the greatest possible meaning: God has revealed himself in history through Jesus Christ. God has supplied the written record of that Christ whom he promised and sent, and who will some day return. God has kept his promises. God will keep his promises. *Maranatha!* Even so, Lord Jesus, come!

SUGGESTIONS FOR FURTHER READING

ALTHAUS, PAUL. *Die Letzen Dinge.* Gütersloh: Bertelsmann, 1949.

BAILLIE, JOHN. *And the Life Everlasting.* New York: Scribner's, 1933.

BRUNNER, EMIL. *The Scandal of Christianity.* Philadelphia: Westminster, 1951.

CULLMANN, OSCAR. *Christ and Time.* Philadelphia: Westminster, 1950.

———. *The Early Church,* trans. A. J. B. HIGGINS. Philadelphia: Westminster, 1956. (Cf. especially chap., "The Proleptic Deliverance of the Body According to the New Testament.")

EICHRODT, WALTER. *Theologie des Alten Testaments.* 3 vols. Berlin: Ev. Verlagsanstalt, 1935.

KÜNNETH, WALTER. *Theologie der Auferstehung.* Munich: Claudius Verlag, 1951.

LATOURETTE, KENNETH SCOTT. *History of the Expansion of Christianity.* 7 vols. New York: Scribner's, 1937–1944.

———. *Christianity in a Revolutionary Age.* New York: Harper's, 1958——.

STAEHELIN, ERNST. *Die Verkundigung des Reiches Gottes in der Kirche Jesu Christi: Zeugnisse aus allen Jahrhunderten und allen Konfessionen,* Vols. 1–3. Basel: Reinhardt, 1951——.

PART TWO

. . . IS LIFE FOR THE CHURCH

Chapter 5

WORSHIP AND LIFE

By H. Grady Davis

CHRISTIAN PRESUPPOSITIONS

A general discussion of worship usually begins with the rather obvious fact that man is a worshiping animal. It seems natural for a human being to stop when his senses come to a closed door and wonder what is beyond. He would hardly be human if he did not believe that there is more beyond, something on which his welfare depends. It may seem no less natural that such a creature should feel a sense of awe and reverence before the unknown, should feel himself dependent on the unseen forces, should believe that there is a way to turn them in his favor, and should try to do it. If this is what worship means, then worship may be thought of as a function of human nature.

Even in such a naturalistic approach to worship as this, it is to be noted that our imaginary human being does not react as a solitary individual. If he is an animist, however primitive, he thinks of spirits as his tribe thinks of spirits, and he calls them by the names his tribe uses. There is never a beginning by an isolated person, for no person is ever isolated. All his thinking and feeling are conditioned by the shared meanings of his group, the equipment of words and concepts common to his tribe. He is not an island, as no man is an island in his worship. Indeed, our animist may be on safer ground than a modern man in one respect, namely, that he does not imagine himself to be a solitary individual.

Worship, understood in this sense, is no doubt a fact of human nature and history. What does not follow is that it is necessarily a valuable or praiseworthy habit in itself. Study of such worship may lead to important conclusions for history, anthropology, psychology, and other sciences of man. It can throw light on the religions of man. It can hardly serve to explain the worship of Christian people.

There is never a fresh beginning in the study of Christian worship either. It is impossible to think intelligently about today's worship without reference to the sixteenth century, and impossible to understand what happened in the sixteenth century without reference to the Middle Ages, the early centuries and the New Testament. It is equally impossible to understand the worship of the first Christians, including the first disciples and Jesus himself, without reference to the Old Testament and the worship of the Jewish people. Christian worship in its simplest form presupposes the whole Bible and biblical history, the whole theology and history of the church, and all persons who have lived and died in Christian faith. All of these are implicit, taken for granted, in the simplest prayer a Christian says alone in his bedroom.

Christian worship presupposes the God who has revealed himself both in his creation and rule of all things and in his Son: the God who has united himself with mankind and performed his redemptive deed in Jesus Christ. It presupposes that God provides a witness to himself not only in his works but also in the Holy Scriptures and in the preaching and teaching and confession of the Church. It presupposes the Church: the shared existence of all those whom the Holy Spirit has joined to Christ in his death and resurrection, as is signified in their baptism. It presupposes that God is present in the human words men speak concerning these things: that he is present here and now and always, making his word good by giving what he offers and performing what he promises. It presupposes that God through his Spirit is striving in men's hearts to get his Word believed wherever it is heard.

FAITH AS WORSHIP

The Word of God, in this sense of a personal self-disclosure and self-commitment, is prerequisite to any Christian worship, even the simplest. Worship is an afterthought, a result of hearing and believing the Word. Worship does not begin with human beings, speaking and acting toward God. It begins with God, speaking and acting toward men. Prayer is not a word, however sincere, spoken in the hope that God will answer. It is an answer to a word God has spoken and now speaks. In Christian theology, worship, like ethics, must be put among the consequences of God's love and favor. Worship is not a way to find God; it is a recognition of the God who has found us. It is not a way to secure God's help, but a grateful acknowledgment of the help he has given us.

This may clarify the idea of worship but it does not make worship cheap or easy. There can of course be no worship of the kind indicated unless there is a God who speaks and acts in his Word. But that is not all. There can be no genuine response to that Word unless it is believed. These are the two indispensable factors in Christian worship: the Word of God and faith. They go together. God speaks to persons capable of hearing and believing, but the Word will be only a human sound until it is heard as God speaking. There will certainly be no response worthy to be called worship until the Word is heard in faith.

When the Word is heard in faith, something always happens. Worship is primarily something done, not something thought or felt or even said. It is a two-way action between God and believers, individually and jointly. God gives and men receive; men give back what God has given, and God accepts it, even though the offering is faulty.

"The trust and faith of the heart alone make both God and an idol," says Luther in his Large Catechism as he explains the first commandment.[1] So in one blinding flash does he illuminate the decisive role of faith in worship. So also does he shatter the illusion that there is anything holy in the natural human inclination to worship something. "A god is that to which we look for all good and in which we find refuge in every time of need."

The thing in which a man puts his faith, on which he relies, and to which he turns for assurance is his god. He makes it his god by regarding it so. This trust and faith are worship. They do not create the thing worshiped, but they do make it his god, the only god he has. The value of worship is determined entirely by the object worshiped, not by the human act of worshiping. The essential character of Christian worship is determined by the God of Christian faith. Worship of anything that is not God is false worship, idolatry. Reverence, devotion, and confidence of the heart directed toward something less than God is a worship of the creature rather than the Creator, and it is an evil and destructive thing. Misdirected worship is death, not life.

Even the true God cannot be God to me until he is made my God by the trust and faith of my heart. God is not God, so far as we are concerned, until he is worshiped as God.

[1] *The Large Catechism*, trans. Robert H. Fischer (Philadelphia: Muhlenberg, 1959), p. 9.

And there can be no halfway measures, no divided purposes in the worship of God. He is to be worshiped because he is God and for no other reason whatever. If an act of worship is performed for any other purpose, it is that other purpose which is served; it is that purpose which is worshiped, and not God.

Seen in this light, worship is an inevitable result of faith, and an indispensable function of a believer's life. It is not only necessary as a means to sustain a life of faith. It is also necessary because faith cannot fail to express itself in worship. As there can be no worship without faith, so there can be no faith without worship. It would perhaps be more correct to say that a life of faith is itself the only true worship of God. Anything less than that is less than worship.

Worship is the acknowledgment of God as God. God must be acknowledged by all Christians together as one Church with one heart and one voice, and he must be acknowledged singly by every Christian for himself in his private mind and conscience. God must be acknowledged in all his works as attested in his Word: as Creator and Giver of all things, as incarnate Redeemer and Lord, and as ever-present Spirit.

All worship is implicit in the first commandment: "I am the Lord thy God, thou shalt have no other gods before me." Whatever else comes within the meaning of worship, it never really gets beyond this. As Luther says further concerning this commandment,

Here you have the true honor and the true worship which please God and which he commands under penalty of eternal wrath, namely, that the heart should know no other consolation or confidence than that in him, nor let itself be torn from him, but for him should risk and disregard everything else on earth.[2]

[2] *Ibid.,* p. 10.

Worship presupposes and requires that God be heard speaking personally in his Word read and preached and taught: that he be heard, believed, and trusted. Thus the reading and hearing of the Word is an important part of all worship, public and private, in the family or in the church service. But worship cannot stop with hearing. One may hear the Word only to speculate about it. But faith is not speculation about the Word or even mental agreement with it. To have faith is to act on the Word, and worship is an acting on the Word. To hear God speak, especially to hear his message of love and hope in the Gospel, and to make no reply is to dishonor God and disregard his Word. Worship requires that we answer him.

God is to be properly recognized. He is to be confessed before men as Father, Son, and Spirit. Christ is to be confessed as Lord before men by every Christian, not once in his life but constantly in witness to the world, as the Lord enjoined. A double confession is to be made before God by the whole Church of Christ and every person in it: a confession of sin and a confession of faith. Only in such a double confession to God can any man recognize himself for what he is, a man at once guilty and forgiven. And only by a constant awareness of this tension in which he lives can any man be prepared either to live or to worship.

Moreover, God is to be praised and glorified. He is to be blessed and thanked for his great glory. He is to be thanked for all his benefits, not the least of which are that he is mighty, that he is holy, and that he expects and commands great things of the children of his love. God is to be spoken to in prayer, for it is his fatherly prerogative to give all good to us and to all men. God is to be obeyed in love and in dread of his displeasure. He is to be served in his good will toward our fellow men, with all we have and all we are.

True worship includes all these things. Nothing short of this can be considered a proper worship of God. Only when all this is truly done is God the God of any human being or of any church. This total, obedient acknowledgment and service is to be rendered to God just because he is God. If people sing or speak or pray or perform acts of worship for any lesser reason, they are not worshiping God.

LIFE AS WORSHIP

It is necessary to insist that worship be understood as this totality of response to God. The commandment leaves no doubt that the wholeness is required. "Thou shalt love the Lord thy God with all thy heart, and with all thy soul, and with all thy mind, and with all thy strength." This is not meant as a catalog of distinct faculties. It points to the unity and integrity of the whole self and the whole life. It means that we cannot serve God with a part of ourselves—part of our time, part of our possessions (ten per cent, for example), part of our interest and loyalty—and serve ourselves or something else with the rest.

Even in this commandment God's concern is for us. He requires that our whole self be centered on him, not because he is jealous for his own honor, but because he is jealous for our good. He has compassion on our divided, fragmentary selves, frustrated and unhappy by reason of the conflicts inside us, so double-minded, triple-minded, multiple-minded that even our prayers cannot be consistent long enough for God to answer them. He wants us concentrated upon him in total worship so that we may stop flying apart, exploding into bits, and destroying ourselves and one another. He knows that nothing less than himself has the power to hold us together, to make us real persons, or to give us integrity.

It follows that worship cannot be something done occasionally whenever we take a notion to do it, nor something done only at a few appointed times as a special item on a busy schedule, nor something done in some separate compartment of ourselves apart from the rest of our lives. It follows also that going through the motions and speaking the words of prayer, praise, or thanksgiving may or may not be worship.

For example, one may say the words of the most perfect prayer ever composed and yet not pray to God. On the other hand, one may pray to God in a few halting syllables or none at all. One may hear the words of an absolution and yet not believe himself forgiven. One may think of his misdeeds and feel guilty about them and yet not confess them to God nor even to himself. On the other hand, one may repent and believe, may confess and know himself forgiven in the secret of his soul, though he may not always find it possible to do this.

This is another way of saying that the life of a Christian believer cannot be split up into categories. The Christian, in all the ramifications of his existence, is to be one person, as his God is one Lord. To think that a part of his life is sacred, related to God, and that another part of his life is secular, not related to God, it to make a distinction where none exists. To think that his worship lies in one area, his moral conduct in another, his family and community relationships in another, and his work at an occupation in still another, is to make certain that none of these will be rightly understood.

No part of any man's life is right until it is recognized as his answer to the call and command of his Maker. But when it is so recognized it becomes a worship of God in the most real sense. This is where work and worship meet: as parts of the one response to the call of God. Here is explained the busy, wearing, confusing complex of activities—the seemingly meaningless round of "birth and copulation and death" (T. S. Eliot, "Fragment of an Agon"). This is where all otherwise senseless activities find meaning.

Moreover, this is where Christ exercises his priestly office through the members of his body on earth. For this purpose he sends them into the world he loves and died to redeem. The Christian's complex relationships with all sorts of people, his place in a family and a neighborhood, his role as a worker and a citizen—these are not accidental. They are the concrete situation in which he is called to worship and serve God. His entanglement with imperfect people like himself is not a misfortune he has to suffer or escape from into "religion." It is precisely within these intricate relationships that he is called to be a Christian.

The Christian is called to exercise Christ's priesthood of love and self-giving in all his various roles: as a parent or child, as a neighbor, as a worker among his fellow workers, as a producer and a steward of goods and wealth, and as a citizen of his country and the world. He is called to be Christ's instrument in every one of these concrete relations, to be that particular member of the body in which alone the Head can act in this particular relation. When he fulfills that calling in the fear of God and the love of Christ, he does it by the endowment of God's Spirit, and nothing he does, not even his menial labor, is of the earth earthly. He worships God with a believing life.

This is the Reformation's legacy to the modern world: the high doctrine of the priesthood of all believers together in the one body of the one Priest and Lord and Redeemer. The nearly complete neglect of the doctrine and the secularization of life that has come to take its place may remind us that even the noblest theological doctrine is useless until it is lived. Indeed, it sometimes seems that the loftier a doctrine is the more liable it is to abuse and perversion, and the more it suffers at the hands of those who talk about it all too glibly.

The theology of worship here suggested is subject to the same abuse. There is danger that someone may despair of ever being able to worship in this high sense, and excuse himself from trying. If the simplest act of worship requires the whole Christian faith, and if God cannot be truly worshiped with anything less than the complete trust of my heart and the undivided loyalty of my life, then what is the use of trying to worship? If worship demands faith and my mind is full of questions and even doubts, how can I worship? Why should I say the words of a prayer when I know I am not praying with my whole heart?

These are valid questions and they should not be dismissed lightly. They point, however, not to the futility of worship, but to its exceedingly great importance. It is the same as with the so-called impossible or absolute ethical demands of Jesus. In worship, as in conduct, God is before us in all his perfect will for us, and he would not have us content with less than that. In worship no less than in conduct, we sin and fall short of his glory. Yet so long as our eyes are on him, he forgives and accepts our fumbling worship as he does our faulty works. The cry of a broken heart is the best prayer.

There is another and perhaps greater danger. Someone may think that a believing and obedient life is worship enough in itself, and may neglect the practice of worship. This is, of course, a form of self-deception. It comes from accepting a too-uncritical standard of obedience and a too-conventional pattern of belief. It is the result of not feeling the pressure of God's holy will and the striving of his Spirit within. It is a complacency that knows neither repentance nor forgiveness.

A man or woman who takes the call to the Christian life seriously will soon discover that it is impossible to sustain one's various roles and discharge one's priestly functions in our intricate relationships with the resources found within himself alone. It is just here, if anywhere, that he will learn the truth of Christ's words: "Apart from me you can do nothing." He is not expected to do anything alone, for he is not alone. He may feel alone, but in that he is mistaken. He is a member of the Church, the community of Christ's presence. He shares the fellowship of the Gospel and the illumination of the Spirit. Wherever he goes, the Church with Christ in its midst goes with him. When he seeks the solitude of some figurative closet, he goes there as a baptized Christian; he prays with the whole Church and the whole Church prays with him.

He may be struggling with his own weakness and sin, but that makes no difference. Or, rather, it may make a difference in his favor. For he is serving a power which manifests itself in weakness and not in strength, and if he were not struggling with his own weakness, he might not be aware of that strength at all. It is just here—in his weakness and insufficiency for the great things he is called to do—that he will learn how he ought to pray. It is just when he turns from confusion and temptations to the words of Holy Scripture that he will learn what it means to hear God speaking in his Word. The creeds and hymns and prayers and other worship materials of the Church will not fail him when he turns to them in this way. They will come alive just here, or never at all anywhere.

It is among the multiplex activities and resultant confusion of a family that a Christian man and woman necessarily come upon the mysteries of life shared. The gift of
life is not in the man and it is not in the woman. The individual does not have it. Here, if anywhere, we must learn
that together we are something which we cannot be apart.
The reverent acknowledgment of this corporate gift and its
Giver is the worship of God and the beginning of wisdom.
It is the image of the Church; rather, it is the Church, the
mystery of existence together as one in the triune God. That
mystery is to be recognized just here, or perhaps never
at all.

Surely, in the intimate contacts and stresses of family life,
nothing but a common acknowledgment of God can give
meaning to it all. In a Christian home, a simple blessing
or thanksgiving or the words of a hymn at the table can
become an act of true worship. In another household it
might have no significance except to the little children, but
here it can bring the entire lives of parents and children
to articulate expression in a moment of time. A passage of
Scripture read by a child, some explanatory words by a
parent, and a prayer which all can understand or say together will demonstrate the fact that the Church is here,
that the Christian priesthood is exercised, and that God is
worshiped.

CORPORATE WORSHIP

The Church must worship together as one because it is
one. It cannot express its true nature except in corporate
worship, corporate life, corporate service. The Church is
not an aggregate of like-minded individuals—God knows!
The Church is not a select group of people who are better
than other people—wiser, holier, more intelligent, or more

moral. The Church is not made one by the mutual love of its members, nor by their common tastes, nor by their common interests, nor by their common aims and hopes as human beings. The Church is not one in its organization, its institution and polity, its biblical or doctrinal theology, nor its preaching and teaching.

The Church is one in spite of apparently hopeless disagreement about all these things. Yet, strangely and inconsistently enough, the Church in its worship always confesses itself to be one. It does so in all its creeds, hymns, and prayers. In this it reflects the New Testament, which does not say that believers ought to be one, but declares that they are one body in union with Jesus Christ. The corporate unity of their existence is like that of a family of brothers and sisters who can fight like cats and dogs but cannot stop being brothers and sisters.

This unity is always affirmed in Christian worship at its best, even if nowhere else. In fact, a good case can be made for the proposition that the Church expresses its unity in its worship materials, especially its hymns and prayers, more clearly than anywhere else. It should not seem strange that this is so. Nowhere else is the Church so truly itself as in the act of recognizing the God who stands in its midst, in the resurrected and exalted Christ and in the power of his Spirit.

The Church which can do this is something more than any of its individual members and more than all of them put together. The Church is the assembly of believers, but believers cannot make the Church by coming together without the presence of Him in whom they believe. The individual Christian is not everything the Church is, even in miniature. The sum-total of his beliefs does not equal the

Church's confession. The force of his doubts and questions does not weaken the Church's faith. Whatever he is as a Christian, he is that in oneness with the Church. Apart from the Church he did not become a Christian. Apart from the corporate union of believers with Jesus Christ, he is no Christian. He is called and chosen to be a branch in the Vine and share the life of the Vine. The life of the Vine is in him, but he has not that life in himself; if the organic connection is broken he withers at once.

This is why the Church's worship must be corporate if it is to be Christian. The congregation in this place is the Church of Jesus Christ, the one holy catholic and apostolic Church, the body with the Lord in the midst of it. It is one body and one Spirit. It has "One Lord, one faith, one baptism, one God and Father of us all, who is above all and through all and in all" (Eph. 4:5)—which implies the Real Presence in this congregation as such, as well as in the Sacrament of the Altar. In its worship, this congregation is one with believers all over the earth, with saints and confessors of all times and places, and with angels and archangels and all the company of heaven.

It is clear that the individual Christian in this congregation, whether he is in the pew or at the altar, can be nothing more than a grateful participant in what the Church is and what it does in its worship of God. Yet this fact does not make him unimportant; it makes him indispensable. As he cannot be the Church without all other believers, so they cannot be the whole Church without him. He is called to perform a function in the priestly ministry of Christ which nobody else on earth but he can perform: to play a part in the life and worship of the Church which nobody else can play. He is called to fulfil the purpose of his existence by adding his heart and voice to the universal prayer and praise and thanksgiving to God by the whole Church and by all creation. No confession of the church is complete without his affirmation; no prayer is the whole Church's prayer without his "Amen."

It is easy to talk about congregational worship. Protestants in general and Lutherans in particular indulge in a good deal of talk about it. We say that the reformers labored diligently to restore congregational worship, and there can be no doubt that they did. We sometimes hear the boast that Protestantism has really given both the Church and its worship back to the people. I am by no means confident that this is true.

The development of the congregational chorale and hymn and their use in the public services of the Church have provided an incalculably valuable means for participation by the people. Books of worship have been greatly enriched by translations of material from all ages, including responsive prayers, litanies, bidding prayers, and other incidental forms. Improved orders for the chief service and daily offices have restored the time-tried structures of the historical liturgies, which give the people a voice in the dialog of worship. All this is undoubtedly true, and its importance cannot be denied.

There is among Lutheran churches ample provision for congregational worship. It does not follow that the congregation is worshiping in spirit and in truth, with the heart and with the understanding. There are too many congregations which play the part only of listeners and spectators, passive listeners not only to the Word read and preached but also to the responses of the choir, the hymns by the organ and choir, and even the prayers of the pastor. There are too many churches in which the people make no response

but to join halfheartedly in a few hymns. There are too
many where they struggle, none too willingly, to "get through"
the service. There are others where they get through it all
too easily and casually, both minister and people.

Something more than provision for congregational worship
is involved here. Indeed, something more than congregational
worship is involved. Corporate worship is at stake, and
corporate worship is more than participation of the people
in the various acts of worship, though it certainly includes
that. The essential character of Christian worship is at stake,
and with it the Church's consciousness of its own nature,
the place of the individual Christian in the Church, and the
function the Christian is called to serve in his life on the
earth. The sense of Church, felt in the bones of Christians,
is involved here in the service of worship. The Church cannot worship as the Church unless it knows itself to be the
Church. Nor can the Christian serve Christ as a member
of his body unless he can find out who he is in the worship
of God along with the other members.

The man or woman who comes to church is congenitally
an individualist, whether rugged or timid. Post-Renaissance
philosophies have not improved his condition. It will take
more than a few pious admonitions and an esthetically satisfying performance of a liturgy to teach him the corporate
character of his existence without betraying him into col-
lectivism.

THE INSTRUMENT OF WORSHIP

In the historical practice of the Lutheran Church, as well
as in its theology, the order of service is a means to an end,
not an end in itself. It exists for the function it performs, as
the organ exists for the music it makes. The organ is not
the only means for making music, but it is one important

means. Just so, the order of worship is not worship. It is an instrument for use in worship. The entire order and each of its parts, everything used in worship, has the importance of an instrument and no other importance. No particular order, no part of a given order, can be indispensable as the one and only way to worship. An order, however, may be a very important instrument for use in worship.

This distinction between worship itself and the instrumental means of worship is always in danger of being lost. A service order, a ceremonial action or object, a vestment, a song of praise, or the wording of a confession or prayer comes to be intimately joined to the experience of worship in the Church, beginning in childhood. The thing grows familiar, venerable, and sacred, and is loved for all its associations and for its own sake. It gets deeply rooted in the self, as indeed it must if it is to be a useful tool for worship. When this happens, it becomes easy to suppose that this thing, this order of service, is worship in and of itself, that it works automatically, that its mere performance is the worship of God. Then the order has ceased to be a means and has become an end in itself, something this side of God, something standing between the soul and God, something one may simply perform instead of worshiping God. Organ music may be effectively used in worship, but listening to an organ is not necessarily worship.

There is also a danger at the other extreme, of supposing that worship will be more spiritual if it lacks fixed or definite form. We are not disembodied spirits. We are creatures of flesh and sensation. Everything we can possibly know, think, or feel takes rise from what we can see, hear, taste, touch, or smell. Nothing is apprehensible to us until it is held in some perceptible form: a concept, a mental picture, a literary or artistic form. All our abstract words begin as metaphors embodying images derived from the five senses. We cannot see God, only his visible works. We truly see and know him only in the Incarnation where he assumes the form and limitations of our creaturely existence and lives with us in our flesh among the things of sense. To try to worship God as the pure Spirit he is, apart from the Incarnation, is to worship, not God, but a mental image of our own fabrication— a false god, an idol which might just as well be made of stone. To imagine that we are worshiping without dependence on some form is to delude ourselves.

Beginning in the sixteenth century, the Lutheran Church has tried to find its way between these extremes—with what success is yet to be seen. Luther and his followers saw no prescribed form of worship or church organization in the New Testament. They insisted that no uniformity of rites and ceremonies is necessary to the existence and unity of the Church. They denied that tradition has divine or prescriptive authority. But they took this to mean that the Church is as free to keep its historical organization and its traditional liturgies as to discard them, and they kept as much as they could.

Lutherans rejected the automatic action of the sacraments, the doctrine that the sacraments work *ex opere operato,* but they held fast to the realism of the sacraments as instrumental means through which God acts in his freedom to do and give what he promises. They rejected the sacrifice of the mass and the doctrine of transubstantiation, but they retained the structure and content of the mass, including its music. They said that absolutely nothing is necessary but the preaching of the Gospel and the administration of the sacraments, but they loved the liturgy (as well as the music and other arts accompanying it) and repudiated all fanatics and radicals who wanted to do away with it.

This, as I see it, is about where we stand today. The situation still poses an unanswered question. The basic question is not whether we shall have formal or informal services. It is not any of the controversial questions about external and marginal things which currently engage the attention of many. It is not a question of how much ritual and ceremonial we will put up with, nor how much and what we dare to borrow, steal, and imitate, nor how impressive we can make our performances (that is, as spectacles).

Nor do I think that the serious question is one of "communication." The biblical speech of our liturgy is indeed strange to the ears of our more sophisticated contemporaries. But why? Is it the language which gives trouble, or is it the thought? I do not think it is the language. We use and love highly technical language about every abstruse subject in which we are interested. This is true not only of our intellectuals but of the general public. Our advertisers could not get along without their mystifying word-magic. Neither could our teen-agers.

I do not think that the genuine mysteries of life and death, of Christ and the Church, of the Word and Sacraments, of the Christian vocation and priesthood, can be put into the jargon of the suburb. I do not think that that is what our people need. The question is whether we can share with them a sense of these mysteries, what the worship of God is, and what the liturgy is for. The answer does not yet appear.

SUGGESTIONS FOR FURTHER READING

ABBA, RAYMOND. *Principles of Christian Worship.* London: Oxford Univ., 1957.

DANIELOU, JEAN, S. J. *The Bible and the Liturgy.* Notre Dame, Ind.: Univ. of Notre Dame, 1956.

EDWALL, P., E. HAYMAN, and W. D. MAXWELL (eds.). *Ways of Worship: The Report of a Theological Commission of Faith and Order.* London: SCM, 1951.

FENDT, LEONHARD. *Einführung in die Liturgiewissenschaft.* Berlin: Alfred Töpelmann, 1958.

KOENKER, E. B. *Worship in Word and Sacrament.* Saint Louis: Concordia, 1959.

MÜLLER, KARL F. "Die Neuordnung des Gottesdienstes in Theologie und Kirche," in *Theologie und Kirche.* Kassel: Johannes Stauda Verlag, 1952. Pp. 197-339.

REED, LUTHER D. *Worship.* Philadelphia: Muhlenberg, 1959.

SHEPHERD, MASSEY H., JR. (ed). *The Liturgical Renewal of the Church.* New York: Oxford Univ., 1960.

VAJTA, VILMOS. *Luther on Worship,* trans. U. S. LEUPOLD. Philadelphia: Muhlenberg, 1958.

Chapter 6

THE CURE OF SOULS

By William E. Hulme

NATURE OF THE ILLNESS

When we speak of the cure of souls we imply that the souls in our care can be sick. It is necessary to know the nature of this sickness before we can speak of the remedy. The traditional religious approach to the nature of the soul's illness is to diagnose it as sin. Theologically speaking this is correct, but what does our generation understand by sin? As a word symbol handed down from one generation to another it has become a generality which has little meaning to the man in the street and strikes very little depth even in the religious. Each age needs its own fresh understanding of sin. This comes from the prophets of the day, the acute and articulate diagnosticians who help us face our ills. These are the highly perceptive seers into the human predicament, who have an equally keen sensitivity to the judgment which rests upon us in this predicament. They demand our attention.

In addressing a group of Lutheran clergymen in London, Bishop Hans Lilje said, "We in the Church need to listen to the existentialists like Heidegger who know where modern man is—who know how to communicate with him because they know how to express his predicament." In addition to our existentialist philosophers and "evangelists," there are our dramatists. Outstanding among these is Arthur Miller.

How does he conceive his task? Says Miller, "One had the right to write because other people needed news of the inner world, and if they went too long without such news they would go mad with the chaos of their lives. With the greatest of presumption I conceived that the great writer was the destroyer of chaos, a man privy to the councils of the hidden gods who administer the hidden laws that bind us all and destroy us if we do not know them." [1] One sees here the perception which created Willy Loman in *Death of a Salesman* and which helped others see themselves in him—the perception of that judgment which befell Willy and may befall us. Eugene O'Neill is another dramatist in this tradition. With cruel clarity he displays his insight into the compulsion we human beings have for the sort of pipe dreams which keep us from reckoning with the "hidden laws" of our existence. By becoming substitutes for sincerity, these pipe dreams bring us to a tragic end, as evidenced in the pathetic figure of Hickey in *The Iceman Cometh*. Across the Atlantic, the British writer John Osborn has shown us the angry young man who knows what torture it is to be a human being.

If we turn in another direction we can listen to our social scientists and cultural analysts who see a sick soul in a sick society. Among these is Fritz Künkel with his peculiar insight into the role of egocentricity in family relationships. He sees not only how the sins of the parents are passed on to their children, but how in varying degrees this transfer can cause each person in the family to lose his identifying role in the family. The extreme of such confusion of roles is the completely reversed family. Künkel describes a family of four in which the members are equally egocentric and the

---

[1] Arthur Miller, "The Shadows of The Gods," *Harper's Magazine,* CCXVII, No. 1299 (August, 1958), 37. Copyright, 1958 by Harper & Brothers. Reprinted by special permission from Harper's Magazine.

ego-image of each is in an opposite place from its rightful one, the father being an egocentric girl, the mother an egocentric boy, one son the egocentric father, and the other the egocentric mother. "They will torture each other," says Künkel, "until all their egocentricity breaks down." [2] These are the sick family relationships which threaten all sense of community and extend their sickness into the vocational, economic, and social life of those involved. As Arthur Miller sees it, "Society is inside of man and man is inside society, and you cannot even create a truthfully drawn psychological entity on the stage until you understand his social relations and their power to make him what he is and to prevent him from being what he is not. The fish is in the water and the water is in the fish." [3] If this understanding is necessary for creating stage characters, how much more necessary is it for an effective pastoral ministry?

How does the sick soul in a sick society experience his sickness? Cultural analyst Karen Horney says he experiences it as emotional isolation from others. When anyone feels emotionally isolated from his neighbors, he develops what Horney believes is the basic anxiety, one which she describes as the feeling of being lonely and helpless in a hostile world. This basic anxiety is "the nutritive soil out of which a definite neurosis may develop at any time." [4]

These writers and many others of our day are perceiving and articulating, in terms modern man recognizes from his own experience in living, what John called "the world"—that which, despite its apparently harmless and even attractive

[2] Fritz Künkel, *In Search of Maturity* (New York: Scribner's, 1943), p. 141.
[3] Miller, *op. cit.*, p. 39.
[4] Karen Horney, *The Neurotic Personality of Our Time* (New York: Norton, 1937), p. 89.

surface, turns out to be a milieu of sickness in which we are all involved. The task of these writers is actually a religious one, for they deal with ultimate questions, questions about man's existence, his purpose, his destiny. Their task is religious because they grapple with good and evil as objective realities in the hidden laws of our existence, and because they concern themselves with the judgment of the gods and the ways of salvation. Eugene O'Neill once said in a press conference, "I am not interested in the relations of man to man, but of man to God." This is God as the discerning seer perceives him in terms of natural revelation. It may be far from the God who has revealed himself in Jesus Christ as the God who is love (*agape*). Yet this awareness of our ills, this judgment upon our society, this perception of the hidden laws in our universe reveals the situation to which we must apply the Christian message of redemption in our day. Because theologian Paul Tillich, for one, has this awareness, he can be particularly helpful as a preacher and as a resource person in the cure of souls.

It was in the interest of applying the Gospel to the peculiar ills of the day that the Lutheran Reformation came into being. Luther's contribution to religious truth was made in the interest of the cure of souls. Because of his keen perception into the nature of his own spiritual ills, he was able to put his finger on the sickness of his society. Luther's own descriptive word for his spiritual suffering—*Anfechtung*—defies translation. Tribulation, temptation, anguish, despair—all are involved, and yet each falls far short as a synonym. In the opinion of Gordon Rupp, *Anfechtung* is an existential word since it concerns man as he grapples with himself and his universe.[5]

[5] Gordon Rupp, *The Righteousness of God* (New York: Philosophical Lib., 1953), p. 106.

It is man's experience of the tortures implied in being a man before God. Out of such inner grappling, Luther was able to express the living truth. In his own words, "A man becomes a theologian by living, by dying, and by being damned, and not by understanding, reading, and speculating." [6]

Luther saw the illness of the soul as the soul curved in upon itself. Since the soul itself is distorted, all that a person does is distorted to some extent by egocentricity. This radical break with the conception of sin which prevailed in the Church of his day is shown by his commentary on the statement from Ecclesiastes, "There is no man who doeth good and sinneth not." Said Luther, this was the same as saying, "There is no man who sinneth not when he does good." [7] Here is a dynamic understanding of sin. To pass on this heritage from the Reformation by living, dying, and being damned is one thing; to pass it on by intellectual propositions describing this heritage is another. So Kierkegaard in his day, in revolt against the dead orthodoxy of a proposition-centered Church, brought forth a fresh insight into the sickness-unto-death and into the revelation of the God-Man as the existential cure.

The ultimate description of human ills centers in the man-God relationship. The image of God in the Judaeo-Christian heritage is understood dynamically as man in communion with God and, within this communion with God, in communion with his neighbors. This communion is broken by the soul's curving in upon itself—by sin. The *imago Dei* is then lost. The contrast between the perfection of God and the sinfulness of man erects a barrier to all fellowship. And so we have emotional isolation instead of communion, sickness instead of wholeness, death instead of life.

[6] *Ibid.*, p. 227.
[7] *Luther's Works*, XXXII, ed. Helmut T. Lehmann (Philadelphia: Muhlenberg, 1958), 183.

SUFFERING

Suffering is the result of sickness. It is a sign or warning that something is wrong with the way things are functioning. We know this to be true of the body. When we have a pain we know something needs attention. So also of the soul when our suffering is spiritual. Although we have drawn a distinction here between body and soul, it is a distinction which can be justified only for purposes of emphasis. Body and soul are vitally interrelated. Sickness and its suffering, whether centered in body or soul, affect the person as a whole.

Suffering, therefore, is for us rather than against us. Something is already wrong when we are suffering. Some of the most deadly ills are those which give little warning in pain until it is too late. We know this in terms of physical ills all too well. So Bernard of Clairvaux can say regarding spiritual ills, "The worst temptation is to have no temptation," [8] that is, to be aware of no temptation. After defining the sickness-unto-death as despair, Kierkegaard says the worst despair is not to be aware that one is in despair. This situation of not being aware of our ills is not one with which the cure of souls in its narrow sense is directly concerned. In its narrow sense the cure of souls pertains to those who know they are in pain—those who either through the ministry of preaching or the tribulations of life are open to the physician of the soul. Yet it is equally true to say that in the course of curing a soul, the sense of pain may be intensified. Conscious pain may be a defense against a greater though unconscious pain, the greater despair. When this is the case the pastoral relationship must help such a person to descend to this greater despair before any genuine healing can take place. The cure of souls

[8] Rupp, *op. cit.*, p. 115.

can be a strenuous experience for both the person suffering and the pastor.

From the perspective of the Gospel, the most important theological insight into the nature of suffering is that suffering is made to serve the redemptive purposes of God. It is part and parcel with that chastening process which the writer of the letter to the Hebrews says is not "joyous but grievous: nevertheless afterward it yieldeth the peaceable fruit of righteousness [to those who] are exercised thereby" (12:11). This is the theology of the Cross in Christian experience. The suffering of the sick soul culminates in the dying of the old, the crucifixion of the flesh, dying with Christ on his cross. Out of this dying comes the cure. We are made whole by rising with Christ from the dead as new men to live a new life. This happens not once, but again and again as we mature in the Christian life.

We can see, then, why Kierkegaard called faith a turbulent thing. It functions within the dynamic of dying and rising. According to Luther, faith is the gift which purges out our sin. In contrast to grace, which establishes our relationship with God, faith is the gift which is given to us on the basis of this grace and is the activator in the battle against the domination of sin.[9]

Faith is always in tension with the trial of faith. Paul said, "We walk by faith, not by sight" (II Cor. 5:7). Instead of contrasting faith and sight as does Paul, we would rather unite them and walk by faith on the *basis* of sight. Sight can be defined as those tangible evidences of faith's reliability, such as prayers that are answered according to our desires, or the emotionally good feeling that comes when people show us

[9] Based on Luther's exegesis of Rom. 5:15; *Luther's Works* (*ibid.*), pp. 227-229.

appreciation, or the success in our endeavors which moves us to "praise God from whom all blessings flow." These are the times when it is easy to believe. The trial of faith occurs when these evidences and assurances of sight are removed. When faith is in tension with its trials, it is being strengthened in its essential character: saying "Yes" to God when all about would encourage us to say "No." In the words of Paul Tillich, "We can stand the Yes and No of life and truth because we participate in the Yes beyond Yes and No, because we are *in* it, as it is *in* us. We are participants of His resurrection; therefore, we say the ultimate Yes, the Amen beyond *our* Yes and *our* No." [10] Obviously there is a direct connection between the cure of souls and the theology of sanctification.

HEALING

The power for healing the sick soul is in the good news of God's *agape*—the redemption from sin and death effected by the life, death, and resurrection of Christ as this is made real to us by the Holy Spirit. It is significant that Jesus' ministry was a healing ministry for the body as well as for the soul. Always, however, it was healing at the level of the God-man relationship. Reconciliation in this relationship is the source of the faith that makes men whole. It is this healing ministry of Christ which the Church through the power of his Holy Spirit carries forth.

There are other healing arts and sciences based upon different premises; prominent among these is psychoanalysis. In psychoanalysis, particularly as it is associated with the orthodox Freudian school, the ills of the soul are interpreted in

---

[10] Paul Tillich, *The New Being* (New York: Scribner's, 1955), p. 104, based on II Cor. 1:19-20: "For the Son of God, Jesus Christ, whom we preached among you . . . was not Yes and No; but in him it is always Yes. For all the promises of God find their Yes in him."

terms of an inevitable tension between biological urges or psychological impulses on the one hand, and social acceptance on the other. There is no conflict between any objective good and evil, nor any Creator-creature relationship within which to evaluate and interpret human frustrations. Resources for healing are assumed to be indigenous in human nature. Through psychoanalysis this potentiality is realized—the ego or self is strengthened to cope with the opposing forces of the biological and psychological urges (the id) and the pressures to conform to standards for social acceptance (the superego).

These basic presuppositions of psychoanalysis have been refined and put into a religious framework by Erich Fromm, who transfers Freud's discoveries from the sphere of sex to that of interpersonal relations. Fromm is both a prophet and a healer. He sees the human problem in terms of the violation of the fundamental laws of human existence. Healing is accomplished by the release or development of the capacity of the human being to love. God for Fromm is simply the word symbol for love, and the religious humanism which he espouses over against theism is the quest for love to one's neighbor and for a society governed by love among its members.

Another of the healing arts and sciences is that represented by drug therapists. According to their point of view, healing is a matter of creating the necessary changes in body chemistry through drugs or other physical devices. This implies that the sickness of the soul is basically physiological. If this were so, then the self would become a purely biological phenomenon. In the opposing camp are the environmentalists. From their vantage point, problems of soul are created by negative forces in society. These negative forces center in poor economic and educational opportunities for some, and in poor interpersonal relationships in the family and beyond it, for others. Obviously, then, healing comes about through improving the economic, the educational, and the interpersonal environment.

Although their understanding of human ills and of the self differs in essence from the Christian position, the Church today by and large recognizes the value of these healing arts and sciences. The Church only challenges their claim to be the whole answer to the human predicament. In so doing the Church is defending human dignity, for when any of these views is accepted as the sole answer, there is little left of human freedom or even of the human self. Christianity welcomes the scientific data and the contribution to human betterment provided by these sciences and arts, but challenges their fundamental motifs. The Church would incorporate their contributions into a theological dimension in which the God-man relationship is a reality and the *agape*-centered, divinely initiated redemption through Jesus Christ is the ultimate good news, the healing power.

Although the Church in its ministry is vitally interested in promoting mental, emotional, and physical health, healing from a Christian point of view is synonymous with none of these, even though there may be and often are correspondences in these areas. When Jesus said, "Thy faith hath made thee whole," to the individuals whom he had healed (Matt. 9:22; Mark 10:52; Luke 17:19), the implication was that a greater issue is at stake than physical health—an issue evident in his warning, "What doth it profit a man if he gain the whole world and lose his own soul?" (Mark 8:36). Healing from a Christian point of view centers in redemption and reconciliation within the man-God relationship, and healing in this area may not always correspond with an empirical emotional stability.

In other words, a pagan may give every evidence of physical, mental, and emotional health. At the same time, a Christian may not. On the other hand, the emotions are a vital element in human living. So also the ways of mental and physical health are interrelated, and neither is dissociated from the cure of souls. What happens in a person's life affects his whole person. Reconciliation with God is not something that happens in the "soul" to the exclusion of the person as a whole. Healing from a Christian point of view has its repercussions in the person's total life. These repercussions are identified in the New Testament as the fruit of the Holy Spirit. "The fruit of the Spirit is love, joy, peace, patience, kindness, goodness, faithfulness, gentleness, self-control" (Gal. 5:22). Certainly these attributes are not without their positive emotional overtones; therefore they do promote general health. But the emphasis is not on the emotion itself, nor must the attribute prove its existence by any empirical emotionality.

PASTORAL THEOLOGY

The branch of theology which deals with the cure of souls is pastoral theology. All branches of theology have the same basis, the Gospel, but they have different frames of reference. Pastoral theology is function- or operation-centered as differentiated from the more logic-centered branches, such as systematic theology. Each branch includes the other's emphasis, at least by implication, but not as its primary emphasis or frame of reference.[11]

The frame of reference in pastoral theology is the uniting of the healing resources of the Gospel with the soul in need. Indigenous to this frame of reference are the Word of God

[11] For a thorough treatment of these differences, see *Preface to Pastoral Theology* by Seward Hiltner, (New York: Abingdon, 1958), especially pp. 15-29.

and the sacraments, with distinct emphasis on the needs of the sick soul and on the minister of the Church as the physician of the soul. Pastoral theology is based on the necessity for a pastoral ministry beyond that of preaching and teaching to assist those in need to receive the Gospel's healing power. In this capacity the pastor is the representative of the fellowship of believers in its sacramental character.

When his disciples pointed to the sacrifices they were making in following him, Jesus said, "Truly, I say to you, there is no one who has left house or brothers or sisters or mother or father or children or lands, for my sake and for the gospel, who will not receive a hundredfold now in this time, houses and brothers and sisters and mothers and children and lands, with persecutions, and in the age to come eternal life" (Mark 10:24-30). This promise is fulfilled in the fellowship of believers, the Church. The Church as the fellowship provides the clothing for Word and Sacrament. It makes tangible the grace of God and, by doing so, works as a counteractive to the offense, the *skandalon,* of the Gospel. The good news may be too good. A love given unconditionally may seem morally wrong to one who has been accustomed to a conditional type of love based upon the law of just deserts. Even though he subscribes to the Gospel intellectually, he may be unable to receive it emotionally. In the fellowship of believers this love of God becomes incarnate, for the Church is the body of Christ. What one may not have been able to receive as a theological abstraction, he can now receive through the concrete demonstration of, or at least a human reflection of, that love within the fellowship. In the cure of souls this fellowship is concentrated in the person of the pastor. It is the highway of personal relationship through

which the Holy Spirit prepares the way for the coming of the
Lord in his scandalous Gospel.

To accomplish its purpose, pastoral theology utilizes the
data of the social and personality sciences. Since it is a
theology which functions through a personal relationship, it
can receive valuable help from those sciences which deal with
interpersonal relationships. There is always the danger, however, that what is incorporated may become the incorporator
—that the price of receiving help from the sciences will be
that the fundamental motif of our pastoral care becomes psychological or sociological rather than theological. To prevent
this the good news of God's redemption in Christ must remain
central in all pastoral activity. When the Gospel is the
dominant motif, all of the elements in the process, regardless
of their origin or past usage, are characterized by this basic
dynamic. Incorporated into a theological framework these
data from the personality sciences serve the purposes of the
Gospel ministry in the cure of souls. The realm of nature
(science) and the realm of grace (revelation) are made one
in Christ.

If pastoral theology differs in its basic motif from the
ideologies of other therapies, it differs also in its aims. The
statement "Thy faith hath made thee whole" implies something beyond healing in its outlook, namely, a faith to live
by. If pastoral theology differs in its aims from other therapies,
so also ought it to differ in its results. Since aims and results
are based on the centrality of redemption in the cure of souls,
aims and results center in a new orientation of the creature
to the Creator which is called the new creation in Christ Jesus.
The new creation, or new being, lives by faith in the living
God, the faith which makes one whole. "Whole" then means
that a human being is not fully a human being until he is in

a fellowship of faith with his Creator. In other words, aims
and results center in the restoration of the divine image, the
imago Dei.

The techniques in the cure of souls are the result of the
aims. On the one hand, these techniques show their indebted-
ness to the personality sciences for an understanding of personal dynamics in the therapeutic relationship. On the other
hand, the same techniques show that they belong to the cure
of souls by virtue of the theological dimension within which
they construe the therapeutic relationship. As an example,
we can take the techniques of pastoral counseling, a specific
and fundamental pastoral ministry in the cure of souls. Pastoral counseling has as its over-all aim the unearthing of the
destructive emotions of guilt, anxiety, hostility, and despair,
and the resolving of them in the Gospel through interpersonal
relationship. To accomplish this over-all aim pastoral counseling has four intermediate aims. The first of these is to
encourage the counselee to share his inner feelings. The appropriate techniques are those methods of pastoral communication which would stimulate this sharing. But the need to
share with the pastor is also the need to share with God. The
second aim is to communicate acceptance to the person who
is sharing. The techniques, accordingly, are methods for
conveying this acceptance. But the need to receive acceptance
from the pastor is the need also to receive acceptance from
God. The third aim is to help in the understanding of the
problem and its solution. The techniques, therefore, are these
methods of communication which encourage the counselee to
bring out into the open that which he is coming to perceive,
even though dimly. But the reception of insight is always
associated with the belief in the presence and guidance of
God. The fourth aim is to establish a personal relationship

which will be an incentive for growth. The techniques in this case are methods which help one to help himself. But the need for a personal bond with the pastor is the need also for union with God. The transfer in the relationship is easily apparent. As a transfer from the pastor to God it is an example of the function of the fellowship of believers as a whole. However, it is not a transfer which dispenses with the human bond, but a transfer, rather, which alters the structure of this bond from that of a dependence which hinders fellowship to that of a dependence within fellowship.

At the basis of the pastoral counseling process is a non-verbal communication of the Gospel which introduces the Gospel by way of human experience. Upon this non-verbal foundation the verbal communication of the Gospel may come about. To say this marks a break with our previous fixation upon verbalization. Here the essential means for communication is the interpersonal relationship. The fact that the minister is a pastor of the Church, a Christian minister representing a Gospel of God's *agape,* does not have to be verbalized by the minister before it can become a determining influence in the character of the relationship. As the counselee communicates his problem to the pastor, the pastor communicates understanding and acceptance to the counselee. The result is a relationship through which the Holy Spirit can work to change the dynamics within the persons. The use of the verbal communication of the Gospel in the interview is a matter of timing, to be decided by the pastor. He must perceive, within the existential moment, when the counselee needs to have the Gospel verbalized and when the counselee is ready for such verbalization.

The point at which contemporary pastoral theology differs most from its predecessors is its formulation as an operation-centered theology. This formulation has tended to add consistency and clarity to the discipline and so the discipline has become easier to teach and to learn. Even though the contemporary approach is identified with the present age, the old familiar landmarks in the cure of souls remain. In fact we may say that the age-old religious therapies have been both enlarged and intensified. We may take, as an example, confession and absolution. If redemption is at the center of the cure of souls, it is necessary that confession and absolution play a leading role in the current approach. Our present understanding of therapeutic communication ought to be a help to us in increasing both the depth and efficiency of confession. In addition, our present understanding both of the nature and value of an acceptive human relationship ought to help us in providing a strong non-verbal buttress to the verbal communication of God's acceptance.

There is also the familiar landmark in the cure of souls known as the "consolation of the brethren." In the current approach this ministry of brotherly comfort is carried out by means of the Word of God and the Sacrament and prayer, as it has been in the past. But now we have the benefit of understanding the person's need to express his feelings, even his resentment, before consolation can be realized. Now we understand, too, the value of an empathetic relationship and the means for establishing it with the person who needs consolation. Finally, we understand better than before how to use the Bible and the Sacrament and prayer in tune with the dynamics of the interview and the person's openness to receive. For the problem is not whether God is willing to give comfort, but whether we are ready to receive it.

PASTORAL ACTS

Since it is a function of the pastoral ministry, the cure of souls is related to traditional pastoral acts, notably, weddings, baptisms, and funerals. Through the wedding the Church and its ministry have the opportunity to establish a bond with the marital union at its beginning. This is most important, since marital discord ranks number one in the problems of a parish. The significance of the pastor to the wedding and of the wedding to the couple helps to create a support which may do much to sustain and to prosper the marriage. The pastor establishes this therapeutic tie not simply by having one or more sessions with the couple in premarital orientation, as important and indispensable as this activity is. He establishes the therapeutic tie, rather, by relating himself as a pastor to the couple both before the wedding and after it, so that the wedding itself orients the marriage to God, and thereby prepares a vital role in the marriage for the Church and its ministry. Not only will this orientation help in the avoidance of marital pitfalls, but it will bring the couple to the resources of the Church and its Gospel should the marriage bond be threatened.

As the sacrament of initiation into the fellowship of reconciliation which is created by the Gospel, baptism is itself inseparable from the fellowship into which the baptized person is received. The practice of infant baptism with its emphasis on the family shows the close connection of the Gospel to the family unit, and of the family unit to the congregation. In baptism the Church and her ministry have a tie with the child and his family. The vows which the sponsors take for the child, to provide for his instruction in the Christian faith, show the interdependence of the sacrament and the Word of God. They also show the ongoing process of Christian nurture which baptism initiates. The family atmosphere of inter-personal relationships is a powerful influence for the development of sick or healthy souls. Consequently the pastoral ministry must have a distinctly family-centered as well as person-centered emphasis. This emphasis is manifested in the administration of baptism, as the child is brought by the family to the Church to be received into the fellowship which unites the family and the Church with one another and with God. Whether it is administered to an infant or an adult, baptism is the focal point of the pastor's ministry in the cure of souls, since as an initiatory means of grace it symbolizes and conveys the reconciliation which heals.

The funeral represents the critical hour for the soul, as the loss of a loved one threatens to be a loss also of life's meaning. The bereaved are confronted with life's ultimate questions. Theirs is the shock of lostness, the anguish of loneliness, and the anxiety of non-being. As the religious ceremony in this time of crisis, the funeral gives to the Church and its Gospel of the Resurrection a dominant place in the issues of life and death. The pastor's ministry of consolation to the bereaved in preparation for the funeral and at the funeral gives the occasion for the pastor's ministry to the grieving following the funeral. We know now, perhaps better than in any other age, how important it is for the grieving to talk out their grief. Grief work, as it is called, cannot be avoided; it can only be postponed. In expressing to the pastor his wounded feelings, the grieving person is sharing with one who represents the very faith which he, the grieving one, needs in order to endure his loss. It is when these obstacles in its way are brought out into the open that the full meaning of the funeral message may take hold.

TEAMWORK

Since the human being is a unity in spite of his diversity
in body, mind, and spirit, human ills cannot be relegated to
any one phase of human existence, but must rather be viewed
in regard to their effect upon the total person. This means
that there may be more than one front at which the battle
against an illness may be waged, even as there may be more
than one area in which the trouble breaks out. Although the
pastor is not the therapist for these other areas in the life of
the human being, he recognizes that therapy in these other
areas is not unrelated to the cure of souls. Nor is his own
ministry to the soul unrelated to the health of the body and
the mind, or to the welfare of one's family, social, and vocational life.

Accordingly it should be obvious that God may well work
through these other non-pastoral therapies in order to benefit
the total person. To recognize this fact involves no surrender
of the pastoral responsibility, but a realization of the complexity of human problems and of our limitations as pastors
to deal with this complexity at every front. Help on any front
by the respective therapist for that problem may benefit the
total person, even in his religious outlook. Since man is a
totality in all of his activities, each of his areas of expression
has a religious significance. The pastor's role in the cure of
souls adds the theological dimension in which the person sees
the whole of life—including what is happening to him in the
other therapies. While the pastor is incapable of dealing with
all the highly specialized ways in which soul sickness may
break out, he is capable and indispensable in ministering at
a theological level, which in turn broadens and unifies the
results of other therapies. So the pastor works together with
the physician, the nurse, the psychiatrist, the clinical psychol-

ogist, and the social and family caseworker in his ministry to people. He looks upon them as members of a healing team of which he is an indispensable member. He recognizes the value of each in his specialty and appreciates their recognition of him as a vital member of the team.

CONCLUSION

We are living in a great day for realizing the Gospel's potential for healing in all areas of living and in all the relationships of life, including the relationship to one's self. The social and personality sciences have been a genuine asset in this realization. But what finally results from our utilizing these sciences will be only a caricature of a healthy soul unless we utilize them within the perspective, the motif, of God's redemptive *agape*. Otherwise, the current approach in the cure of souls will result in the mere assumption of character traits and not in a new person. Only the Gospel can convert a person from his egocentricity to a genuine humility. Out of this basic change in the person develop the changes in attributes: only now do the changes occur at the center, in the motivations and not only in the manifestations.

SUGGESTIONS FOR FURTHER READING

BELGUM, DAVID. *Clinical Pastoral Training*. Philadelphia: Westminster, 1955.

HULME, WILLIAM E. *Counseling and Theology*. Philadelphia: Muhlenberg, 1956.

JOHNSON, PAUL E. *Personality and Religion*. New York: Abingdon, 1957.

OATES, WAYNE. *The Bible in Pastoral Care*. Philadelphia: Westminster, 1953.

OUTLER, ALBERT C. *Psychotherapy and the Christian Message*. New York: Harper, 1954.

WISE, CARROLL. *Pastoral Counseling*. New York: Harper, 1951.

WYNN, J. C. *Pastoral Ministry to Families*. Philadelphia: Westminster, 1957.

Chapter 7

THE SACRAMENTS

By Edward C. Fendt

Throughout Christendom, interest in the sacraments has revived during the last three decades. This revival was certain to come sooner or later. Traditional arguments between Rome and Protestantism were being scrutinized for their theological and historical accuracy and could no longer be pursued as uncritically as before. Research and discussion exposed misunderstandings in both groups and demanded re-evaluation of both sides of the issue.

The sacraments have always, especially since the Reformation, been a subject of intense disagreement. Not only have Protestants rejected the Roman Catholic teachings concerning mass and sacrifice, but they have disagreed among themselves about the importance and function of the Sacrament of the Altar in the life of the Church. Within Protestantism, the baptism of infants has been questioned and, by some, rejected as irrelevant or even unbiblical.

When the ecumenical discussions began several decades ago, the various groups in Protestantism and Eastern Orthodoxy were under compulsion to explain to each other their particular emphases in all areas of doctrine. At no point was there greater divergence than in the area of the sacraments. Compromise and synthesis were impossible. The reasons for disagreement lay deeper than the mere definition of a sacrament or the place assigned to a sacrament by a church. Rather, the disagreements involved the entire areas of christology and soteriology, and more particularly the doctrine of the Church.

It is the restudy of the doctrine of the Church which seems to have set the dogmas of the sacraments in clear focus for our generation. This restudy has resulted in some salutary observations for every church to ponder. Every church is being forced anew to re-examine its understanding of the sacraments in the light of the New Testament and the life of the Early Church, as these have been rediscovered by modern exegetical research.

CHRIST AND THE SACRAMENTS

Modern exegesis of the New Testament has disclosed the inseparable union between Christ and his Church. The Incarnation did not cease with the resurrection or enthronement of our Lord. He remains incarnate forever. The death and resurrection of Christ, as events in New Testament history, are described as those acts by which the risen and ascended Lord continues to accomplish his high priestly function until he returns for the consummation of his kingdom.

The risen and exalted Lord remains the head of his Church on earth as well as in heaven. Through his Spirit he dwells in the Church and makes the Church his instrument for extending his kingdom. He entrusts to the Church the administration of his means of grace, which he himself instituted and through which he conveys and bestows the benefits of his incarnation, cross, resurrection, and ascension. Through the means of grace he acts to bring men into his kingdom and keep them in it. He imparts himself, with all the blessings attending his activity in behalf of men. In this continuing act of giving himself, the sacraments are important channels of bestowal. Without them there would always be a question as to how his grace is personalized and individualized. It is through the sacraments that the grace of God in Christ—addressed to all and to everyman in the Gospel—becomes the personal possession of the individual Christian.

It is "into his death" that the members of the Church were baptized, "so that as Christ was raised from the dead by the glory of the Father, we too might walk in newness of life" (Rom. 6:3, 4). "For as many of you as were baptized into Christ have put on Christ" (Gal. 3:27). The New Testament ascribes more than symbolic significance to baptism. According to the New Testament, baptism is effective in incorporating the person into the organism of Christ and his Church, in which the baptized Christian shares the life of Christ. "For if we have been united with him in a death like his, we shall certainly be united with him in a resurrection like his." (Rom. 6:5). The person baptized is united with Christ and enjoys all the benefits of Christ's incarnation, death, and resurrection.

Baptism is regarded in the New Testament as the rite of initiation into membership in the Church. It is never in question whether a person qualifies for baptism. Every human being, as soon as he comes into existence, is in need of it. In baptism Christ makes a person the beneficiary of a universal atonement, and unless the baptismal covenant is then or later invalidated by the person's unbelief or rejection, it remains in force forever. In baptism, moreover, the Holy Spirit is given. All the activities of the Spirit effecting the redemption and salvation of the person, including the Spirit's bestowal of anticipation "for the glory that is to be revealed," begin for that person in baptism. Thus baptism not only unites with Christ, but also brings the baptized person into the unity of Christ's redemptive work.

The Lord's Supper was given by Christ to his Church as the sacrament of union between himself and all the members of his Church, not only individual communicants but all communicants together, both those in the church triumphant and those in the church militant. Through this sacrament, as he himself instituted it, he continues his presence in the Church in the body broken and the blood shed for the remission of sins (his death and resurrection), and he invites to the common feast all the members of his Church awaiting his return for the consummation of his kingdom.

From the New Testament, the Church receives Christ's witness as to the place and function of the Lord's Supper in the life of the Church. It is the sacrament in which he is to be remembered and received as the One who died on the Cross for the sins of the world and who will come again as the Lord in glory. Thus commemorating and receiving its Lord until he comes again is the Church's privilege and responsibility.

The Sacrament points back to the Cross and the Resurrection and forward to his return in glory to establish "a new earth in which righteousness dwells" (II Pet. 3:13). Through the Sacrament Christ imparts himself to the communicant—as savior and as judge—in the bread and wine used. "The cup of blessing which we bless, is it not a participation in the blood of Christ? The bread which we break, is it not a participation in the body of Christ?" (I Cor. 10:16). It is not only the presence of Christ through the Spirit in the midst of the congregation celebrating the Sacrament, but also the presence of his body and blood in the bread and wine of the Sacrament, on which the New Testament focuses attention.

The presence and gift of Christ's body broken and his blood shed, as these are received in the Sacrament of the Altar,

guarantee and seal the forgiveness of sins and life with him
to every believing communicant. To those united with him,
he thus gives his verdict as their judge as well as his forgiveness and life as their savior.

Another aspect of Christ's judgment is included in the New
Testament description of the Lord's Supper. The unworthy
receive his condemnation. "For any one who eats and drinks
without discerning the body [of the Lord] eats and drinks
judgment upon himself" (I Cor. 11:29). Just as in absolution
there is no forgiveness but only retention of sin for those who
persist in their impenitence and unbelief, so also in the Lord's
Supper. For the person who does not believe the words of
the Lord, "given and shed for you for the remission of sins,"
there is no promise of forgiveness.

The Sacrament of the Altar remains the table of the Lord.
Christ himself is the host. No church can claim the table as
its own and transform the sacramental purpose to suit its own
peculiar ambitions or prejudices without violating the intent
of the host. Yet this is what has happened in Christendom,
and this has become and remains the churches' *skandalon*.

THE CHURCH AND THE SACRAMENT OF BAPTISM

In the case of baptism, the Church soon experienced universal agreement concerning the sacrament's importance and
efficacy. It was generally regarded as the sacrament of initiation and no one was considered a member of the Church
unless and until he had been baptized.

While there is no specific command in the New Testament
to baptize infants, it is very clear from the literature of the
Early Church that infants were baptized. Baptism was regarded as something more than a service of dedication or a
public profession of faith. It was universally regarded as an

act of Christ performed through the Church, uniting with Christ the one who was baptized and thus making him a member of the Church and bestowing upon him all the privileges of that fellowship.

The mode of baptism did not become a controversial issue until the Reformation. Similarly it was not until the Reformation that questions arose about the baptizing of infants. The emphasis on baptism as the sacrament conveying membership in Christ's kingdom remained in the Church's teaching and life until the Reformation. At that time some issues arose concerning baptism, for which Protestantism must plead guilty.

As Protestantism and Rome struggled over the function of faith in the process of salvation, some Protestant extremists interpreted faith as a prerequisite for salvation in such a way that they questioned whether infants could qualify. Such reasoning led to two alternatives, either: (1) to delay baptism until the candidate was old enough both to believe what was taught him and to give expression to his faith, or (2) to assert that the infant did in fact qualify for baptism by virtue of the faith which baptism created in him. Both viewpoints shifted the emphasis in baptism. Instead of the Lord's promise and bestowal of grace, which demand central attention, the candidate's personal qualification assumed the position of prominence.

Conversely, the emphasis on faith was to detract from the importance of grace, thus calling into question the whole matter of sacramental grace. The sacraments soon were regarded as symbolic of grace otherwise received, rather than as effective conveyors of grace hereby bestowed. The emphasis shifted from the divine initiative and divine activity in the sacraments to the believer's reception of and reaction to the

Lord's command and promise regarding the sacraments. In some Protestant groups, baptism was no longer regarded as necessary for membership in the Church because faith in Christ, the one thing necessary, could be effected through hearing the Gospel. The Lord's Supper became a memorial rite, and an annual observance of it was considered sufficient compliance with the Lord's command.

In the Lutheran tradition, the necessity of baptism for incorporation into the body of Christ has remained intact, as has the baptism of infants. When compelling voices in other Protestant circles questioned the propriety of baptizing infants who had no prospect of Christian nurture and discipline by their parents, the Lutheran answer was clear: Responsibility centers in the congregation where the baptism takes place and the Church under whose auspices it is performed. The ancient custom of having sponsors, men and women in good standing in the congregation (in addition to the parents themselves), was retained to insure proper rearing of the baptized children. Such sponsors not only speak for the child at the service of baptism, but promise to see that the child, as soon as it can learn what a solemn promise has been made in its name, will be reared in the baptismal covenant.

This practice of having sponsors at the baptism of infants has undergone some changes in recent years. In some Lutheran parishes, the parents themselves may be the sponsors. Or the parents may stand alongside other sponsors and answer the questions addressed to the sponsors. In some of the older churches, the sponsors present the child for baptism and the parents remain in the background.

Two fundamental aspects of the Church's practice in the baptism of infants remain as important considerations: (1) The parents, whether formally serving as sponsors or not, are obligated to rear their baptized child in the Christian faith, and (2) the congregation in which the baptism takes place must consider the baptized infant a member who comes under the congregation's pastoral care.

The Church provides instruction in the Christian faith and life from early childhood to the age of confirmation. In the rite of confirmation the baptized child makes his own confession of faith and promise of faithfulness as a member of the Church. Preconfirmation instruction and confirmation continue in the Lutheran churches' program of pastoral care for baptized children. The roots of this practice lie deep in the Old Testament tradition of the covenant people. The Church of the New Testament continued that tradition. The Lutheran Church has found no good reason to deviate from the biblical precedent.

In the Lutheran tradition the rite of confirmation has never assumed sacramental character. However, it has always been a problem in liturgics how to confirm both those confirmands who have previously been baptized and, along with them in the same service, those unbaptized confirmands who must now first be baptized. The danger in such a service is that baptism may appear to be but a means to confirmation, whereas it is baptism itself which must always remain primary.

THE CHURCH AND THE SACRAMENT OF THE ALTAR

The Lord's Supper has remained the culmination of congregational worship in the common service on Sundays and holidays. In some places and periods Lutherans have imitated their Protestant neighbors by disassociating Communion from most of the Sunday services and limiting the observance of the Sacrament to certain days on the church's calendar. In other places the tradition has persisted of having Communion on every Lord's day and holy day. In recent times, throughout Lutheranism, there has been a steady trend toward more frequent observance.

In the Lutheran churches, the custom has persisted of preceding or at least combining the service of Holy Communion with a service of confession and absolution. This custom has provoked some interesting theological questions. Is the purpose of the absolution to make the communicant worthy to receive the sacrament, or is absolution part of the sacrament itself? Why is it necessary to receive the absolution in two forms, verbal and sacramental? Is the reception of the Lord's Supper, in such an arrangement, climax or anticlimax?

The Lutheran dogma on these matters is pertinent. It is the same God who acts in both absolution and Communion, bestowing the same grace of forgiveness in different forms. In the absolution his forgiveness is spoken; in the Sacrament of the Altar it is bestowed through the body and blood of Christ. A generous God conveys his forgiveness to the worshiper in several ways, and the penitent believer never receives the pardoning grace of God too often.

The authority to absolve members of the Church from their sins was given by Christ to his Church. "If you forgive the sins of any, they are forgiven; if you retain the sins of any, they are retained" (John 20:23). It is not clear from the New Testament whether the exercise of this authority was limited to the pastoral office or was made incumbent on every member of the Church. It was given to the Church, the *una sancta,* "the universal priesthood of believers," but the development of the administration of this power was left to the Church. There are instances in apostolic times where absolution belonged to the pastoral office, but there is also good reason to conclude that any Christian was authorized to absolve another.

Absolution soon came to be regarded as a sacrament in the post-apostolic era. Thus it became a fixed function exercised primarily through the clergy. It became one of the chief duties of those performing pastoral care. Even though Lutherans do not regard absolution as a sacrament on a level with baptism and Holy Communion, they have retained it in their liturgy, and the administration of absolution centers in the ordained clergy.

After the prayer of confession, in the order for public confession, the pastor says: "As a Minister of the Church of Christ, and by his authority, I therefore declare unto you who do truly repent and believe in him, the entire forgiveness of all your sins . . . On the other hand, by the same authority, I declare unto the impenitent and unbelieving, that so long as they continue in their impenitence, God hath not forgiven their sins, and will assuredly visit their iniquities upon them, if they turn not from their evil ways, and come to true repentance and faith in Christ, ere the day of grace be ended." [1]

Intercommunion remains a problem. For Lutherans, "It becomes very doubtful whether any theory that falls short of the Lutheran doctrine . . . will adequately explain the utterance of St. Paul in reference to the Eucharist." [2] Lutherans are reluctant to compromise their understanding of the purpose and essence of the Sacrament by joining in its celebration with other, doctrinally different Christian groups. Anglicans are concerned that the Sacrament be administered legitimately, and to safeguard legitimacy there is the apostolic succession. Lutherans, on the other hand, are more concerned with the correct doctrine of the Sacrament. They regard unity of faith

---

[1] *Service Book and Hymnal of the Lutheran Church in America* (Philadelphia, 1958), p. 252.

[2] Principal Andrews as quoted in P. T. Forsyth, *The Church and the Sacraments* (London: Independent, 1953), p. 163.

(in the Lord's promises in this sacrament) and agreement in doctrine as essential to sacramental participation.

Anders Nygren has written an apt comment on the entire problem of intercommunion in Christendom:

> We must not exaggerate the extent of this division. Even where two Church communions refuse the fellowship of the Lord's Supper to one another and believe themselves unable to meet with one another at the Lord's Table, they yet cannot dissolve the fellowship that exists in the fact that both—each for itself—partake of the one loaf: "Because there is one loaf, we who are many are one body, for we all partake of the same loaf" (I Cor. 10:17). . . . The *skandalon* of Christendom consists, not in its lack of fellowship in holy communion, for this exists and can never be broken, but in the lack of actualization of this fellowship in the life of the Church. That the unity exists, but that we ourselves retard and hinder it from actualization, this is our *skandalon*.[3]

In the past quarter century, noteworthy developments have taken place in the intercommunion of some Lutheran churches with other Protestant Churches. The Lutheran churches in India contributed to the agreements which the Church of South India reached in formulating its liturgy. The Lutheran and Reformed churches in the Netherlands have established intercommunion. The (Lutheran) Church of Denmark and the Church of Scotland have agreed on a basis of intercommunion. A recent report from theologians in the Lutheran, Reformed, and Union Churches in Germany suggests a theological basis for intercommunion among these churches. In all of these developments the emphasis has remained on the sacramental character of the Lord's Supper, wherein Christ imparts himself to the communicant within the congregation of believers ready to receive him. The theses for intercommunion stress the positive and usually omit any rejection of

---

[3] Anders Nygren, *Christ and His Church,* trans. Alan Carlsten (Philadelphia: Westminster, 1956), pp. 122-123. Used by permission.

doctrinal positions previously held by the negotiating groups. By the ultraconservatives this method is questioned, but by the more ecumenically minded this method is welcomed as a fruit of the Spirit's work in the unity of the Church.

CONCLUSION

For Lutherans, the significance of the sacraments in the life of the Church may be characterized, in general terms, as evangelical and ecclesiastical. Evangelically, the sacraments are the bestowal and reception of the grace of God in Christ. They point to the "Christ for us" who through the sacraments becomes the "Christ in us."

In discussions of Holy Communion among ecumenical gatherings, there is increasing interest in designating it as sacrifice. Lutheran theologians always relate this term to the death of Christ on Calvary. The Savior who sacrificed himself, who became the sacrifice to God for the sins of the world, still comes as that sacrifice to each communicant at the Communion table, giving him his body and blood in which he accomplished the redemption of mankind. The emphasis is not on what the communicants present as a sacrifice, but on his sacrifice sacramentally given.

The promises of Christ and the New Testament witness regarding both sacraments are taken seriously, and every effort is made to exclude addition to or departures from the *ipsissima verba,* the words of institution, in either sacrament. This loyalty to the Lord also underlies the decisions regarding the elements used in both sacraments, to use what Christ himself used or assumed would be used when he instituted the sacraments—water in baptism and unleavened bread and wine in Holy Communion. Lutheran congregations find it difficult to substitute other bread or unfermented grape juice for that which was customary and used by the Lord.

The concern for the sacraments is also ecclesiastical. The sacraments were given by the Lord to the Church. They are not the possession of individual Christians nor do they belong only to certain Christians. They belong to the whole Church and to each congregation of believers in the Church. The administration of the sacraments in the Lutheran tradition is therefore placed within the congregation. Unless a sacrament is administered under the auspices or supervision of an established congregation there is a question about proper observance or responsible pastoral care. It does not seem likely that the Lutheran position will change to advocate baptisms under private or personal auspices, apart from congregational responsibility, or to initiate and participate in the administration of Holy Communion under highly questionable conditions. Lutherans do not regard the Eucharist as the means or the goal of Christian unity. Agreement in the Gospel and the right administration of the sacraments remain the road on which Lutherans prefer to travel toward Christian unity.

SUGGESTIONS FOR FURTHER READING

ALTHAUS, PAUL. *Was ist die Taufe?* Göttingen: Vandenhoeck und Ruprecht, 1950.

AULÉN, GUSTAF. *Eucharist and Sacrifice,* trans. ERIC H. WAHLSTROM. Philadelphia: Muhlenberg, 1958.

BAILLIE, DONALD. *The Theology of the Sacraments.* New York: Scribner's, 1957.

BARTH, KARL. *The Teaching of the Church Regarding Baptism,* trans. ERNEST PAYNE. London: SCM, 1948.

BRILIOTH, YNGVE. *Eucharistic Faith and Practice,* trans. A. G. HEBERT. London: SPCK, 1930.

CULLMANN, OSCAR. *Baptism in the New Testament,* trans. J. K. S. REID. Chicago: Regnery, 1950.

SASSE, HERMANN. *This Is My Body.* Minneapolis: Augsburg, 1959.

WORLD COUNCIL OF CHURCHES COMMISSION ON FAITH AND ORDER. *One Lord, One Baptism.* Minneapolis: Augsburg, 1960.

Chapter 8

THE MISSION OF THE CHURCH

By Fredrik A. Schiotz

It was a fearful and hopeless group of disciples our Lord found when he rose from the dead. He proceeded to release them from their paralysis through a search of the Scriptures. Luke reports from the conversation with Cleopas and his friend on the road to Emmaus that "beginning with Moses and all the prophets, [Jesus] interpreted to them in all the scriptures the things concerning himself" (Luke 24:27).

'MISSION IN THE OLD TESTAMENT

We have no record of the details of Jesus' explication to Cleopas and his friend, but its essential outline is easily discernible in the Old Testament. The conflict between righteousness and unrighteousness began with the story of creation and the Fall. The failure of mankind to respond to the divine promises moved God to call Abraham and to enter into a covenant with him. The covenant became the foundation for the doctrine of Israel as the people of God. God, the Ruler and King, the Powerful One, brought them out of Egypt and made them his peculiar people.

But Israel was disobedient and provoked God to judgment. The peculiar people now became "the remnant," an eschatological community who would survive the judgment on Israel. The prophets identified this new community with the

132

coming of the Messiah. The rabbinic exegesis of the Old Testament interpreted the prophetic predictions as pointing to the "days of the Messiah," the expected time when God would visit his people with judgment and blessing. Jeremiah, in speaking of the new covenant by which the true Israel is to be constituted, said: ". . . they shall all know me, from the least of them to the greatest, says the Lord" (Jer. 31:34). In Isaiah, the prophet cried out: "Awake, awake; put on thy strength, O Zion; put on thy beautiful garments, O Jerusalem, . . . Ye have sold yourselves for nought; and ye shall be redeemed without money. . . . Therefore my people shall know my name: therefore they shall know in that day that I am he that doth speak: behold, it is I" (Isa. 52:1, 3, 6 A.V.). This "I am he" becomes Jesus' solemn affirmation of the finality of the Christ (John 8:28; 13:19).

The call to Abraham restricted the covenant community. The Gentiles stood on the outside and could enter only as proselytes. But this very constriction was to the end that all might be reached. God's concern for all people was comprehended in the very call which created a covenant Israel: ". . . in thee shall all families of the earth be blessed."

This concern for *all* people while the plan of salvation unfolds in Israel is frequently reflected in the Old Testament. It may be seen in the stories of Ruth and Jonah. In Solomon's prayer dedicating the temple, the compassion for the Gentile overflows. Such Psalms as 2, 67, and 72 are similarly clear and specific. The prophets, too, give frequent voice to a compassion that looks beyond Israel. See Isa. 45:22; 52:10; 55:5; Jer. 16:19; Zech. 9:10; Mal. 1:11.

MISSION IN THE NEW TESTAMENT

Archibald Hunter has characterized the theme of the New

Testament as "'Heilsgeschichte,' the story of salvation."[1] This story, he has pointed out, is chiefly three things: a savior, a saved people, and the means of salvation.

The New Testament calls the story of salvation the "kerygma," the proclamation of the coming of God's redemptive rule in Jesus Christ. The word kerygma may signify either the act of proclamation or the thing proclaimed. The second meaning is the more common in the New Testament. The Gospel is the proclamation of an event: the coming of Christ, his death and resurrection and redemptive rule.

In this New Testament story of salvation, the proclamation of a Savior and a message of salvation imply a saved community, the people of God, the *ecclesia.* Whether or not Jesus actually used the Aramaic equivalent of *ecclesia,* his words and action indicated an intent to create a new "people of God."

The new people of God is implied in Jesus' frequent reference to himself as the Good Shepherd. The Gospels show him as one who is concerned with a "flock," whose mission is to gather "lost sheep." He willingly lays down his life for the sheep (John 10:15). The purpose of his dying is "to gather into one the children of God who are scattered abroad" (John 11:52). The teaching about the shepherd and his sheep was clearly grasped by the apostles. Peter observes, "For you were straying like sheep, but have now returned to the Shepherd and Guardian of your souls" (I Pet. 2:25). The writer of Hebrews explicitly points to the death of the shepherd as the foundation for a new covenant (Heb. 13:20).

Perhaps the most concrete evidence of Jesus' activity in creating the new people of God was the calling of the twelve

---

[1] Archibald M. Hunter, *Message of the New Testament* (Philadelphia: Westminster, 1944), p. 11.

apostles. In the very number twelve—the number of the tribes of Israel—Jews were alerted to the messianic program. The twelve were taught and commissioned to go forth to others. In the Last Supper the new covenant was formally proclaimed: "And he took the cup, and when he had given thanks, he gave it to them: and they all drank of it. And he said unto them, This is my blood of the new testament, which is shed for many" (Mark 14:23-24 A.V.). The twelve now became the core community of the new Israel, the *ecclesia* of God.

After the death and resurrection of Jesus, the core community became a growing flock to which the Lord added daily "such as should be saved" (Acts 2:47 A.V.). No longer does one have to infer that believers are the new community. The first chapter of Acts calls the followers of Christ the *ecclesia*. Hunter concludes, "The Christians' choice of that word expressed their claim to be the true people of God at once old and new." [2]

The identification of the followers of Christ with the Church, found in Acts, is accepted and elaborated by Paul. He believed that life in the Spirit marked the Church as being the true "Israel of God" (Gal. 6:15-16). The supernatural messianic community promised by the prophets for the last days (Isa. 4:3-5; Ezek. 37:12-14; Mal. 3:16-17; 4:1-2) was fulfilled in the Church.

We have observed that the messianic community promised by the prophets is fulfilled in the New Testament Church. In the Church the concern for all people which shimmers across the pages of the Old Testament breaks out in the full-orbed light of the New Testament. To be sure, Jesus' teaching and healing were pretty well confined to the Jews. Except for the Samaritan woman at the well of Sychar, the Gentiles who

² *Ibid.*, p. 68.

received his attention got it only by seeking him out. But his concern for the Gentiles was never in doubt. Nicodemus was reminded that "God so loved the *world* . . . that *whosoever* believeth in him should . . . have everlasting life" (John 3:16 A.V.) (italics added). As Jesus looked to the end of history, he taught "that many shall come from the east and west, and shall sit down with Abraham, and Isaac, and Jacob, in the kingdom of heaven" (Matt. 8:11 A.V.). Observe further the reference to the Ninevites, the Queen of Sheba, Tyre and Sidon, and the Land of Sodom (Matt. 11:20-24; 12:41-42). The great judgment scene in Matthew, chapter 25, pictures "all nations" as gathered before His throne.

As Jesus approached his Passion, the full scope of God's concern for the Gentiles unfolded. All the Gospels show that the mission to the Gentiles follows the death and resurrection of the Messiah. In the last chapter of each of the Four Gospels, the object of concern is all people. Jesus made this unmistakably clear in his instruction of Cleopas and his friend: "Then opened he their understanding, that they might understand the scriptures, And said unto them, Thus it is written, and thus it behoved Christ to suffer, and to rise from the dead the third day: And that repentance and remission of sins should be preached in his name among *all nations,* beginning at Jerusalem" (Luke 24:45-47) (italics added).

The initial response of the disciples to this broad outreach to all people was hesitant and faltering. But it was definitely there from the day of Pentecost. In his sermon on that day Peter declares: "The promise is unto you, and to your children," and then adds, "and to *all that are afar off,* even as many as the Lord our God shall call" (Acts 2:39 A.V.). (italics added). Whatever hesitance there may have been on Peter's part to accept the full significance of his own words was washed out in the vision granted him on the housetop of Simon the tanner in Joppa (Acts 10:9-48).

Paul never doubted that the mission of the *ecclesia* was to all people. While he retained the idea that some "advantage" accrued to the Jew (Rom. 3:1) and that salvation was for "the Jew first" (Rom. 1:16), he would tolerate no limitations on who might participate in the Church of God. "There is neither Jew nor Greek, there is neither slave nor free, there is neither male nor female; for you are all one in Christ Jesus" (Gal. 3:28).

Perhaps the simplest statement of mission, applicable to all times, is Jesus' word to the disciples: "As the Father has sent me, even so send I you" (John 20:21). Regin Prenter has stated well the implications of this word: "In the New Testament the Church is the means whereby Jesus' ministry is continued after his ascension." [3]

If anyone has any doubt about the specifics involved in the Father's sending of the Son, let him carefully weigh Jesus' announcement at Nazareth: "The Spirit of the Lord is upon me, because he has anointed me to preach good news to the poor. He has sent me to proclaim release to the captives and recovering of sight to the blind, to set at liberty those who are oppressed, to proclaim the acceptable year of the Lord" (Luke 4:18-19). Here is an outlook that makes proclamation of the Gospel the primary mission, but it does not stop there. The welfare of the whole man is also Jesus' concern.

THE CHURCH'S MISSION: LUTHERAN THINKING

If there is any contemporary formulation of thought about the Church's mission which may be designated "Lutheran,"

[3] Regin Prenter in an address to a pastoral conference of the Scandinavian Churches held at Aarhus, Denmark and reported in *Kristelig Dagblad,* August 4, 1959.

presumably it must be gleaned from the reports and papers of meetings where the Lutheran Churches of the world have been substantially represented. The only contemporary meetings which qualify for this designation are the three Assemblies of the Lutheran World Federation.

The Third Assembly (Minneapolis, 1957) met under the theme "Christ Frees and Unites." This theme did not address itself specifically to our topic, the Church's mission. Nevertheless, the fifty-one theses which came out of the Assembly discussion groups said some specific things about Church and about mission.

In a brief, two-sentence thesis the scriptural revelation about the Church was affirmed:

> Through all ages there is one holy catholic and apostolic church, whose head is Jesus Christ. In Him the Father was revealed and to Him the Holy Spirit bears witness, guiding us into all the truth.[4]

The holy catholic and apostolic Church, the body of believers, must be given a form through which it can work, through which its mission can be accomplished. The Minneapolis Assembly declared that the Lutherans find this form in the Lutheran Church:

> The Lutheran confessions claim our allegiance because they not only proclaimed the Gospel in a crucial age of the church's life in accordance with the Scriptures, but they continue to direct us in our understanding of the Scriptures consistent with apostolic tradition (p. 110).

"The church lives by faith in Jesus Christ" (p. 117). The Spirit has been given to the Christian as a "down payment" of his inheritance. The power of the Spirit's presence shows itself "most clearly in the essential activities of the church:

---

[4] *Messages of the Third Assembly, The Lutheran World Federation* (Minneapolis: Augsburg, 1957), p. 109.

worship, mission and *service* to our fellowmen" (p. 118).
The Church's mission is to witness to the Gospel:

Whenever the witness to the Gospel invades the domain of demonic
powers, idolatry and militant or creeping atheism, the ultimate victory
of the Lord is foreshadowed (p. 118).

The Church's mission is also service:

Christ came to the world as a servant. Justified by Him through
faith, we are made free to serve one another by love, and he to whom
much is forgiven, loves much. Christian faith is active in love. "Our
Lord put off the form of God and took on the form of a servant,
that He might draw down our love for him and fasten it on our
neighbor" (Luther) (p. 113).

. . . we are called to translate love and compassion into the structures of justice. In matters of civil liberties and racial integration, of
concern for the uprooted and for people in areas of rapid social
change, and of care for the mentally and physically disabled, our love
fails if it does not materialize in recognition of human rights (pp.
113-114).

THE CHURCH'S MISSION: THE RESPONSE OF THE LUTHERAN CHURCH IN CONTEMPORARY AMERICA

The years since World War II have brought a many-sided
upheaval in American life. Population shifts have been continuous: from the rural sections to the cities, from the inner
city to the suburbs, and from one region of the country to
another. Many city areas have been confronted with an influx
of colored people for the first time. Established congregations
in rural communities and in the inner city have been weakened
and some have been dissolved.

To this welter of change the Church has responded on
many fronts. Commissions and departments of evangelism
have been organized. Through their efforts congregations and
pastors have been sensitized to the need for planned, co-ordinated calling on the unchurched. The September, 1959, meet-

ing of the inter-synodical Lutheran Evangelism Council emphasized that the congregation is alive to its mission when:

1. It recognizes that it is a part of the community;
2. It has a concern for the total well-being of the community;
3. It determines its evangelism approach on the basis of the social and cultural level of the community;
4. It grows and changes with the community.[5]

The implementation of the congregation's missionary concern has received fruitful assistance through the Preaching-Teaching-Reaching missions sponsored by evangelism departments. The P-T-R movement has been studied and put to frequent use outside of the Lutheran family.

Stewardship departments have moved away from the concept that their primary responsibility is to raise the benevolence budgets of the Church. Increasingly the emphasis is on biblical education: a confrontation with the truth that we have been bought with a price. What we are and own belongs to the Head of the Church. In order that this commitment shall not be forgotten, systematic proportionate giving is encouraged. Counselors, usually laymen, are made available to congregations to assist in evangelical self-analysis of mission response.

The call for justice in racial integration and civil liberties received strong support at the annual meeting of the National Lutheran Council in February, 1958. An eight-paragraph "Christian Affirmation on Human Relations" was approved for use in the eight participating churches of the Council.[6] Some Lutheran congregations now include a paragraph in

---

[5] *Minutes of Lutheran Evangelism Council,* Sept. 1-2, 1959 (St. Louis, 1959), p. 3.

[6] *American Missions Together,* Division of American Missions, National Lutheran Council, XII, No. 1 (May, 1958), 11.

letters of call requiring the pastor to minister to all people, irrespective of racial origin.

In states with a substantial Lutheran population, inter-synodical Lutheran welfare societies stimulate interest in the works of *diakonia* and co-ordinate the efforts of the churches in this field. National Lutheran Council churches and the Lutheran Church–Missouri Synod work together in a large overseas Lutheran relief program. Refugee resettlement work has alerted the churches to the necessity of continuing service to immigrants.

The population flux in the cities across the land has called for careful study and analysis. This necessity prompted the Division of American Missions of the National Lutheran Council to set up a staff for urban church planning. Area studies and congregational self-studies have been conducted in a number of communities. An "Urban Church Effectiveness Study" was developed by the Council staff, and has become the pattern for similar studies by six different denominations.[7]

Changing land use and the resulting population shift to the cities moved the Division of American Missions to set up, more than a decade ago, a staff on the Church in town and country. Interpretative pamphlets have been prepared and distributed, consultation service has been provided, and area study conferences have been organized. This sense of mission to rural communities has arrested, and in many instances stopped, the erosion of congregational strength. A study of eighteen counties in Minnesota showed a population decrease of 13,239 between 1940 and 1950. Yet during the years 1951-56, the Lutheran Church in these counties showed a membership increase of 12,562.[8]

[7] *Ibid.*, p. 3.
[8] *Lutheran Church in the Timberland Area*, Rural Church Program, National Lutheran Council, Chicago (1958), Section 2, p. 9.

THE CHURCH'S MISSION: THE RESPONSE OF THE LUTHERAN CHURCH IN CONTEMPORARY AFRICA AND ASIA

World War II did more damage and provoked more dislocation of work for the Lutheran Church than for any other Protestant communion. Communication between supporting mission societies in Denmark, Finland, Norway, and Germany and the churches receiving their support in Africa and Asia was broken. This imposed a sizable fire-brigade responsibility on the Lutheran churches of North America, Sweden, and Australia.

To meet postwar reconstruction obligations adequately required the calling of a deliberative assembly. Lutheran churches in all parts of the world were invited to send representatives to a convention which would consider the organization of an international federation. The convention met at Lund, Sweden, June 30–July 6, 1947, and out of its deliberations the Lutheran World Federation was born.

The Lund Assembly gave considerable attention to the Church's mission in Africa and Asia. Out of Section II of the Assembly's three working groups a significant body of guidance emerged:

1. "The obligation to carry the Gospel to every human being is a sacred responsibility entrusted to all Christians. All the Lutherans of the world should co-operate in the discharge of this responsibility. And Lutherans hold this trust in common with all other Christian groups." [9]

2. There should be " a unified approach of the Lutheran Church in its world mission. It is the purpose of the Lutheran World Federation to foster this unified approach" (p. 73).

[9] *Proceedings of the Lutheran World Federation Assembly, Lund, Sweden, June 30—July 6, 1947*, p. 71.

3. Wherever possible, missions should be united and resources pooled (p. 75).

4. "The sovereignty and equality of voice and responsibility of all churches, younger and older, should be achieved as soon as possible and should be fully recognized. There should also be a recognition of our interdependence upon each other" (p. 75).

5. "The present Lutheran mission crisis . . . is the common responsibility of all Lutherans in the world. Missions and younger churches that are left without a supporting agency should be helped by the churches of the whole world federation of Lutheranism. . . . where help must be given, it should be given with the purpose of building self-supporting, self-governing, and self-propagating Lutheran churches" (p. 76).

6. "While this *ad interim* help is given, it is with the hope that all 'orphaned missions' will be restored to their original supporting agencies as soon as possible. All programs of present aid should be geared into such a plan, the return to be speeded to the utmost" (p. 77).

Section III of the Assembly submitted two very important and relevant guiding principles:

1. "Men of every race, language, and nationality are one in nature and of equal worth in the sight of God. Christ died for all men. No group is inherently superior or inferior to any other. The existence of recognized inequalities gives added responsibility, not added privilege, to those who are in favored positions" (p. 88).

2. "If there is to be peace in our time, imperialistic practices must be stopped" (p. 89).

How well was the consensus of Lund invested in action? In

many and varied ways. The Lund Assembly had authorized the organization of a Commission on World Mission. Six members were appointed who met at Oxford, England, for organization in July, 1949. Mission board and mission society representatives were invited to attend at their own expense. Fear that the Commission might become a super-mission society was conspicuously present at Oxford. To allay these fears a set of resolutions was adopted, defining the Commission's area of responsibility and action.

The Commission moved quickly to get representation by nationals from Africa and Asia. The Hannover Assembly (1952) was petitioned to provide the new Commission with three representatives from the Occident and three from the Orient, and this petition was gladly granted. In 1956 the Commission decided that at least every five years an annual meeting must be held in Africa or Asia. This concern for partnership has given the Commission excellent rapport with churches of the East and West. The fears of Oxford have been replaced by a confidence remarkable both for its persistence and its depth.

An early test of the Commission's essential unity and its ability to provide creative counsel in critical situations occurred in India in 1950. The Gossner Evangelical Lutheran Church in North India became autonomous during World War I. It was jealous of this distinction. After World War II, when the fervor for political independence swept India, suspicions arose in the Gossner church that their independence might be subtly undermined by the missionaries who had been invited to work in the church. Their *Mahasabha* (convention) therefore adopted a statement entitled "Terms of Reference Given to Individual Missionaries Working in the Gossner Church." This statement gave to those missionaries who had become members of the church the right to speak in the *Mahasabha,* but no vote.

The Commission's discussion of the Gossner action revealed a consensus that no member in good standing can be deprived of the right to vote because of his race or home background. On the other hand, it was acknowledged that in a period when nationalistic feeling is extreme, a missionary might, for the sake of the kingdom, forego exercising the right to vote. This discussion led the Gossner Church to revise the "Terms of Reference" so that Christian truth was obeyed and suspicion of the "designs" of the missionaries was removed.

In New Guinea, the unification of work and the pooling of resources have been realized to a larger degree than anywhere else in Africa or Asia. The American Lutheran Church and the United Evangelical Lutheran Church of Australia took over the work of the Neuendettelsau Society of Bavaria after the Japanese evacuation. Postwar negotiations with the Australian government opened the door for the return of Neuendettelsau missionaries. It was then agreed to unite the work of the three groups. Missionaries are assigned to specific pieces of work and places on the field by officials who are elected by the missionaries. In the difficult area of salary it has been agreed that a common schedule will prevail for all missionaries. American missionaries, who have larger expense commitments at the home base, receive appropriate supplementation from their home churches.

Tanganyika, East Africa, provides a rich illustration of application to the Church's mission as defined for the contemporary scene by the Lund Assembly. Prior to the war, three German societies were at work in five areas of Tanganyika. During the war, German missionaries were deported and mission properties were placed under the care of the custodian of enemy properties.

After the war, the government returned the properties with two stipulations: (1) that the title be held by the National Lutheran Council, an American corporation, and (2) that the German societies should never again be allowed to return to administer work in Tanganyika. The news of these conditions was broken to the representatives of the German societies and the German Evangelical Missionary Council at a meeting in Neuendettelsau in Bavaria in August, 1949. It takes little imagination to understand what a blow this was to the German representatives. For a long time there was no spoken reaction. At last old Dr. Knak, director of the Berlin Mission Society, rose, paused a long time, and then slowly spoke these words: "It is clear that we face a new day, and we must walk in God's new way."

Dr. Knak's determination to thrust away the temptation to despair was justified, and his belief that God would make a new day out of present defeat was prophetic. In due time the government relaxed its strictures against German workers. Today a great international team, with missionaries from the American churches of the National Lutheran Council and from Denmark, Finland, Norway, Sweden, the Netherlands, Germany, and India, is at work in Tanganyika. The five area churches have had a phenomenal growth. The Northern Area church became the first continental African church to become a member of the Lutheran World Federation. This same church has recently elected an African pastor as its president. In Dar es Salaam, an interracial Lutheran center and hostel is now in process of erection. One former German mission director who visited Tanganyika and observed the international teamwork and the solid progress in racial understanding was moved to say, "Here I see Christian ecumenicity in action."

The application of the Batak Christian Protestant Church of Indonesia in 1949 for membership in the Lutheran World Federation confronted the Federation with a delicate task. No constitution accompanied the application although the LWF constitution required that a church applying for membership must submit its constitution for examination. The delicate element in this situation lay in the fact that representatives of the LWF had visited the Batak church in the fall of 1948 and had explained the requirements for membership. They had counseled the church to discuss the matter in each of its districts and, if desire for membership persisted, to file an application in time for consideration at the Hannover Assembly in 1952. However, the Bataks knew that an application could also receive action at the hands of the Executive Committee, which would be meeting in the summer of 1949. This posed a situation in which refusal of membership might be interpreted to mean that the Batak church was not considered an independent and self-governing body. Such a thought would have been an affront, especially since Indonesia was then in the midst of a war of rebellion against the Netherlands.

The Executive Committee of the Federation decided that to deal with the Batak church as a mature, self-governing church would require that no action be taken on their application until a constitution had been filed. In January, 1950, a consultation between representatives of the Federation and of the Batak church was conducted at Rajamundry in India. Thereafter nothing was heard from the Batak church until a few months before the Hannover Assembly met in July, 1952. The application for membership was then resubmitted. Accompanying the application was a constitution and a confessional statement, both of which had been prepared by the Bataks without Western help.

The LWF constitution required subscription to the Augsburg Confession. The Hannover committee, examining the Batak confession and constitution, found no reference to the Augsburg Confession. This was called to the attention of the Batak delegation. Pastor Sitompul, then secretary of the Batak church, replied: "Our people are not acquainted with the Augsburg Confession, but we mean to go that way." [10] Here was an honest answer and a straightforward declaration of purpose. Bishop Meiser of Bavaria, chairman of the committee, said in a committee caucus, "It is clear that we cannot deal with a younger church as we do with the older churches of the West." Thereafter Bishop Meiser reached his hand across the table and clasped that of Secretary Sitompul, with the words, "I give you the right hand of fraternal fellowship." After the subcommittee's report, the Assembly unanimously received the Batak church as a member of the Lutheran World Federation.

The Church's mission is the same in all ages: "taking part in the action of God, in fulfilling His plan for the coming of His Kingdom by bringing about obedience of the faith in Jesus Christ our Lord among the nations." [11] The method of approach and work must vary according to the circumstances in each age.

SUGGESTIONS FOR FURTHER READING

ALLEN, DEREK W. "Christ's Teaching about Missions," *International Review of Missions,* April, 1958.

[10] The Batak Church is the result of the missionary labor of the Rhenish Mission Society, a German union society. However, most of the missionaries who had been sent to the Bataks were Lutheran, and Luther's Catechism had been the basic tool of instruction in Christian doctrine.

[11] Walter Freytag, "Changes in the Patterns of Western Missions," *International Review of Missions,* April, 1958.

DODD, C. H. *The Apostolic Preaching and Its Developments.* New York: Harper, 1954.

KERSBERGEN, LYDWINE VAN. "Growth of the Lay Apostolate," *The Commonweal,* Vol. LXVII, No. 15 (January 10, 1958).

KLOETZLI, WALTER, and ARTHUR HILLMAN. *Urban Church Planning.* Philadelphia: Muhlenberg, 1958.

NEWBIGIN, LESSLIE. "One Body, One Gospel, One World," *Ecumenical Review,* January, 1959.

————. "Summons to Christian Mission Today," *International Review of Missions,* April, 1958.

TILLICH, PAUL J. "The Theology of Missions," *Christianity and Crisis,* Vol. XV, No. 5 (April 4, 1955).

WEBSTER, DOUGLAS. "The Missionary Appeal Today," *International Review of Missions,* July, 1958.

PART THREE

AND THE CHURCH FOR LIFE . . .

Chapter 9

THE CHURCH AND SOCIAL ACTION

By Karl H. Hertz

Every attempt to clarify the theological foundations of social action on the basis of the biblical record must recognize that neither the Gospels nor the other writings of the New Testament contain any sayings or events which can be construed literally as "social action." The Early Church accepted its surroundings as the milieu into which God had placed it, within which its members carried on the duties of their stations in life, but it certainly never launched any reform movements and apparently never felt the urge to do so.

Thus we cannot define any direct relation between Christian faith and social action in biblical terms. This is not, of course, to deny that there have been Christian theologies with strong impulses towards social action, but their starting point has typically been a particular doctrine—e.g., the superiority of the spiritual sword over the temporal, the millennial rule of the saints, the calling of the Christian to particular employments, or, most sweepingly, the orders of creation themselves.

What is here proposed is not a concession to quietism but the assertion that the Christian stance over against the world today must in some sense always draw upon and be continuous with the life of the Early Church. Two preliminary propositions will help clarify the meaning of this assertion. First, the opening paragraph is intended as a statement of the prima-facie content of the New Testament, not as an interpretation of these writings. Second, to make this prima-facie content normative in a literal sense is to reduce what was addressed to the urgencies and exigencies of a particular moment to a code which imprisons present-day Christianity within the framework of its first-century expression.

The distinction between the theological and the biblical is simply the distinction between the set of doctrinal statements which give a systematic account of the meanings of the original sayings and events and those sayings and events themselves. This difference is sometimes not clearly articulated. Consequently, the legitimation of social action has often been a "secondhand" operation, being deduced from a doctrine and thus only mediately related to the biblical source materials. My contention is simply that this is not good enough. The derivation of social action from a theological doctrine, no matter how skillful, always looks suspiciously like a piece of intellectual sleight of hand, smuggling the necessary ethical rabbits into the doctrinal hat in order to produce them with a flourish at the proper moment.

The New Testament writings themselves provide in their sayings and events a picture of Christian involvement in the world. They delineate the actual life situations of a number of the small assemblies of believers caught in the midst of various problems and predicaments, debating discipline and policy (about the problem of meat originally offered to idols, about Christians' responsibilities to the Roman administrators, and the like). In the debate and controversy we can see the development of an image of the relationships existing between the churches and their surroundings. Similarly we see the individual Christian both in his life of worship within the congregation and in his questionings about the meaning of his continued existence within a complex network of social relationships. (What were his obligations to an unconverted spouse? What did he now owe the empire and its magistrates?)

Since I am not charged with an exposition of the New Testament world in all its rich detail, I offer only a quick summary of "the social involvements" of early Christianity.

SOCIAL INVOLVEMENT OF THE NEW TESTAMENT CHRISTIANS

There was no withdrawal from the world. Except for a few random personal observations Paul made about matrimony—always with an eye to what was possible—Christians were expected, urged, and instructed to remain where they had been. While this may be disheartening to certain reforming temperaments, we must see this requirement against the background of later Christian asceticism and the flight from the world into the monastery. Considering how rapidly another kind of practice developed in the life of the Church, the clarity of the New Testament witness to continued involvement in the total life of society is really remarkable.

The early Christians' involvement was not unconscious, but deliberate, in the light of a clearly drawn picture of the structure and meaning of their social surroundings. The complex of social institutions within which they carried out their daily routines was both man-made—the product of history—and divinely established. What was given was the result of human effort; it therefore belonged to time and history. At the same time, God was seen as providentially and redemptively active, not openly (except to the eyes of faith) but as the hidden, unknown Father who mercifully sustains the whole complex of human existence from day to day.

This Christian appraisal of the existing social order represented no first-century doctrinal innovation; it simply continued the long-familiar teachings of Old Testament prophecy that all order, natural, social, and political, rests in God's merciful will and serves his ends. It was the faith which affirmed God's action when the Assyrian came down like a wolf on the fold and affirmed it still when Pontius Pilate was procurator in Jerusalem.

Obviously then what was given, although it rested on God's ordinance, was not unqualifiedly good. Far from it. Any early Christian familiar with the prophetic tradition could distinguish between the fact that the empires of the ancient world received their authority over man as part of the providential order of God in his loving care for his creatures and the fact of the moral perversion and flagrant abuse of what God had given. The Christian knew in fact that, from the perspective of its alienation from God, the creation had become "the world." The powers which ruled the creation, although existing by God's ordinance, were powers of "the world": oblivious of God, either by original ignorance or deliberate intent—depending upon how one wishes to construe these "principalities and powers"—they sought to go their own way. This independence of God, this claim to autonomy, here as elsewhere, is the essence of sinful corruption. To this kind of a world a Christian could not be "conformed." He recognized the legitimacy of the historically given as part of God's mercy; he could not grant its autonomy.

Within the historically given institutions, the Christian was to act responsibly. His actions did not justify him in Church or society. Nor did they count as part of his "sanctification," if the term means a measurable progress in "religious" life, quantitatively computable as discrete bits of "obedient" conduct. Christian sanctification is qualitative. As the new man lives the life of faith, the entirely new characteristics of his way of life shine through the old forms and customary routines. He is differently related and rooted.

His responsibilities existed as a part of the Christian participation in the realization of the will of God. For God ordered the existing social structures as the instruments of his care for his creation. Not by imposing order on his creation from the outside, nor by natural law, nor even by establishing rigid, immovable social institutions but through the creation itself— in, with, and under the historically given forms of custom and work, marriage practices and political authority—the Creator pressed for the fulfilment of his merciful purposes. Consequently the Christian was called to obey the magistrates, to honor the emperor, and—most difficult—to pay his taxes.

Such obedience was never routine, for "the principalities and powers of this world" constantly asserted their autonomy. Sin was always lurking in them; corruption was endemic; demonic perversion was not impossible. So Christian existence always involved tensions, conflicts, and temptations. Daily existence was a matter of daily decisions. Christians were to conduct themselves faithfully, no matter what the cost. They could not claim immunity from criticism nor escape punishment for misconduct. "After all, it is no credit to you if you are patient in bearing a punishment which you have richly deserved! But if you do your duty and are punished for it and can still accept it patiently, you are doing something worthwhile in God's sight. Indeed this is part of your calling," as Phillips paraphrases I Pet. 2:20.

Christian existence in this life was thus God-given. This present life was indeed a period of strangeness, of estrangement and pilgrimage. But let us remember that a pilgrim is not a tourist; he does not simply gawk about in the world, straining his eyes to discover the latest curiosities or sensations: a pilgrim is a man with a purpose. Furthermore, the pilgrimage goes through this world—not around it by some ascetic detour, or over it in some jet-propelled pentecostal trance, but through it—vale and mountain, light and shadow.

The Christian thus lived an exposed life, out in the world, open to all the possibilities of wrongdoing. He could not run away; nor could he passively accept "the world," resignedly twiddling a pair of pious thumbs and shaking his head self-righteously over human wickedness. He had duties to perform.

His first loyalty in the performance of these duties was not, however, to the institutions of his society. He was subject to man-made authority *"for the Lord's sake"* (I Pet. 2:13) (italics added). Involvement in the social order was not a matter merely or primarily of civic duty; it was obedience to the Lord. The Christian worked, served, and obeyed, but not just as a member of society involved with others in a complex of activities necessary for the continuation of the social order. He obeyed as a man of faith, as one who saw what was hidden from the eyes of others, namely, that the social order existed as part of the meaningful providence of God.

The life of faith had two dimensions: a relationship to the other man and an embodiment in the fellowship.

The Christian approached his fellow man with an entirely new perspective. Much has been made of the new dignity which the Gospel bestows on the individual person. Most frequently this person has been seen in isolation, or only in his relationship to God. The result has been a self-centered individualism, concentrating on the relationship to God and on personal piety and devotion, introspectively anxiety-ridden, morally inner-directed, and seeing each Christian as com-

mitted to the same pious self-sanctification, as if we were all
Leibnitzian windowless monads without vital relationship to
one another. This is not the Christian image of man, before
or after faith. The Christian doctrine of man is the doctrine
of man as "the other," as the neighbor in need.

From beginning to end the biblical concepts of man are
relational concepts, concepts which speak of man as "image,"
"creature," "rebel," and "child"; or, with reference to other
men, as "brother," "neighbor," and "fellow-believer." Man is
related to God as creature and redeemable prodigal; to his
fellow man he is related as one in need or as one who can
serve the other's need. The center of his life is never in himself. In fact, the biblical requirement is the complete opposite.
"If any man would come after me, let him deny himself and
take up his cross [daily] and follow me" (Matt. 16:24).

The stress, therefore, falls not on my view of myself but on
my view of my fellow man, the one who is my neighbor, to
whom I owe compassion. No matter who he is. "I was in
prison . . . naked . . . hungry" (Matt. 25:34-40). Wherever
suffering and oppression exist, there I am called to respond,
without setting moralistic conditions, even in the instance of
enemies. The dignity of the human personality, as the Gospel
sees it, is the dignity of the other, the neighbor.

For this is the kind of God revealed in Jesus Christ, the
associate of outcasts, the companion of corrupt officials, the
friend of the Samaritans. The life of faith is the life of concern for others—of all kinds and conditions, of all colors,
races, and creeds, pious and impious. For God's rainfall
waters not only the fields of the faithful; it also reaches the
fields of the unfaithful. God's love encompasses all of his
creation; his salvation is intended for all. As a Christian I
can draw no boundary line whatsoever.

My life is thus directed outward, not inward. Monasticism and asceticism in most forms are foreign to the spirit of the New Testament: in any form, they generally involve preoccupation with my own righteousness, not with my neighbor's need; they involve efforts to appropriate spiritual gifts for myself, not the New Testament impulse to serve others. The revolutionary, even scandalous quality of the New Testament assertions about the life God enables the redeemed to live is rooted in this other-centeredness. How sharply this is conceived can be understood by serious attention to New Testament descriptions of the process. To be a Christian requires first of all that I die, that I become transformed, that I receive a "new life in Christ." No wonder it takes the gracious action of God in Christ to make a Christian, for every Christian is the result of a death and a resurrection.

In this outward-directed life of seeing Christ in every person in need, the Christian does not operate as a lonely philanthropist. Not only does the Gospel make me see my neighbor in a new light, but it brings me into a new set of relationships. The Christian Church is no aggregate of pious atoms, each splendidly isolated from the other; it is a *koinonia,* a fellowship.

True, a good part of the Christian world has at many times and places forgotten the reality of this fellowship. In many accounts of Christian devotion, the life of faith has been described without reference to the companionship of faith. Furthermore, fellowship has often been corrupted into a form of sociability or limited by a false aloofness or separation from the world. Still the fellowship exists; amid all the brokenness of human existence, I do not stand alone. I am part of a company of the faithful whom God has bound to one another in Christ and set at their tasks in the world.

This fellowship is at the same time a kingdom; it is under the rule of Christ. This too is a present reality. The kingdom is hidden. To identify it with any denominational or empirical religious association is to do violence to its nature. The eye of faith can indeed recognize the Body of Christ; in the Sacrament of eating and drinking, it is both mysteriously hidden and mysteriously revealed. But the unbeliever cannot know it. In the present age this body is a broken one, burdened by the Cross, manifesting itself by proclamation and suffering.

Thus the Christian is thrust into the world, but he is not alone. He is part of a colony of Heaven. Almost anonymously he accepts the responsibilities of the situation which confronts him, acting faithfully, knowing that the fellowship of believers surrounds and supports him.

No theocracy is implied in any of this, nor any organization of separatist Christian political parties. The Church as church exists visibly in the world in the Word and Sacrament; it is a place of proclamation. But the members of the Church, each in his own way and place, knowing themselves undergirded by the community of the Word and Sacrament, act responsibly, obediently, and compassionately to carry out the will of their Lord. The Christian knows that—although the "principalities and powers" may still be present and active—God has placed the whole creation under the Lord Christ, and it is in faithfulness to Him that he now lives in this world.

All of this is obvious from the New Testament record. I believe that implicit in it is something much more dynamic than a quietistic resignation to existence in a world corrupted by sin. The Christian knows the corruption for what it is, alienation from God, but beyond and beneath the corruption he sees God at work. For this very reason his life in this world is not a life of withdrawal, but one of involvement; not a life of passive acceptance of "the way the world is run," but one of constant decision-making; not a life of aimless drift, but one with direction, to serve "the other" through the given structures of the world.

Naturally no Christian lives this life perfectly. At no point can the Christian feel himself free from the judgment of sin. In fact, since his choices will always lie between greater and lesser evil—for "the world" is caught in sin—his every act has to be seen in a double perspective (as sin when measured against the absolute requirements of God, and as righteousness when seen as part of the life of faith.) The Christian lives, therefore, with an uneasy conscience; his responsibility is greater than simply fulfilling public duties.

What is true of the Christian in his public life is also true of his personal life; it is equally ambiguous, subject to the same double perspective. Thus the distinction which Troeltsch ascribes to Luther of a double morality of *Amt* and *Person* simply does not hold. For in his office the Christian is just as responsible to God as in his private life. The moral pressures and responsibilities of public office may indeed be greater, the temptations may be more alluring, but does any sober and realistic person believe that the private relations, primary and intimate, between persons (whether in marriage or in friendship) are free of perversions of responsibility? A day spent in a family counseling center should disillusion even the most idealistic. Quietism as a way of escape from sin is a form of self-deception; it is abdication of duty under the illusion that one can be a better Christian in private than in public life. Withdrawal from public life as a form of resistance to injustice may of course be another matter.

There is, in addition, an inherent relativism in the Christian view of social institutions. The Scriptures expound no doctrine of the State and make no attempt to offer any systematic explanation of its origin. There is only recognition of "existing powers" and their "tasks." What exists is indeed described as resting on God's ordinance; this does not make it divine. It is man-made, transient, variable, subject to perversion and destruction. In contemporary application both the Soviet Union and the United States are historically given, the products of human endeavor, and at the same time they manifest the mysterious ways in which God's providential care is exercised. They are equally subject to the dangers of corruption and of demonic perversion.

NEW TESTAMENT IMPLICATIONS FOR THE CHURCH IN SOCIETY

This analysis suggests certain consequences. (1) There is no Christian blueprint for a social order; there are no Christian principles or theories of the State or the economic order. In this sense a biblical theology is not doctrinaire, but "unprincipled" in the best sense of the word. Christian people must decide in the freedom of the Gospel to what courses of action their involvement in social structures may lead them. (2) Christians must not take the actual decisions made in the first century as normative for all generations. Those decisions were made in specific contexts, in a given historical configuration. The structures of life are different today (partly as the result of the Christian leaven); our involvements, opportunities, and responsibilities are different. Moreover, the Church consisted then of a few scattered congregations, made up to a considerable degree of the politically powerless and the socially insignificant. Today the situation is different, at least in many parts of Western Europe, the British Commonwealth, and the United States. We must act within the context of the situation in which God has placed us. The emphasis here is always on what God does for us (in having called us into his kingdom at just this juncture in history) and with us (confronting us with specific opportunities for action). Our decisions are rooted in his deeds. Our response may be described as obedience, provided we do not reduce the meaning of obedience to codes and principles. We do what in faith we must do. This will differ from one context to another. How shall a Christian working in East Germany interpret "Be subject to man-made authorities for the Lord's sake"? How shall the president of a state Farm Bureau Federation respond? Both are involved, committed to acting "for the Lord's sake," and confronted with decisions. Each decision is by its very nature a form of Christian social action.

What is the role of the Church as church in these affairs? Two answers seem obvious.

First, the Church is to proclaim this biblical stance to its members. The Word must be made known and understood; Christians must be reminded that they are not to run away from life, from involvement and responsibility. The content of the proclamation of the Word at this point will always include the proclamation of the compassionate concern for others as a part of the life of faith.

I must therefore seek justice, expect the state to be just, and indeed where opportunities exist, advocate justice. I do so, not because justice will save my neighbor's soul or bring him into my church, but simply because God has ordained the structures of life for the securing of justice.

Precisely because I am a Christian the driving force behind my passion for justice will be compassion for the other. What my neighbor needs for the sustenance of his life is what I must do, for in my neighbor I meet the Lord himself. He is still incarnate, still suffering—and still confronting me in the lowliest and most despised of men.

My compassion, moreover, will seek channels of effective help. If one compares the Christmas basket charity, or the pious insistence that love must be a person-to-person relationship, with social action and its concerns for social structure and political involvement, then what is here suggested may appear heretical. So it may appear—to the person for whom Christian piety is an inner self-development and an accumulation of pious habits. But his view of personal piety certainly finds no support in the classic biblical illustration of compassion, the parable of the Good Samaritan. The help the Samaritan offered was no one-time injection of benevolence, but continuing care. Furthermore, he used the only structure of society at his disposal, the inn, whose keeper (by reputation, at least, in the first century) was probably as corrupt and mercenary as any contemporary politician.

The first duty of the Church, then, is simply to proclaim the Word of compassionate concern and to urge that Christians work responsibly within the given structures of society.

This proclamation is by its very nature a political act, for it defines the relationship between the Church and the "existing powers." Under certain circumstances it could be a highly dangerous political act. But although proclamation is a political act, the Church must not use it for "political" ends, i.e., to secure partisan objectives, to seek political power openly or secretly, or to support political or economic vested interests. The proclamation is Gospel, the love and mercy of God manifest in the structures of society and the life of faith made possible by that love and mercy.

The second task of the Church is to draw attention to the nature of the responsibilities and tasks attached to public life.

In specific instances, especially when Christians have been neglectful of their duties, the Church may find it necessary to speak directly and bluntly. More frequently, the task of the Church will be directed to a more general content. It will urge Christians to discuss and deliberate freely, motivated by their awareness of responsibility. Indeed, since Christians have no blueprints for an ideal social order, they may even be called upon to do some hard and painful thinking.

There is, however, another dimension to the witness of the Church. For as "the elect [people] of God," the Church knows itself to be "the new humanity." To the Church is entrusted a sense of the meaning of life which can never be derived from the examination of the historically given. Thus the Church can face the fact that all that is historically given will pass away. (Need anything more be said about the relativity of "the powers that now exist"?) The form of the new humanity is not given, except in negatives. The present order of things offers no blueprints. Nor does the Church have any. But it knows that in the perspective of God's purposes the status quo, including the American way of life, is not sacrosanct.

What now exists, furthermore, is under the authority of Christ. Without rejecting the valid insights of the doctrine of "the orders of creation," especially their emphasis on God's care for what he has made, I think we need this radical New Testament perspective. Christ rules over all. He does not rule in the political sense of the misguided zealots who would amend the United States Constitution to this effect. This is not a political program. It means simply that the eyes of faith now see all history, all structures and institutions, from the vantage point of their "new being." We are Christ's men wherever we are; there is no place available to us where we are free to act as non-Christians. In all things we must live life with a due sense of responsibility.

SOME SAMPLES OF THE CHRISTIAN STANCE

The specific applications could lead to endless debate. I wish only to define the Christian stance in certain areas.

In political life I am bound to the obligations of citizenship, not merely passively but actively. This is a Christian responsibility "for the Lord's sake." The how of my participation will vary with opportunity, education, talent, and interest, as it will vary with the political constitution of the nation in which I reside, but I cannot reject my involvement. In a democracy, involvement may include holding public office, taking part in the affairs of a political party, signing petitions, or simply keeping myself informed. God may use any or all of these in fulfilling his merciful intention of caring for his creation.

This participation will not be without its conflicts and tensions. Naturally. That is no excuse for shirking responsibility. It may bring me some strange bedfellows. So be it. God's care is not limited to the saints; nor is God limited to the employment of pious men in achieving his ends. This too is part of his mercy. Thus as his servant, I do not concern myself much with external consistency, with principles of political righteousness, or with whether my companions have clean hands or wear freshly laundered white shirts. I simply ask how in this situation I may give the most effective and permanent help to "the other man," the man in need, in whom the Christ appears to me.

Race problems offer an excellent illustration of the opportunity for faithful response and responsibility. Perhaps God has put me just where I am right now that in this place and time I may proclaim by my action that the love of God has no strings tied to it, that his mercy is not conditioned by color or hair texture or ancestry. This is not a matter of an edict from "the ecclesiastical hierarchy." No such convenient excuse will work. It is simply a question of how each of us in faith responds to what God requires of us. We are responsible to him, even when this means to bear the cross of economic boycott, of social ostracism, or perhaps even of violence. Each of us must also ask himself whether to refuse the cross is not a betrayal of the citizenship God has bestowed upon him.

But this is not all. Negro Americans, Christian and non-Christian alike, have suffered more, much more. For the white person to talk about "the cross" of persecution in this respect is almost blasphemous. What is needed here, above all, is the sense of fellowship in the faith. These patient, suffering people, even to the most anonymous and insignificant, are my companions in the faith, "fellow citizens" with the saints, joint heirs of Christ. To them at this time above all I must give the hand of fellowship, giving reality to the *koinonia,* helping them bear their burdens by assistance and support of all kinds. Every believer, no matter what his color or congregation, is involved; none is free of responsibility or opportunity. This is what it means to be part of God's elect people, his chosen race.

What is true within the fellowship is equally true in the world. Wherever the Christian sees oppression and injustice, he must act in whatever way he can. Strategies will vary with contexts. God has not bound himself to a single pattern in his care for his creation. Physical differences of race and cultural differences of custom are historically given, but within this framework, as elsewhere, sinful perversion occurs— plunder, pillage, rape, exploitation, oppression. Therefore in the Lord's name and for the Lord's sake, we must protest, no matter what the cost. For this is my neighbor in need, and I must simply ask, "What is it that I can do right now?" Furthermore, how can I make certain that my help is no temporary palliative but effective, continuing assistance. Thus I am committed to justice, to involvement in the structural arrangements of my community—in school and shop, in stores and playgrounds, in the courthouse and in the church.

All of this does not mean that we reduce life to the dead level of a moralistic uniformity "for the Lord's sake." We are richer for creative variety in equality. No Christian is called upon to limit the grace and mercy of God to the narrow platform of a particular faction or creed. He is called upon to think and act responsibly, creatively, come hell or high water.

The Christian action which flows from my situation may be on one occasion conservative, on another radical. Neither is a priori determinable. God cares for his creation, and by his mercy he has established structures through which his care is exercised—the home, the school, the courtroom, and the workshop, to name but a few. To defend good order in all these activities of life, for the purpose of protecting the life, the freedom, and the well-being of others, is conservatism in the best sense. When "the powers that now exist" pervert these so that life and freedom are threatened, and injustice and oppression abound, then the Christian cannot passively withdraw. He has no place to go—in this world. He must witness by his life; he does witness by what he does or leaves undone. To be silent or resigned or withdrawn is to say, in effect, that what is going on is the will of God.

In economic and political life, therefore, just as in the other relations of life, the Christian must accept responsible involvement. Two major considerations would appear to dominate in this involvement. (1) God's merciful care for his creation, the fact that He fosters good and forestalls evil, cannot be trivialized by equating it with the policeman's night stick. (Although to insist on respect for law and order in contemporary America is no minor witness.) The provision of a decent minimum level of wages and decent housing, health, and school facilities to the hard-core minorities—migrant labor, Puerto Rican immigrants, or unskilled Negro workers—may do more to reduce divorce, delinquency, drunkenness, disease, and other problems than all the pious sermons preached in all the Protestant churches in America, urging the poor to repent and to work hard without complaining, so that they can become like their respectable middle-class Christian friends. (2) The promotion of every social program involves a risk, the risk that we confuse means and ends. This is the legitimate element in the criticism of the welfare state. For when a particular organization of society is made absolute, when the limited and transient is made ultimate, then "the powers that now exist" are put in the place of God. Some of our experience with the over-concentration of power in the hands of the few, whether ecclesiastical hierarchs, capitalist entrepreneurs, labor racketeers, political messiahs, or overweening bureaucrats, ought to suggest that "the powers that be" become increasingly subject to demonic perversion as they manage to occupy more and more of the available social space by themselves. We must, in addition, reject any view which reduces man to a bit of hedonistic protoplasm or a manipulatable commodity—but to do so as a pious, self-sufficient individualistic monad is itself a betrayal of the Creator.

ONE FINAL WORD: ONE FINAL LORD

One final word. In a period of major social transformation, God's care for his creation may also express itself by the disappearance or radical alteration of some social structures and the appearance of others. Radical criticism of the affluent society and its presuppositions needs honest Christian examination. Christian involvement in man-made institutions requires no permanent allegiance to the status quo. It may be the best expression of Christian compassion and faithfulness to give responsible leadership in the construction of the new —not as a better approximation of the kingdom of God, but as a more responsible exercise of compassion in the present circumstances of human existence. Only the Christian aware of the transience of the historically given, only the Christian committed to doing all "for the Lord's sake" will be able to have the perspective which allows him to see the old order pass and a new order come into being. Whatever comes, we shall be involved as a fellowship of the compassionately concerned. Whatever comes, through faithful service within the structures of society, we shall proclaim in deed as well as word that "Jesus Christ is Lord to the glory of God the Father."

SUGGESTIONS FOR FURTHER READING

BENNETT, JOHN C. *Christians and the State.* New York: Scribner's, 1958.

CARLSON, EDGAR. *The Church and the Public Conscience.* Philadelphia: Muhlenberg, 1956.

CULLMANN, OSCAR. *The State in the New Testament.* New York: Scribner's, 1956.

DOMBOIS, HANS and ERWIN WILKENS (eds.). *Macht und Recht: Beiträge zur lutherischen Staatslehre der Gegenwart.* Berlin: Lutherisches Verlagshaus, 1956.

Chapter 10

THE FAMILY

By Carl F. Reuss

The family is recognized widely as the basic unit in society. In their understanding of it, however, theologians bring in an additional dimension. They declare that God created man to live in community, that God ordained marriage and the family as the training ground for community living, and that God's will can be accomplished through patterns of family living pleasing to him. From time to time theologians have set forth what they believe to be God's purposes and patterns for marriage and the family. Their views have been regarded as binding upon the devout and served as a measure of how far short the godless fell.

Purely profane, secular influences have also operated at times to affect standards for family life. They have challenged the validity of the sacred, eternal truths set forth by the theologians. The present is an era of such challenge, testing, and inquiry. Traditional forms and functions of family life are being affected or drastically altered by the impact of social, economic, political, and other forces.

Old restraints are being relaxed, and new freedoms accepted. Former patterns and structures are in the process of disorganization. Reorganization of the family is occurring to enable it the more effectively to function amid changed conditions. What message can theologians bring to the crisis of family life? What response would God have them make to the current confusing realities of family disorganization and reorganization?

Conclusive, generally accepted, fresh, and vital answers are not yet at hand. Few theologians seem to have attempted an integrated, systematic theology of the twentieth-century family. This is not to say that church bodies have been indifferent to the pressures assailing the family. Far from it! Individual communions, such as the Anglican,[1] Lutheran,[2] and Presbyterian,[3] have responded to the challenge with serious studies and significant reports. In 1961 the National Council of Churches held its North American Conference on the Church in family life. The World Council of Churches has studied the areas of rapid social change and is pointing out those major problems of family life which emerge from such change.[4] A study conference under World Council of Churches auspices, held in April, 1959, expressed itself on "the population explosion" and on contraception.[5]

Religious leaders are aware of the pressures which cultural changes are exerting upon the family. It is to be hoped that

[1] *The Lambeth Conference, 1958* (London: SPCK, 1958; Greenwich, Conn.: Seabury, 1958) contains not only the encyclical letter of the bishops but the report of a committee on the family in contemporary society.

[2] Lutheran interest in the subject is typified by the following projects: the Family-Life Research project of The Lutheran Church–Missouri Synod; Lutheran Youth Research, sponsored jointly by youth boards of the major Lutheran bodies in America; section meetings at the 1957 Lutheran World Conference on Social Responsibility dealing with marriage, parenthood, and family; and the report of the Commission on Education of the Lutheran World Federation to the 1957 Assembly on "The Family in Christian Education."

[3] The Office of Family Education Research, Board of Christian Education of The United Presbyterian Church in the USA presented a preliminary report of its research to the 171st General Assembly.

[4] *The Common Christian Responsibility Toward Areas of Rapid Social Change* (Geneva: WCC, Dept. on Church and Society, 1958) reports progress of the study from 1955 to 1958.

[5] *Chicago Daily News,* October 7, 1959; *Ecumenical Review,* October, 1959.

theologians will analyze the trends of the times, sift the mass of data available from social and psychological research, and study the scriptural record anew. Such a re-examination and reappraisal of all that is taught as valid and normative for marriage and family relationships would be valuable in giving relevant counsel to men and women hungering for timeless truths amid swiftly shifting settings.

CURRENT TRENDS AFFECTING THE FAMILY

Some current trends and pressures affecting the family in a significant way deserve attention and comment in the light of theological emphases. None of these trends exists in isolation. All are interacting and interrelated. All challenge, either directly or indirectly, traditional teachings and widely held assumptions.

1. *Personal foundation for marriage.* From being primarily a socially oriented arrangement for satisfying personal needs, marriage has shifted to a personally oriented arrangement for satisfying social needs. The emphasis is placed not on institutional obligations but on personal freedom to choose a marriage partner, on personal happiness in marriage, and on personal satisfactions.

Congenial companionship is, of course, a legitimate expectation from marriage. Companionship, however, does not merely take; it shares. Moreover, marriage is also a social and a religious relationship. It must manifest a balance between proper personal aspirations and the valid claims of the community. Young people need reliable guides and trustworthy criteria in their personal choice of a marriage partner, which they have a right to expect not only from parents but also from their church. Traditional religious teachings have emphasized parental approval of the person chosen as marriage partner. Is this a remnant of parent-arranged marriages, or is it a counsel of practical wisdom? A significant volume by the Family Life Committee of The Lutheran Church–Missouri Synod deals courageously with the broad subject of engagement and marriage.[6]

2. *Acceptance of divorce.* Given the expectations held for marriage, divorce is an acceptable "solution" for many persons. According to this line of reasoning, "A person has the right to a happy marriage, and if he doesn't find it with one person he should try another." Divorce statistics suggest that such a view is widely held. Moreover, divorced persons now are accepted in social and other circles where formerly they were excluded.

Religious teachings remain clear that marriage should be in fidelity to one partner for life and that divorce is wrong, the consequence of sin. Applying these truths to specific cases, however, raises vexing problems.

3. *Distortedly physical emphasis on sex.* Satisfying sexual curiosity and sexual appetites would seem to be major goals of American life, judging from many of the mass communication media. Sex and love are falsely equated. Sex, moreover, is associated almost exclusively with busts or hairy chests, hips, legs, and the genital organs. Sexual experimentation and sexual expression outside of marriage are encouraged. Popular songs, magazines and books, the theater and motion pictures, radio and television tend to accentuate such stunted, immature concepts of the real nature of sex in human life. Much of this emphasis is a revolt against earlier taboos which virtually forbade any mention of sex.

Church leaders until recently have accepted the notion,

[6] *Engagement and Marriage: A Sociological, Historical, and Theological Investigation* (St. Louis: Concordia, 1959).

prevalent in the Puritan and Victorian eras but originating in the early Christian era, that sex is innately evil and to be tolerated as an awkward, if at times pleasurable, necessity for the perpetuation of the race. In recent years they have begun to redress the balances,[7] recognizing that physical sex is a powerful force—but not the only ground for or bond in marriage. They emphasize the good and beauty of sex when it is used as God intended, but also the damage which results when sex becomes a commodity for sale or purchase. Sex is not merely a biological phenomenon or drive. Sex carries also psychological, emotional, and spiritual qualities which affect the entire male or female personality. Such qualities set human sexuality far apart from the reproductive sex of the animal kingdom. They give deep meaning to the biblical verse "male and female created he them."

4. *Changing roles of men and women.* Traditional definitions of what is expected of men and what of women are no longer accurately descriptive. Women have won a greater freedom to decide upon careers and roles, and also a status much closer to that of equality with men. Chivalry or special deference to "the weaker sex" has virtually disappeared, a casualty of "equal rights." As wives have become gainfully employed outside the home, husbands have found themselves expected to share in household duties. The patriarchal family has been replaced by the equalitarian, or even the matriarchal.

[7] Cf. William Graham Cole, *Sex and Love in the Bible* (New York: Association, 1959) and *Sex in Christianity and Psychoanalysis* (New York: Oxford Univ., 1955); Roland H. Bainton, *What Christianity Says about Sex, Love, and Marriage* ("Reflection Books" [New York: Association, 1957]); W. Clark Ellzey, *Romance in Christian Marriage* (*Ibid.,* 1958); and Seward Hiltner, *Sex and the Christian Life* (*Ibid.,* 1957). See also Harold Haas' splendid essay, "Christian Faith and Family Life," in *Christian Social Responsibility,* ed. Harold C. Letts, Vol. III (Philadelphia: Muhlenberg, 1957), prepared for ULCA Board of Social Missions, and *God, Sex, and Youth* by William E. Hulme (Englewood Cliffs: Prentice-Hall, 1959).

These trends run contrary to the usual theological emphasis on the husband's role as head of the household. There has been a softening of this emphasis, reducing his role to ruling "in love" rather than "by authority." These trends run the risk of overlooking fundamental male-female differences, and of ignoring the creation account of the two sexes as being complementary rather than competitive. The trends are constructive in that they encourage the development and use of the talents and abilities of women as persons. The range of vocational response and of stewardship opportunities open to women has been considerably enlarged.

5. *Rights and freedoms of children.* Americans today tend to believe that children are entitled to rights, freedoms, and privileges, with a minimum of duties, obligations, and responsibilities. The years of education and dependency are lengthened, child labor laws discourage early entrance into the employment market, life is made as attractive and easy as possible, and parents run errands for their children to spare them that effort. Children are wanted, not merely accepted, by their parents. In consequence, however, children often dominate their elders. Their whims and wishes become commands for their parents, especially if the objects of their wishes are things that can be purchased.

Theologians stress, rather than the rights of children, the status of parents as God's especially appointed representatives, and the duties children owe to parents and to all in authority. A nation dominated by its children is a theological scandal. Children are viewed as God's blessing upon marriage. Parents owe their children care and nurture, in spiritual matters as well as in the more mundane matters of speech, health care and nutrition, relations of the sexes, and the many other elements in balanced nurture. Parents also owe their children an example to be emulated. When parents are old, they can expect that their children will provide for their care and keeping.

6. *High standard of spending.* Families these days have available for their comfort and enjoyment a treasure-store of things, all requiring a high level of cash income. Automobile, television, electricity, automatic washers and dryers, built-in ranges and refrigerators, vacation trips, dancing lessons, and many other conveniences and luxuries—all calling for cash or credit—can contribute either to family enrichment and solidarity, or to a poverty of spirit in the midst of material plenty. Things and the desire for more things may well be the reason Mother seeks gainful employment. She labors for labor-saving devices!

Material comforts can indeed be enjoyed, but not made the end and goal of life. Persons can thankfully accept and recognize them as blessings from God, as the "daily bread" he gives. The ever-present danger, though, is that men will idolize these products of their hands and forget their true Source. Theological insights warn men that where their treasure is, there their hearts will also be. Theology reminds men, too, that covetousness is sheer idolatry. On the other hand, theology has not yet dealt adequately with the fact of relative abundance as Americans experience it. Theological roots and assumptions presuppose poverty to be the typical lot and material comfort the exception.

7. *Industrialization and specialization.* The home is no longer the center of economic productivity. The place a man works has long since been shifted from the home to the factory, shop, office, or store. Few families are united around a common economic center, or in a family business. Work divides the family, each gainfully employed member going to a differ-

ent place of employment. Moreover, much of the economic order is industrialized, commercialized, specialized, and concentrated in a limited number of power centers. Family and
domestic interests normally are subordinated to the impersonal
demands of the machines, the hours of the shift, and the other
devices whereby individuals with differing abilities and spe-
cialities are co-ordinated into a smoothly operating system.

Theologians have protested, with increasing success, the
dehumanization of the person in modern industrial and com-
mercial processes. They have pleaded for recognition of family
values, with some success. For the most part, however, the
impact of industrialization upon family values, as distinguished
from effects upon the person, has not received the same theological attention.

8. *Urbanization.* The concentration of people in cities, a
world-wide trend, has had profound effects upon the family.
Problems of housing, of maintaining family standards in a
heterogeneous community, of participating effectively in
social institutions, and of finding an acceptable self-identity
in the anonymity and impersonality characteristic of a large
city are among the problems affecting the family. At the same
time, the advantages and opportunities of urban living should
not be minimized.

For the most part theologians have given little critical attention to urban living. What attention they have given has
been on the side of the superiority of rural values and their
preservation in a metropolitan setting. Support for this is
drawn from the rural imagery in the Bible, and from biblical
condemnation of such cities as Sodom, Gomorrah, and Baby-
lon and of the injustices emanating from cities of Israel. A
theological approach to the positive values of urbanization,
particularly as these enrich family life, would be an interesting

and rewarding exercise. It might begin with the reminder that "the New Jerusalem" is a city!

9. *Widespread mobility.* Americans are a mobile people, both horizontally and vertically. For families, mobility usually means separation from the larger family of parents, siblings, cousins, and other relatives. Ties are broken and the small family of husband, wife, and children must accept an enforced independence. Uprooted by geographical or social mobility, family groups are likely to seek a sense of belonging and stability wherever they can find it. Mixed marriages usually are a product of mobility.

Mobility is a topic churchmen have approached mostly from the viewpoint of its effects upon the institutional church. Few seek seriously to study the great migrations and mobility recorded in the Bible in terms of their effects upon people and nations as well as their working out of God's purposes in history. Much careful attention should be given also to the many implications of the growing incidence of mixed marriages—marriages mixed religiously, socially, economically, and even racially.

10. *Freedom for inquiry.* Compared with some earlier generations, today's generation has ample opportunity to inquire into and to discuss openly a wide range of questions connected with marriage and family life. Men and women are free to use the objectivity and the methods of social science research to seek answers to questions which, until recently, they dared not even ask. The findings of such research are often widely circulated. Mass circulation magazines, in particular those edited for women, devote much space to topics in this broad field, doing so with a frankness and forthrightness once reserved for professional journals.

Despite the fact that the Bible deals openly and honestly

with sex, marriage, and the family, many church people remain reluctant to have these topics discussed openly in the churches. In part they fear that public discussion cheapens and degrades what should be private and sacred. In failing to discuss the issues, however, they leave the field to counselors and discussion leaders who are not religiously oriented. Research methods, fortunately, are accepted and used in the family life field by some of the research projects of the churches. The old era of shamed silence about questions of family life is passing from the Lutheran scene in America.

Trends and factors other than the foregoing might have been elaborated. For example, one might mention the increase in leisure time and the competition for this time, the widespread acceptance of contraception and the increasing acceptance of artificial insemination, the current willingness to discuss and to seek treatment for deviant sexual behavior, the large number of parents without partners and of single persons beyond normal marrying age, the decreasing age at first marriage, and the separation of family members into age and sex groupings.

FUNDAMENTAL FUNCTIONS OF THE FAMILY

Awareness of the pressures exerted by social changes and the realization that family structures are changing can be unnerving. A sense of perspective is helpful in appraising developments such as those discussed in the preceding section. It becomes helpful to seek out what purposes the family may serve in God's order of creation.

Form and structure, after all, are but means for accomplishing ends and purposes. They are not sacred in their own right. Their genuine validity depends upon how well they serve to fulfil the desired purposes. A number of forms and structures may each serve almost equally well in the fulfilment of essentially similar objectives. In this spirit we submit that the particular patterns and authority structures a people uses to regulate its family life are secondary in God's regime to how well they accomplish the fundamental purposes he desires the family to fulfil. Change in forms and structures of family life, in response to changed cultural conditions, he countenances, but his fundamental purposes for the family remain central, universal, and unchanging.

One ventures but timidly, and with full recognition of culturally imposed biases, to suggest what appear to be the family's fundamental purposes in the divine order of creation. Five such purposes seem to warrant special consideration:

(1) to answer the need for companionship and for loving and being loved:

(2) to foster the richness and fullness inherent in the fact of a two-sex creation;

(3) to insure orderly procreation of the race, including maternal protection and infant care;

(4) to prepare the child through rearing and nurture to live in effective community with his fellow men;

(5) to provide status and identity, alike in relation to self, to neighbors, and to God.

This catalog is different from the more usual one which names companionship, procreation, and control of sex drives as basic functions of the family. It is different from the sociological listing of the affectional, biological, economic, educational, protective, recreational, and religious functions the family is felt to fill. Nor does it confine itself to the four wishes: recognition, response, security, and new experience. Rather, the five fundamental functions suggested above represent somewhat of a composite of the usual theological, sociological, and psychological emphases.

1. *Answering the need for companionship.* "It is not good that the man should be alone; I will make him an help meet for him." So, in Genesis 2:18, God soliloquizes at creation. Man was created for companionship. The family properly serves this function before any other agency, and more effectively.

Closely related to companionship is loving—having someone whose interests we wish genuinely to serve and knowing that another person is sincerely and wholeheartedly interested in our well-being. It is in the family that the supreme virtue of love is, or should be, most clearly expressed.

2. *Fostering richness of sex.* God created the human race male and female. Sex colors the whole of personality; it does not merely determine the roles in the reproductive process. Distinctively male qualities and distinctively female qualities add richness and variety to human life. A one-sex community is but a partial human community; the important qualities characteristic of the other sex are missing.

Marriage, of course, is founded on sex differences. It provides not only a means, negatively, of preventing gross sexual sins, but also a means, positively, of elevating and giving spiritual tone and qualities to the sexual relationship between husband and wife. Through the family the children gain their first training in male-female roles and their first experience with the meaning of sex in human life.

3. *Insuring orderly procreation.* Sex drives being what they are in human beings, reproduction of the race in one way or another is fairly certain. The family, however, is a means for insuring that this process will be carried out in an orderly manner. Indeed, the family raises this process above the ani-

mal level, for reproduction is made a participation with God in the mysteries of creation of new life. It becomes an acceptance of God's blessings of fruitfulness.

Pregnancy and lactation impose temporary disabilities upon the mother. The extreme helplessness of the infant and the consequent care needed from its mother—or a mother substitute—require protections. A well-ordered family system insures the mother and the infant of the care, help, and protection they need in their period of dependency.

4. *Preparing for community living.* Families are the first schools in which children are taught to live with their fellow human beings. The rudiments, at least, of language and communication, of standards of morality and integrity, of respect for persons and property, of understanding of the purpose and meaning of work, of use of time and energies, and of many other areas of human relationships, are learned—well or ill—in the family.

5. *Providing status and identity.* A clear, consistent picture of one's self, one's purpose in life, and one's destiny is needed for a wholesome, balanced youth and adulthood. Self-understanding and self-acceptance, of both strengths and weaknesses, is important as a basis for harmonious relationships with one's fellows. "Take heed to thyself, and keep thy soul diligently" (Deut. 4:9 A.V.) and St. Paul's words in Romans 12:3, II Corinthians 3:5, and Galatians 6:3-5 remind us of the importance of a realistic appraisal of self in relationship to others.

The family is the typical agency through which the child first achieves his status in the group and his identity and recognition as a unique, distinctive personality. Where the family fails to effect the needed balance between the rightful expectations of the person and the proper claims of the community, troubles arise sooner or later.

Religious training, too, begins in the family, as Ephesians 6:4 declares. Children need training in sensing and appreciating both the beauties and the mysteries of God's world. They need to hear and be made to think about God and the meaning of his mighty acts for them and all persons. The breadth of coverage of the religious education of children, and the many opportunities during the day for it, are suggested especially in Deuteronomy 6:7-8. Non-Christian families, and families completely untouched by Christianity, typically provide their young with some orientation to the gods they worship and the means of satisfying these gods' demands.

The foregoing are functions basic to all families. They fill needs with which God endowed man, and which the family is uniquely equipped to meet. Precisely what structures and patterns any particular society uses to accomplish these purposes is relatively immaterial. It may well use agencies and forms which we in our Western small-family structure would not label "family." We, in turn, lacking the strengths and supports of the larger family, turn to schools, clubs and sociability groups, and commercialized resources for meeting personality needs and institutional functions which in other cultures can be provided by the family.

Christian family life differs from non-Christian not in the specifics but in the spirit. Its structure is not different, nor are its functions. Its distinctiveness lies in its orientation toward Christ and its conscious awareness of his reconciling ministry. It becomes a warm loving relationship in which husband and wife, parents and children, are blended through Jesus Christ into a living unity. It wants his transforming presence to strengthen the members for living at peace with themselves and with their neighbors because they are at peace with God.

SOME TROUBLESOME QUESTIONS

Against this broad background of fundamental functions, specific, troublesome questions arise. Perhaps these issues arise at least in part because the theologically based answers of the Church and the pragmatic answers of the world come into conflict. This is inevitable, for Church and world do not share common loyalties and objectives. Rather arbitrarily five such issues are singled out as fields in which theologically oriented help would be useful. These are: parental authority, juvenile delinquency, wives working outside the home, planned parenthood, and divorce.

1. *Parental authority.* As was suggested earlier, American thought has downgraded parents and elevated children in status and authority. This situation carries destructive possibilities. Of course the old patriarchal pattern where father ruled with iron will and quick hand is not one which many would wish to reinstate. A balance between the extremes of rigid paternalism and child-dominated authority is desirable.

Scripture seems to indicate such a balance especially clearly in the beginning verses of the sixth chapter of Ephesians. Children are counseled to obey their parents, with the reminder of the message and the promise of the Fourth Commandment. On the other hand, parents, too, are admonished. They are warned against provoking children to justified anger; directed to rear them in conformity with the Lord's precepts.

In the Lutheran tradition, parenthood has an elevated, even sacred, status dating from Luther's teachings on the meaning of the Fourth Commandment. In his Large Catechism he wrote: "For God has exalted the estate of parents above all others; yea, he has appointed it in place of himself upon earth." Moreover, Luther believed that "all authority has its root and warrant in parental authority." On this essential premise he based his teachings about the honor and respect which are due the civil authorities and all others in positions of responsibility.

Honor or power or authority is given, according to Luther, not for homage but rather that, in obedience to God, its bearer will conscientiously discharge all the duties of his office. Parenthood thus imposes obligations. Parents conscious of their status as God's special agents are more likely to take their authority seriously, and less likely either to abuse it or abdicate it, than are parents who do not recognize the sacred office they bear.

Parental authority is wielded under the principles of fairness, justice, equity, and integrity. Mercy tempers justice, among human fathers as with God the Father. Parents must set rules and expectations, as does the Father in heaven. The child needs to know that the world is an orderly place which expects persons to discipline themselves, to live up to their responsibilities, and to accept the consequences of their actions. Parents need to establish and to maintain a consistent, but moderate, discipline as a means to cultivating in their children a sense of responsibility, a willingness to accept their duties, and the formation of consistent and orderly habits.

Schools, clubs and associations, government agencies, churches and Sunday schools today are bearing some of the authority vested in parents. This authority, however, is only delegated, not abdicated. The basic responsibility for the nurture, rearing, and discipline of the children remains with the parents.

2. *Juvenile delinquency.* One way of looking at juvenile delinquency is to see it as rebellion against parental authority. It is similar in essence to the rebellion of created man against his Creator. Adam and Eve disobeyed God's authority, setting their will above his. Cain slew Abel. Absalom revolted against his father. Illustrations could be multiplied. At the root of juvenile delinquency is a conflict of wills, the youth's wanting his way in defiance of or in opposition to that of prescribed authority. The fault, fundamentally, is sin.

Parents may bring about rebellious behavior by the way they treat their offspring. Joseph's brothers reacted against both the insufferable superiority of the boy and the obvious favoritism of the father. Eli and Samuel, both religious leaders, failed in rearing their sons and saw them go astray. The parable of the prodigal son reveals an indulgent father as well as a selfish son and a resentful brother. "He that spareth his rod hateth his son: but he that loveth him chasteneth him betimes" (Prov. 13:24 A. V.). These words are as true today as when the biblical writer penned them.

Controls upon and correction of juvenile delinquency require a clearer understanding of its causes in specific cases than is generally apparent. Dealing with the delinquent must not foster in him the impression that the way to get recognition and attention is to become troublesome. At the same time, it must leave room for the genuine possibility of remorse, repentance, and the sincere effort to mend evil ways. The resources of the larger fellowship can strengthen and support such a desire for a better life.

When parental failure is grossly evident as a decisive factor in juvenile delinquency, it may become necessary that the state step in to abrogate parental rights. In the interests both of the child or children and of the community, the state necessarily, if reluctantly, must assume its role as God's agent to prevent further evil and to promote the well-being of child and community. Gross abuse of direct parental authority requires intervention by a broader authority.

3. *Gainfully employed wives.* The opportunity now open to wives and mothers to hold paying jobs outside the home poses problems. The traditional view held that woman's place was in the home with her husband and children and her outside interests were in the church. The older picture, too, was of the family as an economic unit, with the wife providing economic services in gardening, preserving foodstuffs, sewing, and other ways. The prime difference between the traditional and the present view perhaps is that now the wife and mother adds her economic contribution in cash earned outside the home rather than in services within the home.

Of course this presents difficulties, especially when the children are young. Excessive absence of either parent, or both parents, may be damaging to the children. This is as true when parental absence is occasioned by outside employment as when it results from excessive participation in church, civic, or social activities. In either case parents may be neglecting the regular and consistent confidence, supervision, care, guidance, and control which they ought to provide as stewards accountable to God.

Another problem is that outside employment may so cause the family to desire material things that it forfeits its awareness of the non-material values in life. In families where the wife and mother is working primarily for goods and possessions, the warning to Timothy may require frequent repetition (I Tim. 6:6-11, 17-19). There are opportunities aplenty for constructive, spiritually rewarding but economically unremunerated service. Such opportunities find fewer volunteers as women take up paying positions in commerce, industry, and the service professions.

There is a danger, however, that the liabilities in this trend will be exaggerated and its assets minimized. Actually many families are able to use this new pattern constructively, to their own benefit, in enlarged service to God and neighbor, and in an enriched quality of living.

4. *Planned parenthood.* One reason married women have been able to hold gainful employment outside the home has been the availability of means for planning parenthood. The number of children and the spacing of their births have come to be regarded as matters of parental decision rather than of chance. Children are desired as a normal fruit of marriage and an evidence of God's blessing. In planning their families, married couples would wisely heed the psalmist who pointed out the special blessings which may accrue to larger families and the rich joys from children born in one's youth (Ps. 127:4-5). They are then more likely to experience the truth that "grandchildren are the crown of the aged" (Prov. 17:6).

The first corporate American Lutheran expression on planned parenthood was a statement on "Responsible Parenthood" submitted by the Commission on Social Relations to the 1954 (final) convention of the American Lutheran Conference. This statement was referred by the Conference to its participating bodies for consideration and possible action. In slightly altered form it was adopted by the Board for Christian Social Action of the American Lutheran Church and by the Los Angeles convention of the Augustana Lutheran Church. The United Lutheran Church at its 1956 convention adopted thirteen "Summary Statements on Marriage and Family Life," of which one dealt directly with the planning of parenthood. A more complete "Study on Marriage and Family Life" submitted by the Board of Social Missions dealt with these topics at some length.[8]

From these several Lutheran statements and actions certain areas of agreement can be seen. So long as it causes no harm to those involved, either immediately or over an extended period, the means used for controlling pregnancy is a matter of personal choice guided by medical counsel. Both voluntary childlessness and an unrestrained production of children without realistic regard for parental responsibilities are brought into question. Artificial insemination with semen from someone other than the husband, as a means of overcoming involuntary childlessness, is so fraught with moral, legal, social, biological, and psychological implications that a Christian will be extremely wary of using this method. The closing paragraph of the statement by the Commission on Social Relations summarizes the point of view inherent in its approach:

Any planning for the number and spacing of the births of their children must be practiced prayerfully in accord with the fruits of the Spirit rather than in indulgence of the lusts of the flesh, and in the full freedom of the redeemed believer who feels his stewardship responsibility to his Lord. When so practiced it can bring the conscientious Christian husband and wife a deep appreciation for God's gracious blessings, a greater joy in the responsibility which parenthood brings, and a richer satisfaction over their partnership with God in His creation of each new life entrusted to them.

Not all Lutherans accept this general point of view. Some prefer, instead, the point of view expressed by Dr. W. A. Maier, who in his volume *For Better—Not for Worse* condemned contraception as vigorously as do Roman Catholics.

5. *Divorce and remarriage.* Traditional Lutheran teachings permit divorce on the grounds of adultery or willful de-

---

[8] Copies of the statements approved by the three groups are available from their respective headquarters. Alfred M. Rehwinkel develops a similar view carefully in *Planned Parenthood* (St. Louis: Concordia, 1959).

sertion. In a divorce granted on such grounds, viewed as scriptural grounds, the "innocent" party has traditionally been permitted to remarry.

This teaching increasingly is being called into question. It is challenged on the grounds that any divorce is incompatible with the divine will, that the exception clause in Matthew's Gospel is a later interpolation, that to name only two valid grounds for divorce and no others makes Jesus' and Paul's words legislative rather than normative, that rarely if ever is one party to a divorce entirely innocent and the other wholly guilty, that a second marriage prayerfully entered may be a wholesome preventive of grosser sins, and that the handling of issues involved in divorce and remarriage is a matter, not for ecclesiastical legislation, but for pastoral action.

Two church bodies, the American Lutheran Church and the United Lutheran Church, at their 1956 conventions adopted statements of guidance to pastors and congregations. The weight of their argument was on the side of the objections cited above to the traditional Lutheran position. Needless to say, there was considerable debate at the two conventions. Opponents saw in the statements a relaxing of standards!

Mobility of peoples, intensified mission work which draws into the Christian fellowship persons previously divorced and remarried, recognition of the benefits a wholesome marriage confers, and popular acceptance of divorce have compelled reconsideration of Lutheran views on divorce and remarriage.

FURTHER ATTENTION NEEDED

Lutheran theologians are increasingly aware of the realities of the cultural climate within which they study marriage and family questions. They have grown particularly sensitive to the psychodynamics of personality development. They are re-examining central theological concepts and terms, with their implications for personality fulfilment and mental health.

An area for further exploration is the family as the laboratory for Christian living. How the family evidences reconciliation, forgiveness, the impact of justification by faith, faith active in love, stewardship, vocation, God's grace, his continuing creation, and the battleground between sin and Satan on the one hand and God's will and power on the other is an area worthy of competent theological analysis.

The fact that chapters on the family and on social action are included in this symposium is an indication of progress. For long, Lutherans were so concerned with purity of doctrine that they could not concern themselves with the mundane issues of life. Now they recognize that correct doctrine is immensely relevant to the realities of life.

SUGGESTIONS FOR FURTHER READING

BURGESS, ERNEST W., and HARVEY J. LOCKE. *The Family: From Institution to Companionship.* New York: American Book, 1953.

DUVALL, EVELYN M., and SYLVANUS DUVALL (eds.). *Sex Ways in Fact and Faith.* New York: Association, 1961.

FAIRCHILD, ROY W., and JOHN CHARLES WYNN. *Families in the Church: A Protestant Survey.* New York: Association, 1961.

FEUCHT, OSCAR E. (ed.). *Helping Families Through the Church.* St. Louis: Concordia, 1957.

HULME, WILLIAM E. *The Pastoral Care of Families.* Nashville: Abingdon, 1962.

Marriage and Family Living. Quarterly journal of National Council on Family Relations. Minneapolis.

MARTINSON, FLOYD M. *Marriage and the American Ideal.* New York: Dodd, Mead, 1960.

WALLER, WILLARD. *The Family: A Dynamic Interpretation,* rev. Reuben Hill. New York: Dryden, 1951.

Chapter 11

THE CHURCH AND EDUCATION

By Edgar M. Carlson

THE PLACE OF EDUCATION IN A THEOLOGICAL VIEW OF EXISTENCE

In a volume devoted to theology, a discussion of education presents some problems. The simple fact is that not much discussion of education takes place at the level of theological principles.

Even a cursory glance at the literature on education will make this clear. Volumes dealing with the philosophy of education concern themselves primarily with the goals of education, theories of knowledge, the learning process, moral and spiritual values in education, and other matters of theory as distinguished from practice. Where an attempt is made to give a distinctly "Christian" character to the philosophy of education the discussion centers around the content of teaching, a Christian world-view, a Protestant theory of education, and the relation of faith and reason.[1] While these are all valid and important considerations, there appears to be a prior theological question which is seldom asked. To most educational theorists it may seem at best an academic question, hardly deserving consideration. But if one is to deal with education theologically, it would seem to be the basic question.

[1] E.g., *Toward a Christian Philosophy of Higher Education,* ed. John P. von Grueningen (Philadelphia: Westminster, 1957).

Let us put the question this way: What is the place of education in a theological view of existence? That this is a strange way of speaking about education may be indicated by the fact that the phrase "a theological view of existence" will almost surely need to be explained. It defines a view of existence which accepts the primacy of God, with all else derived from and responsible to him. He is the Creator; all else is created. The world of things and men and relations in the natural and social order both throw light on the activity of God and are illumined by God's action. For any theology which would claim Christian association, the action of God is decisively revealed in the person of Jesus, who is the definitive "revelation" of God.

Our question is: What is the place of education in a view of existence such as that outlined above? Is education a part of the inherent functioning of the order and process of life as God created it, or is it something which the human spirit has devised to attain certain desired ends? To put it in another way: Is the school a basic human institution like the family or government, inherent in the nature of creation and having its own intrinsic function and authority, or is it a product of human decision with a delegated function and delegated authority?

It is characteristic of Luther and the theological tradition which derives from him to speak of three basic institutions or "orders." The first is the family. One cannot conceive of human existence without some form of the family. The perpetuation of the race demands it. The relation of the creature to a Creator gives a religious dimension to life which has its counterpart in the Church. The existence of several families requires some form of extra-familial government to maintain order and secure justice. The family, the Church, and the

State are, therefore, inherent in the very nature of the created world. Sometimes a fourth relationship is spoken of as being of the same basic character, i.e., the economic one. The existence of more than one family unit implies, almost of necessity, some kind of relationship among families and between families and the soil or other sources of sustenance.

Can the school claim an equally basic relationship to the created order? Surely it can be claimed that education in the sense of the transmission of culture—insight, experience, standards, mores, ideals—is an inherent function of ongoing human life. Each generation does not begin *de novo*. The learning process yields something which can be accumulated from one generation to another and passed on to the young. But it is equally clear that the basic channel for this transmission is the family. Education belongs to the responsibilities of parenthood. In much of primitive society the home is the major, if not sole, educational unit. The school appears to be a device by which the families take advantage of the knowledge of the better informed members of the community for instructing the children of all, especially in areas calling for more specialized training than the majority are likely to have. They therefore delegate some of their responsibility for the transmission of culture to a school with qualified teachers. As civilization develops and the deposit of knowledge becomes larger and more complex, the school comes to play an increasingly important role. It may even become unconscious of the delegated character of its authority and the representative character of its function.

When the educational needs exceed the family resources, so that some portion of the educational function must be delegated to another agency, alternatives are open. One is a free association of families establishing a private school. A second is the government which has jurisdiction over the total citizenry of the community involved. The third is the Church. Since in a "state of nature" the function belongs to the family, it does not appear that one can claim divine sanction for any one of these above the others. Each is thoroughly legitimate, though advantages may be claimed for each of them. If one accepts the premise that the function belongs inherently to the family, one must grant to families the full freedom to delegate the function as they will.

It may be argued that the content of education, the nature of the culture to be transmitted, dictates that one or the other of these alternatives is right and the others wrong. Since the private school can be anything which those who have delegated the educational assignment wish to make it, the issue here is really between government and the Church as suitable instruments to carry out the program of educating the young. Each has an inherent character of its own, independent of its educational activities. It may be claimed, for instance, that the Church makes certain affirmations about the Creator and the creation which prevent it from being objective and open-minded, and hence is not well suited to the educational task. This hardly seems convincing, since most learning involves transmitting the conclusive experience of the past. Whatever the limitations of such conclusions may be they are not unique to the field of religious dogma. Of more importance, and to the Church's credit, would seem to be the universality of its interest. It is no breach of its character to seek out the secrets of the atom or the functioning of the nervous system. Neither is it a breach of the character of government to accept responsibility for at least a part of the task of cultural transmission. The maintenance of order requires an enlightened citizenry. Where government has become the instrument by which the total community seeks to provide for the common welfare, as in most modern nations, it is clear that education occupies a large place among the common concerns. While the maintenance of order may only require minimum standards of education, the common welfare will often seem to dictate high subsidies for the most advanced training and research.

Moreover, to whatever extent it is a duty for citizens to be enlightened and to develop their potentialities for contributing to the common welfare, government seems to be a logical vehicle for securing performance of this duty. It has coercive functions, by virtue of its intrinsic nature, and can, therefore, compel compliance. It can require that all children go to school until they are sixteen, without parental consent. At least, there does not seem to be any disposition in our country to question the jurisdiction of government in this regard. Government can also provide the means for supporting an educational program through its power to tax. When education becomes widespread and extended, taxation is the generally accepted method of providing the necessary economic resources.

We have asserted that in a "state of nature," education is a function of the family. When performed by either the Church or the State it must be understood to be a delegated function. Either or both can properly accept this delegated function and responsibility without violating their essential character. It is apparent, however, that the educational assignment will not be identical in the two cases. The educational program will partake of the character of the sponsoring "order." For instance, the Church can offer education but it cannot require it. To do so would conflict with the free response which is essential to the existence of the Church. An educational program under the sponsorship of the Church would necessarily have a certain voluntary character to it. On the other hand, the coercive element in the State makes compulsory education entirely normal when education is under the auspices of the government.

Furthermore, Church-sponsored education can be without restriction as to subject matter, since whatever concerns the Creator or the creation is within its sphere of interest, even though it is outside of its authority. A State-sponsored education is not well suited to the transmission of religious elements in its culture for at least two reasons. The first is the variety of religious interpretations and convictions which are to be found in most societies. It is conceivable that there could be such a measure of unanimity regarding religion in a nation that it would be acceptable to all the citizens to use public channels for the transmission of religious culture, but it is highly unlikely. Even a folk-church or State church must provide for some recognition of the dissenters. In a pluralistic society, with free churches, the complications are much greater. Agreement on the content of religious teaching calls for such a reduction and abstraction of religious beliefs as to satisfy no one. The result would be the creation of another religious viewpoint which would have no actual counterpart in the existing religious life.

However, even if it were possible to produce such a generalized version of specific religions, there is another reason public education would not be well suited to its transmission. The religious outlook which would be dispensed through State-sponsored education would partake of the compulsory, nonvoluntary character of the State. To this extent the religious culture transmitted would be compromised. At the very least, it would appear that some provision would have to be made to exempt the dissenter from this part of the educational program.

The provision which obtains in the United States, whereby the government determines the minimum standards of education required of all citizens, with public provision for full educational development for all, and with the permission—even encouragement—of private and Church institutions, recognizes that education is really a delegated function and that parents and citizens have the right to determine whether they prefer an education under the auspices of the Church, the State, or a private association of families.

EDUCATION AND THE DIVINE LAW

We have tried above to find an answer to the question: "What is the place of education in a religious view of existence?" If we are to deal theologically with education we must now ask a further question: "What is the nature and function of education from a theological point of view?" Presumably there is a religious interpretation of education even when it is conducted under the auspices of the State. Not infrequently, we criticize public education for not achieving what, on the basis of a religious interpretation of its functions, we could have no reason for expecting it to achieve. The same may be true of education under the auspices of the Church.

It may be helpful to use the theological distinction between Law and Gospel in this connection. It will be especially pertinent for a Lutheran approach to the question. The position to be taken here is that the function of education is properly to be understood as a part of the activity of God designated by the term Law, and that this is the case even when education is carried on under the auspices of the Church.

First it will be desirable to make sure that we agree on the meaning of the term Law as it will be used in the following discussion. By Law we shall mean the discipline which God imposes upon us by virtue of the nature of man and the structure of the world as God has created and established them. Creation, including man, is the product of God's action. This is not to be understood as restricted to the first moment of time but as the continuing, dynamic action of God in the present. If one may use a crude analogy, God's creative power is at work in the world as electrical energy is at work in the lighted lamp or the running motor. At every moment, the light and the movement depend as much upon the electrical impulse as is the case when the light goes on or the motor starts. Thus God sustains the world in being throughout every moment of history. If he were to cease to create, the world would cease to be. Law describes the consistent action according to which creation takes place. Its consistency is most evident in the physical realm—so evident that the physical sciences have frequently been tempted to describe the operation of the physical world in mechanistic terms. The mind, too, operates in an orderly fashion which makes it possible to speak of "laws of learning" or "axioms" in the fields of logic and mathematics. We have already referred to the fixed structures in society, the "created orders," which are inherent in existence because the world is made that way. There are also moral laws, governing human behavior; these are not the result of social mores and customs but have an inherent relationship to the way life must be lived in this kind of world.

The primary function of education is to transmit the knowledge society has acquired regarding man, things, society, human relations, and the whole created world. Whatever insights have been gained regarding "things as they are," that is, the discipline which is imposed upon us by reality, each generation must seek to pass on to the next. Since we are constantly acquiring new knowledge and correcting or supplementing previous conclusions, there is never a completely fixed body of knowledge to transmit in the simple manner suggested above. The student undertakes exploration and investigation, choosing or being convinced about alternate interpretations and sometimes making new discoveries for himself.

To a large degree, the educational assignment is descriptive. It seeks to acquaint students with "what the facts are." In certain areas, however, interpretation plays a conspicuous role. The relation of facts to one another, the meaning which is to be given to a set of facts, may be as important as the facts themselves. In some fields, education must also deal with values and goals, or the subjective judgment of the learner as he responds to the world around him. Directly or indirectly, education is then seeking to provide norms for behavior or appraisal. While it is somewhat of an oversimplification, it is generally true that the natural sciences are chiefly descriptive, the social sciences are also interpretative, and the humanities are also normative.

All of this can be comprehended under the term "Law." Education is a matter of acquainting people with things as they are. Truth, in the sense of conformity with reality, is the only valid test which can be applied. If either government or Church establishes some other basis for learning, it is corrupting education. The hard discipline of truth is the yoke assumed by every teacher and every student in any program of learning worthy of the name.

At this point it must be acknowledged that the approach indicated above is not the popular approach in modern American education. It is more characteristic to define the purposes of education in terms of the sort of person we should like to produce or the sort of society we should like to create. Thus we speak of "personal adjustment" or "personal development" and the "culture-moulding process." This represents a significant shift from an earlier conception of the function of education. Instead of being oriented toward the past, it is oriented toward the future. We decide what kind of people and what kind of society we want to produce, and we establish the curriculum content and the methods of instruction which will achieve the desired result. Of course, in the present state of knowledge, where so much more is known than any single person can ever learn, we must make some selection of what knowledge is important in view of the demands life places upon us. But when we are told that "social or cultural change" [2] is the basic fact about our time and that "problems of social control are rightly becoming the chief concern of our time" [3] and the teacher is assigned the task of being "the guide in the culture-moulding process," [4] I become somewhat apprehensive. Are educators per se equipped to make the judgments involved in shaping the future of either an individual or a society? Is truth safe if it becomes an instrument with which to manipulate people so that they will have the attitudes and outlook we want them to have and will accept the kind of culture we think should prevail in the future?

There has been great stress in modern education on the free development of the individual. This has sometimes taken the form of virtually undisciplined inquiry without the benefit of what others have learned. The mind was to be developed and this could best be done by learning at first hand, un-

[2] Harold Rugg and William Withers, *Social Foundations of Education* (Englewood Cliffs: Prentice-Hall, 1955), p. 7.
[3] *Ibid*, p. v.
[4] *Ibid.*, p. 26.

trammeled by the conclusions of others. Now we seem to be moving toward the discipline of a desired outcome, and we are trying to find ways of assuring that result through the educational system.

The definition of our educational assignment in terms of Law, of things as they are, the deposit of knowledge and insight with which the past provides us, is a surer safeguard of both the discipline and the freedom which is essential if man is to be what God intended him to be. Knowledge of the way things are, according to the best judgment of the past and in the light of the highest values the past has produced, is the prime requisite for freedom. We do not release the individual from making responsible decisions beyond making available to him the fruits of historical experience. As soon as an attempt is made to "condition" personal reactions, we are limiting the area of responsible freedom and insofar depersonalizing the learner.

What has been said above may seem to be begging the question in that it assumes a degree of certainty about the way things really are which does not conform with the facts. Are there not as many interpretations of what is right and wrong, for instance, as there are people? How does this square with the relativism which is the prevailing mood in much of the world of learning, especially in the social sciences?

Perhaps we have here an inadvertent outcome of the "secularization" of education. We have noted the limitations upon education when the transmission of religious culture is conducted under the auspices of the State. It must not be assumed that education under the auspices of the Church knows more —has more objective truth—than education under the State. But the Church can profess a relative knowledge of the Absolute, whereas the State does not have the freedom to affirm a

religious ultimate or Absolute. To do so is to become involved
in conflict with the religious pluralism of our society. Education under the State may, therefore, have to content itself
with a "relative knowledge of the relative."

Is the situation otherwise in the church college? Let us
reaffirm our position that the hard discipline of truth is the
yoke assumed by every teacher and every student in any program of learning worthy of the name. This means that the
church college must be willing to submit its teaching to all
the tests of truth which have reasonable claim to validity. It
thus exposes itself to the same measure of skepticism or relativism with respect to the facts as does any other kind of educational institution. It does not have an infallible textbook
which exempts it from the necessity of investigation and
verification of all the facts. The descriptive function of
education, and consequently the measure of skepticism concerning the facts, cannot be much different in the church
college from what it is in the public institution. But it will
differ significantly in the interpretative and normative functions. This will be so for two reasons: (1) its uninhibited use
of Christian sources and ideas in providing the frame of
reference within which the interpretation is made, and (2)
its affirmations of faith and its dedication to values and norms
which are inherent in the Christian view. Such affirmations
and dedication cannot be merely assumed by the teacher in
a church college for the purposes of instruction; he must have
them before they can become effective in his teaching. But,
if he has them, he is free to use them in the church college in
a manner and to a degree which is not possible in the public
institution. Since these are basically aspects of faith, they
cannot be translated into absolute knowledge; even the faithful church college teacher will acknowledge that he has at

best a relative knowledge of the Absolute. This is, nonetheless, something quite different from a "relative knowledge of the relative."

EDUCATION AND THE GOSPEL

Thus far we have been investigating the nature of education in terms of the theological concept of law. We have noted the broad similarity between education under the auspices of the State and of the Church except for the freedom which the Church has to use a more comprehensive range of sources of insight, specifically those connected with the Christian faith, in the interpretative and normative elements of the educational task. Now we would approach the question from the viewpoint of the theological concept of Gospel.

The Gospel is the gracious message of God's reconciling deed in Christ by which men are released from the bondage of their guilty self-centeredness and brought into the relationship of faith in and obedience to God. It is the mission of the Church to declare this Gospel to all men at all times and in every circumstance. The teaching of Law is not irrelevant to this central mission of the Church. Indeed, Christian theology understands that a vivid awareness of the necessity which is laid upon creatures by the Creator and of their failure to conform to this Will of God is an important preparation for receiving the Gospel. This refers primarily to relationships in which the human will is a factor, as distinguished from cause and effect relationships in the physical world.

Is the educational process a channel through which the Church can carry on its work of reconciliation through the Gospel? Surely this cannot be the case with public education at any level. The lack of unanimity in the community with regard to both the meaning of the Gospel and the desirability of declaring it, as well as the compulsive character of government, prevent it. Even the preparatory function of the Law is largely nullified by the elimination of specifically religious elements from the content of public education. To be sure, there may be inadvertent and unintended religious consequences from public instruction and some of these may be favorable to religious growth and positive faith. The church college, on the other hand, can intentionally and purposely undermine the sense of self-sufficiency and self-centeredness by teaching the discipline of Law in all areas, against the background of its positive affirmations regarding God as Creator and Lord. In addition, the church college can provide innumerable opportunities for declaring the Gospel within its curriculum, in personal counseling, in common worship, and in the total impact which it seeks to make upon the student.

There is a Gospel ministry to be performed for students in the public educational system. At the elementary and secondary level this is performed through the home and the local congregation. At the level of higher education it is usually performed by a kind of home mission activity which is adapted to the community of learners. The activity may include religious foundations, campus churches, and religious workers around or in the educational community. It does not affect the education being offered within the institution, but it is, nonetheless, an exceedingly important service to the people attending it. For many students away from home it constitutes a major link with the living and serving Church.

The community of teachers and learners has always been a major concern of the Church. This is inevitable because the Church must be concerned with truth. Its treasure is a Gospel, a Message, a Word of God, and this must be communicated. While faith can never be reduced to ideas or propositions, neither can it be dissolved into moods and attitudes independent of sound understanding. Anti-intellectualism, however pious or patriotic, can be no part of the Church's posture as it confronts the world. This is particularly true today. The man of learning is being restored to the position which he has characteristically held during most of human history and from which he was temporarily dislodged by the man of action. The mechanics and technicians of our industrial civilization have now become the nuclear physicists, the biochemists and mathematicians, whose abstract and theoretical discoveries alter the character of our world beyond our wildest dreams. They shape the future far more than the managers of men or machines. The Church cannot resign itself to a diminishing role in education unless it is willing to accept a weakened voice in the future.

THE CHURCH AND THE CHURCH'S SCHOOLS

We must now attempt a more definitive and comprehensive statement of the nature and role of the Church's program of education with particular reference to its provisions in the field of higher education. We have tried above to view the church college as a part of the total program of education which has been delegated by parents to private, public, and church institutions. We will now inquire into the relationship between the Church's own institutions of learning and the Church.

It is not adequate to think of the Church's colleges and seminaries solely as agencies of the Church through which certain common functions of the constituent congregations or church bodies are carried on. They have a certain independent character, not entirely unlike that of the local congregation. The college is an inquiring community, set apart for a particular task. It must expose itself to all the sources of insight, all the stimuli for learning, the whole realm of truth. It consists of a dedicated and committed faculty, fully trained to distinguish truth from error, at least in the field of instruction, and a community of students qualified to pursue studies at the level of higher education. The Church entrusts to this community the conceptualizing of its own faith and life, the clarification of its own intellectual outlook, and the formulation of appropriate and effective methods of communicating its faith through the learning process. In a Christian institution, the faith to be conceptualized and clarified is the Christian faith. In a Lutheran institution, it is that faith as understood from a Lutheran perspective. If this is understood to be restrictive it is misunderstood, since every Lutheran position subordinates itself to an objective Christian norm. That is, the Lutheran position affirms the priority of the truth of the Gospel over every statement or definition of that truth.

The Church's institutions of learning have both a priestly and a prophetic function. They are vehicles through which the Church serves its members and society at large by performing a part of the educational assignment, putting all of its resources of insight and commitment to work for the common good. Seminaries, of course, have the specific professional assignment of preparing pastors to serve the congregations. Colleges and seminaries are teaching arms of the Church. They serve the Church by serving others. But they are also, in a real sense, teachers of the Church. They have the responsibility of keeping the Church intellectually alert and alive. They must interpret the world to the Church as well as the Church to the world. Unless the Church understands the world to whom its Gospel is addressed, it will not be able to communicate with it. As the physical sciences, psychology, the social sciences, etc., disclose the nature of modern man and his environment and relationships, the Church's institution of learning should transmit its knowledge about the world to the functioning Church in all its branches and activities. Through the community of scholars working under its auspices, the Church dips into the currents and cross-currents of contemporary culture and learning in order to increase the effectiveness of its contemporary witness. At the same time, through the same community of scholars, it is extending its witness into the world of learning beyond its own institutions. The educational enterprise carried on under the auspices of the Church has intimate relationships with the whole world of learning. Its sociologists, psychologists, and philosophers are spokesmen for the Church in their broader professional associations.

Education under the auspices of the Church is not a sheltered and protected activity. On the one side, it is exposed to the whole range of secular thought, its error as well as its truth; on the other side, it is exposed to the full range of religious reality and influence. It is the function of its educational program to screen and absorb and impart truth coming to it from all directions. The teacher, especially, must translate and transmute all these raw materials into a Christian view of life and the world. He must be constantly analyzing and restating his own Christian understanding of things so that it is meaningful in the world of ideas with which he is working, and must help his students to do the same. He must relate the "data" to his Christian frame of reference, so that the truth about the world is not denied and so that the truth about God is affirmed.

In this encounter with the frontiers of knowledge, the Christian teacher may find it necessary to talk about the Christian faith in ways which are not entirely identical with what has been said by others in other times and places. The nature of his assignment makes it almost inevitable. The dialogue between the Church and the world takes place in education in an acute and intense form. The issues arise here before they must be faced in the pulpit. Here they can be lifted up, examined, analyzed, submitted to tests of logic and history, evaluated in the light of their presuppositions and their implications. Ideally, this is where the evangelistic weapons of the Church should be forged; or, if this is claiming too much— since the real weapons of evangelism must always remain the Word and the sacraments—this is where they should be kept sharp and burnished.

The Church's institutions of learning are a kind of advance guard, a pilot project, an explorer contingent for its encounter with contemporary culture. It is almost inevitable, therefore, that a certain tension should normally exist between the Church and its educational institutions. They live along the frontiers of learning and this is always a somewhat hazardous existence. They may get new ideas which seem to put established patterns of thought in jeopardy. There is a great responsibility resting upon the representatives of the Church in the field of learning to be faithful to its message and mission. The Church is wise to keep the ties between it and its institutions close, so that those who teach may never forget that they are emissaries of the Church in the field of learning, and, equally important, that the Church may profit from the intellectual ferment which is the proper environment for an institution of learning.

The Lutheran Church has kept these ties close and stands to profit from this wisdom. Perhaps it has sometimes been motivated as much by the desire to protect the inquiring students as by the desire to free the inquiring mind. But this would not be true today. Lutheran colleges and seminaries are moving into positions of significant leadership in wide fields. There are indications, too, that they are increasingly conscious of their specifically Christian task, and that the Church is responding with genuine understanding and substantial support.

SUGGESTIONS FOR FURTHER READING

BRETSCHER, PAUL M. "Toward a Lutheran Philosophy of Education," *Concordia Theological Monthly, XIV* (February, 1943), 81-95.

DAVIES, RUPERT E. *An Approach to Christian Education.* New York: Philosophical Lib., 1956.

FERRE, NELS F. S. *Christian Faith and Higher Education.* New York: Abingdon, 1954.

FORELL, GEORGE W. *Faith Active in Love: An Investigation of the Principles Underlying Luther's Social Ethics.* New York: American, 1954.

FROER, KURT. *Theologie im Dienst des Unterrichts.* Munich: Chr. Kaiser Verlag, 1950.

———. *Erziehung und Kerygma.* Munich: Chr. Kaiser Verlag, 1952.

GAEBELEIN, FRANK E. *Christian Education in a Democracy.* New York: Oxford Univ., 1951.

LUECKE, RICHARD H. "Truth and Freedom in Christian Schools," *Lutheran Education, XCI* (October, 1955), 78-85.

TINGELSTAD, O. A. "A Lutheran Philosophy of Education," *The Lutheran Outlook* (April, 1949), pp. 1-8.

PART FOUR

. . . IS THE CHURCH FOR THEOLOGY

Chapter 12

THE MINISTRY OF THE WORD

By Richard R. Caemmerer

"Theology in the life of the Church" is not theory apart from the life of the Church, but the force by which the Church really lives. We can say this if by "theology" we mean literally the "Word of God," God's action communicated to God's people and by them to each other. In practice the life of the Church can be a counterfeit, engendered and sustained by forces other than theology. This chapter proposes to discuss the agency by which the theology of the Church becomes practically realized in the life of the Church. That agency is the ministry of the Word.

Such counterfeiting of the life of the Church occurs when the ministry of the Word fails to function. That failure may come about when the world conquers the Church and stops its ears to the Word. It may be due also to a perverting of the Word, so that the Word becomes no longer the working of God in men through the grace of God in Christ but rather a collection of sentences to be said, debated, or subscribed to, or a secular message which is the word of men instead of God. But this failure may be due also to a perverting of the ministry.

Throughout history the churches have been concerned about the ministry of the Word in their midst. Some have accentuated the authority of their professional ministers, and to that end have employed an episcopal polity. Others have been less concerned for "order" and more for the Word which Christians are to minister to each other. Often the sides in this controversy have been taken by established or official churches on the one hand and the "free" or dissident churches on the other. These European points of view have been bequeathed to American successors. Actually every Christian communion must face at any time and in every place the question of the nature of its ministry. For the life of the Church depends on the functioning of its ministry of the Word.

THE THEOLOGY OF THE MINISTRY OF THE WORD

Basic to the theology of the ministry is the theology of the Church. It is the gathering of people who have been drawn into a community in Christ. This community can be thought of as universal, throughout the world, as well as local, in the given place. The source of this community and the power which draws its members together and sustains them in community is the call from God, his word to each of them and all of them that he has redeemed them through his son Jesus Christ to be his people. The community of this people involves their common faith in this God and his Christ, and their common experience of the Spirit of God through whom they can call Jesus, Lord.[1]

The New Testament *koinonia*, rendered "community" in the preceding paragraph, implies much more than a collection of like-minded people. It refers to an aggregate of individuals bound severally to Christ by faith, but it means that they

---

[1] The simplest summary of Paul's doctrine of Church and ministry is Eph. 4:1-16; a counterpart employing chiefly Old Testament language is I Pet. 2:1-10. First Corinthians, chapter 12, is an important discussion in terms of the functioning of the Holy Spirit.

share this faith mutually. They are drawn into a living process in which each one reaches out to the other because of and for the sake of what all have in common, namely this faith in Christ. They are one, whether it be two or three Christians in a family, or two or three hundred in a congregation, or two or three million in a denomination. They are one, not just statistically as a collection of individuals, but as a household and family bound together by intimate relationships, as a troop of soldiers buckling each other's armor on, as members of a body in which each conveys life toward every other or serves every other, and as a building erected for holy purposes in which each rank of stones supports the next.[2]

Mutual service is vital because the members of the Christian community are under constant threat. To their dying day, they are threatened by the world, the aggregate of men without Christ, which eagerly invites them to share the community of its desires and experiences without Christ. The Devil, the arch-conspirator and co-ordinator of things against God, ceaselessly expedites the attrition and erosion of their faith in Christ. This is the function of the body of Christ, that its members sustain one another in the midst of peril and failure, that the strong succor the weak. Hence in practical fact the overarching objective of the Church everywhere is to be the company of those who watch for one another's edification and upbuilding in Christ.[3]

The one tool for edification, in the radical sense of sustaining spiritual life, is the Word of God. The Word of God is

[2] The outstanding exposition of *koinonia* in the New Testament, the First Letter of John, does not employ the term *ekklesia*. Note Paul's discussion in First Corinthians, chapters 10–15, and Romans, chapters 12–15. For a remarkable study of the biblical materials see Paul S. Minear, *Horizons of Christian Community* (St. Louis: Bethany, 1959).

[3] Compare the sayings of Jesus assembled in Matthew, chapter 18, and in Matt. 25:31-46. The first and sixth chapters of Ephesians are vivid in this respect.

simultaneously the speech or the communication of God, and the acts of God. The Word of God sustains the universe in its course and the galaxies in their orbits; it melts the snow (Heb. 1:3; Ps. 147). The Word of God speaks the wrath of God over man's rebellion and His judgment over man's sin (Heb. 4:12-13). But the Word of God by which Christians are sustained and edified in their community is not God's power in general nor the dread voice of his judgment. Rather is it the saving and freeing act of God in Christ, himself the Word of God, through whom God at the cost of his suffering and death redeemed the world to himself (John 1:14; 14: 6-11). That act of God in Christ, visibly transpiring in Palestine at the turn of the Christian era, becomes contemporary in our own life and age as Christians, members of the redeemed company, speak the Word of Christ to one another (II Cor. 5:17-21; Eph. 4:14-16).

That Christians speak the Word of Christ to one another does not mean simply that they engage in religious exercises, although these can be a setting for it; nor that they quote Scripture to each other and sing sacred hymns, although these acts may help in the process. It means that human beings who believe in Christ become agents for the powerful Word and work of God toward their fellowmen. They seek to recall in the minds of their hearers and companions that saving act of God in Christ by which he originally called them to be his own. As they succeed, God's own power and Spirit works in them what only the Spirit can do: they find new heart to have faith in the Lord Jesus Christ, and their hands find new strength to serve each other and all men.[4]

---

[4] The most comprehensive statement of the process is Col. 3:1-17 (Eph. 5:8-21 is parallel); with special reference to common worship, First Corinthians, chapter 14; with application to its force for mutual upbuilding in Christian life, Heb. 10:19-25.

This mutual speaking of the Word of God and purveying of the life stream of the Church the New Testament terms the ministry.[5] Here we are calling it the ministry of the Word. Where it languishes, the members of the Church grow feeble. St. Paul told the Corinthians that their spiritual life was ebbing because they were perverting the Sacrament, intended to be the signal of God's forgiveness of his people's sins, into a token of class distinction and an occasion for drunkenness. He told the Galatians, as he encouraged them to accept responsibility for each other's spiritual life, that they would produce precisely the yield they labored for: if they planted the passions of pride and theological self-righteousness, they would reap a harvest of death; if they would seek to cultivate the Spirit and his works in one another, that would be the crop (I Cor. 11:18-30; Gal. 6:1-10). Ministry means service. For that, Jesus said, he came into the world, and this sustaining of the spiritual life of the fellow Christian is to be the one main task of his disciples (Matt. 20:20-28; John 13: 12-20).

THE CHURCH'S MINISTRY OF THE WORD

"Minister" is a term which has become pre-empted for professional preachers of the Gospel, and pastors. In the plan of God, however, every Christian is a minister of the Word of God. This applies to his witness to the world about him outside of the Church, and to the manner in which he sustains his fellow Christians inside the Church. St. Paul describes the many functions with which Christians are entrusted by the Spirit for the edification of the Church. Some involve one

[5] The King James version allows Eph. 4:12 to look like an expression for the functions of the Church's professionals, whereas it might be rendered more aptly: "So that they should equip the saints for their task of service, namely to edify the body of Christ."

sort of activity, some another, but all have this in common: They are given by the Spirit of God, and they are for the sake of the spiritual life of the fellow members of the body of Christ (I Cor. 12).

The insight into this fact is perennially hampered. Christians have always viewed the Old Testament people of God as a sort of visual aid in understanding their own Church on its pilgrimage. Israel had its special order of priests who administrated worship and "served" God; rapidly New Testament Christians identified the rank of their leaders of worship with that of the priestly caste, and ordination with its indelible stamp served to exalt the rank. Throughout the Middle Ages, climaxing in the Reformation, a reaction to this caste was the accent on the royal priesthood of all believers. In the course of time, the reaction gained this stress: the Christian does not need the help of an intermediary, a priest, but can go straight to God for forgiveness because of the great high priest, Jesus himself. This stress is valuable; but it is unfortunate that it was termed "the royal priesthood." In the scheme of God's call to his Old Testament people, all of them were to be kings and priests, and the officiants at their sacrifices were not intermediaries, but helpers for the worship and sacrifices of all of them (Exod. 19:6). Thus the royal priesthood of God's people in this age is likewise the bringing of sacrifices by all of them, for the sake of all of them. It is indeed a term for the ministry of the Word, for the one way by which the Christian can sacrifice himself and his brother to God is by speaking the helping Word of God to his brother always (I Pet. 2:1-10; 4:10-11).

In the first centuries after the Reformation, Lutheranism, with its stress on *das Predigtamt,* tended to make the Word and absolution spoken by the pastor the one means of spiritual edification practiced in the Church. Calvinism placed much stress on the lay elder; yet even there the lay ministry became an oligarchy instead of including the whole laity. Some of the free churches have historically stressed lay preaching; again, the result has tended to be the enhancement of a lay elite. The liturgical revival, Roman and Protestant, has placed a splendid accent on lay participation in worship; yet often it has been accompanied by a parallel elevation of the dignity of the officiant and a weakening of the primary responsibility of the worshiper.

The chief obstacle for the exercise of the ministry of the Word by every Christian toward his brother has been one of omission rather than commission. It has been the simple neglect of the horizontal dimension in the body of Christ. Most denominations are stressing the rehabilitation of family life, and with it the restoration of household worship. Curiously the stress on mutual sharing of the Word of God, as well as common reaching up in adoration to God, remains weak. Likewise in the attempt to revive intelligent and conscious participation in group and liturgical worship, the horizontal values of ministry from worshiper to worshiper, so richly affirmed in the New Testament, receive meager articulation. The years of material prosperity have enlarged the Church's activities in fund raising, plant construction, public relations, and evangelism. Lay participation in all of these has been stimulated well. Yet the privilege and duty of each Christian to speak the saving Word to his brother first, for the sake of his upbuilding in faith, has often been left untouched.

These lags in the understanding of the ministry of the Word as primarily the task of every Christian, and a first response of his faith, are obviously more than theoretical or abstract in importance. They involve the functioning of the Church. They also hamper an understanding of the functioning of the special ministers, the pastors.

"GIFTS" TO THE CHURCH'S MINISTRY

All Christians are ministers of the Word, "speaking the truth in love." The New Testament itself, however, makes clear the place and function of special servants of the Word. St. Paul twice lists special functionaries—he refers to them as "gifts"—who stand in a special relation to the church (I Cor. 12:28; Eph. 4:11). Such persons were the apostles, among whom he included the twelve, himself, Barnabas, Apollos, Silas, and Timothy.[6] They were the first to reach the scene in the proclamation of the New Testament Gospel. With them were associated the prophets, who proclaimed special revelations to the Early Church, and the evangelists, early associated with the apostles in the proclamation of the Gospel, whether itinerantly like Philip or in residence like Timothy (II Tim. 4:5).

Paul also uses a designation which has become contemporary: pastors and teachers. Evidently this is one category. The two terms in conjunction outline an ongoing nurture of a group of Christians in a given place. The New Testament function of the pastor is clear. In accord with its metaphor, the term implies feeding the flock.[7] This feeding implies the ministry of the Word of God, the provision of the Gospel. The term "teacher" bracketed with this title stresses the continuing, upbuilding nurture in the Word of God.

For that task, still termed the pastorate among us, the New

[6] Acts 14:14; I Cor. 4:6-9; I Thess. 1:1, 5; 2:6. Note the term "apostles of the churches" in II Cor. 8:23.
[7] Acts 20:28; note that this passage incorporates also the concept of overseer.

Testament employs also the terms "elder" or presbyter, and "overseer" (in the King James version) or bishop. Early in its history, the Church developed a graded series of functionaries — deacons, presbyters, and bishops — but in the New Testament itself the terms seem to be used interchangeably.[8] The leaders of the church at Ephesus were termed both elders and bishops, and St. Peter could term himself an elder as well as a bishop (Acts 20:17-29; I Pet. 1:1; 5:1).

The other synonym for the pastorate, "overseer," is instructive. It incorporates the accent that the pastor was to equip the people, the ministers of Christ, for their task of mutual edification. This concept accords well with the picture of the body of Christ. Each member of the Church is to serve every other member in the mutual supply of spiritual life. The pastor is to help each member to accomplish this task. The pastor is not only a feeder of the rest, but a co-ordinator among them, a trainer and a playing coach, a servant of servants with and for the sake of the Word and its ministry. All members of the Church have mutually ministering and helping functions; a few have the business of equipping and guiding the rest.

Paul fills out the pattern of the pastoral function with two words, "helps, governments" (I Cor. 12:28); more literally, "aids" and "steersmen." In their close proximity to the discussion of the Spirit as the one great gift, these titles imply the function of helping the Spirit work richly in others.

In their original bearing, these designations correlate closely with the concept of the Church as the body of Christ, which nourishes its children with the Word of God. Historically, the

---

[8] The Pastoral Epistles are thought to suggest the later hierarchical development; it remains a question whether they cannot be understood to express the normal Pauline equations.

Church has had difficulty in maintaining their significance. Practically, that difficulty is always present, in a variety of situations ranging from anticlericalism to *Pfaffenherrschaft*, the rule by the clergy. The simple picture of the shepherd breaks down into pasturage and guidance by force.[9] The Early Church spoke of its teachers and pastors as leaders, men presiding as the father in the household; the accent on dignity and authority could easily enter (I Tim. 3:4-5, 12; 5:17; Heb. 13:7, 18, 24).

The term "bishop," particularly, embarked upon a career in which it took to itself authority quite different from that of the helping pastor. The Pastoral Epistles suggest that one "overseer" is to assume the care of others and the guidance of them in their duties.[10] Very early bishops regarded themselves as authorized—on the authority of Scripture—to demand obedience from churches.[11] Parallel to the feudal system, the bishop—and sometimes a secular authority—had the "authority of jurisdiction" and the "authority of order," namely the right to appoint the clergy who would administrate the sacraments. Basic to this development are the questions: What makes a pastor a pastor? Who gives him his authority? The various answers to these questions are the labels for many denominational differences. Yet, more pertinently, they lie at the heart of the Church's ministry of the Word. They may be summarized as follows:

(1) The authority of the ministry goes back to Jesus and his award of the right to forgive or to retain sins, "the

---

[9] A possible impulse to this end, though stoutly resisted in I Pet. 5:3, may have been the element of force in the designation of the exalted Christ as shepherd, Rev. 2:27; 12:5; 19:15.

[10] Titus 1:5; possibly I Tim. 5:22; but this may imply a ceremony of receiving into church membership; similarly I Tim. 4:14; II Tim. 1:6.

[11] Ignatius of Antioch, "Letter to the Philadelphians," in *Apostolic Fathers,* ed. Kirsopp Lake (London: Heinemann, 1919), I.

keys" (Matt. 18:18; John 20:22-23). He gave this right to the disciples. Hence only those clergy have the right who have received it from the apostles or their successors.[12]

(2) The Lord gave the keys to his people, his Christians; all of them have the right of the keys. When they assign the right to an individual, by appointment, he has the authority.[13]

(3) The ministry is not an authority, but a service. Christ, the Lord of the Church, gives it as a gift to the Church which is his body. His call comes to his men in various ways, through different human hands.

These three answers all claim prestige of Scripture and churchly tradition. The Reformation attacked the first of them on theological grounds, claiming that the keys were given to the Church. The second answer was one of the ways by which Protestants sought to supplant the hoary authority of bishops.[14] All the people called and chose, or at least ratified the appointment of, their pastors, through the act of ordination. The third answer is the one which the Church is still trying to give. As it does so, it finds the Scriptures speaking in many different ways of the appointment of the clergy. It utilizes the fellowship of the Church and the churches to bring to light the impulses and gifts of its men for the many kinds of special ministries which it needs. It sets up, in every situa-

[12] Apostolic succession is regarded by most churches in the episcopal tradition as essential. For some churches, recognizing an apostolic succession of their ministry is not regarded as essential, but nevertheless is symbolic of continuity.

[13] The term *cheirotoneo,* in Acts 14:23 or II Cor. 8:19, is said by some to imply a vote by people present.

[14] Thus the Augsburg Confession uses the term bishop simply as the person who has the ministry of Word and Sacrament, and narrows the medieval *potestates* to "forgive sins, judge doctrines, reject doctrines contrary to the Gospel, and exclude from the communion of the Church wicked men whose wickedness is known . . . simply by the Word," Art. XXVIII, 20-21. *Concordia Triglotta* (St. Louis: Concordia, 1921), p. 87; cf. also the Apology, XIV, 13 (*ibid.,* p. 447). In *Book of Concord,* trans. and ed. Theodore G. Tappert (Philadelphia: Muhlenberg Press, 1959), the pages are 84 and 283.

tion, agencies and methods by which pastors and teachers are available and supplied.[15] It does not belittle the inner sense of calling which impels many prospective pastors to seek, or to prepare for becoming engaged in, the service of the church, but it does not make that inner call the entire criterion for fitness. In the Apostolic Age, it became the responsibility of those already in charge of the teaching ministry to ascertain and foster aptness for teaching (I Tim. 3:2; II Tim. 2:24).

Naturally the churches with a congregational or informal polity sense a greater need for clarifying the meaning of the pastoral office and the place of ordination than those for whom the questions are already answered in an episcopal tradition. Yet even if all disputes on "order" were composed, the chief concern would still remain: that the Church's pastors and teachers actually be servants of the Word. The New Testament is broad in stressing simultaneously the responsibility of pastors and teachers to Christ and their responsibility to the people; our time must keep clear that this responsibility is that of serving, of conveying the vitality of God's grace and Spirit by means of the Christian Gospel and the Word of forgiveness (II Cor. 4:5; Eph. 4:7-12). A number of situations conspire to keep this concern sensitive. The European established churches are hampered by undermanning of parishes and a preponderance of formal, almost secretarial duties as contrasted with the ministration of the Word. In America, the accents on plant and funding place a premium on administration and public relations as the most important skills of the pastor. His theological competence and his skills of shep-

---

[15] A splendid illustration of the Church seeking to call itself to a biblical foundation, but to leave the road clear from human accretion for the best mutual service, is H. Grady Davis' "The Ministry in the New Testament," *Chicago Lutheran Theological Seminary Record,* Maywood, Illinois, Vol. 57, No. 3 (July 1952).

herding and teaching suffer loss.[16] Ultimately a vicious cycle develops, for pastors are not going to serve their people with the Word of God unless their people demand it, and their people are not going to demand it unless they have been fed. Theologically it is a good time to be alive in biblical studies and in the rediscovery of the theology of the Word. These advantages are illusory unless the Word reaches the people and is spoken by the people to themselves and their world.

SPECIAL MINISTRIES OF THE WORD

If the terminology of Eph. 4:11 be granted and every Christian be called a minister of the Word, then the pastor is already a "special minister," a servant out of the ordinary. In this section the title special ministries will be used, however, to comprehend the posts of the many functionaries other than the pastors themselves whom the Church puts to work, in the course of time, for specific tasks of teaching and edification through the Word. Where the pastorate has been elevated to a position of solitary eminence, these posts have been termed assistantships to the pastors. Although assistantships exist, as in multiple pastorates in a given parish, or in secretaryships for pastors, they are, like the many other posts, basically the service "of the Word" for the people, and not for the pastors.

Illuminating is the office termed by students of Acts 6 a diaconate. Deacons were appointed to implement the daily "serving" of the poor in the Christian congregation at Jerusalem, in order to free the time of the apostles for the "serving of the Word." [17] Their qualifications implied competence not

---

[16] See Joseph Sittler, *The Ecology of Faith* (Philadelphia: Muhlenberg, 1961).

[17] Acts 6:1-7; on the subsequent careers of Stephen and Philip, note chapters 8 and 9.

so much in social work per se as in the edification of the
Church above all, and at least two of their number were
preachers. Paul frequently applied the term servant or deacon
to himself and to his co-workers (Eph. 3:7; Col. 1:6-8, 23,
25; 4:7; I Thess. 3:2; I Tim. 4:6; cf. Rom. 11:13). What
contrast was there between the functions of bishop and those
of "servant" or *diakonos?* (I Tim. 3:8 ff.; cf. 3:1-7). The
Church early set up a gradation of deacon, priest, and bishop,
who differed in rank according to the number of sacraments
each was authorized to perform.

In Protestant churches, the male "deacon" has usually been
regarded as a lay official or functionary of a congregation,
parallel to the popular meaning of the term elder. In the
Lutheran churches of Europe, the male diaconate has a status
of distinction, although its functions comprise chiefly services
auxiliary to the management of the church and the care of the
needy. In American churches, the counterpart of the European deacon is at work, although seldom with the name
deacon. The overloading of the pastorate and the accent on
business administration is beginning to lead to the development of posts of business assistants, business managers, parish
secretaries, and lay administrators of colleges and missions.

A parallel can be noted in the employment of women in
auxiliary positions. Whether the term servant in Rom. 16:1
is simply a description of a helpful and charitable woman, or
a title for a special office, is unclear, but the Early Church
soon employed the title officially. The female diaconate seems
to have flourished until it was absorbed in the vocation of the
religious. Lutherans in Europe and America have revived the
institution under a variety of disciplines and for a broad range
of purposes.

Hitherto a leading argument for the fostering of the diaconate has been: "Let the Christian Church discern, encourage, and capitalize on the many fruits of the Spirit in its midst." Certainly it is good stewardship of the abilities at the disposal of the Church to deploy them and train them. The important question remains whether the Church is properly fostering, in these and other callings, the ministry of the Word. Does a business administratorship classify as "ministry of the Word" just because it is the adjunct of a parish or a religious institution? Is the special service rendered to the Church by a nonreligious function to be given status only if it can be called a ministry of the Word? Some of the difficulty on the popular level underlying this discussion is seen in the sluggishness in distinguishing between evangelism and pre-evangelism: "I can preach Christ just by doing a good job at my daily labor." A half-truth is involved here. The daily labor may be a splendid opportunity for putting the individual into a situation in which he can effectively speak the Word of God to people, even though the labor itself does not do it. The labor is not a special ministry of the Word, however, but a setting for the ministry of the Word in which every Christian engages.[18]

Precision in this matter is not merely academic. For it aims at safeguarding, in the thought and action of the Church, the ministration of the Word of God. The concern for the spiritual quality and potential of the helpers of the apostles, implying a crucial demand for their services concerning the Word itself, is suggestive for contemporary policy. In the mind of worker and client alike, "servant of the Word" may assume the dimensions of "position related to the Church." It is important, to the contrary, that the true servant of the Word always

[18] Cf. in Acts 5:12-16 and I Pet. 4:10-11 the close relation of service and speech.

retain ministering the Word to the next man as the center of his task.

Noteworthy in this regard is the activity of a teacher in a church-related school. Many of these teachers are trained in church-related schools, and many have training qualifying them for the pastorate. It is a curious imprecision to grant ministerial status to such a position in terms of previous training for or experience in the pastorate, rather than in terms of the task itself. It is equally imprecise to accord "Word" status to the teaching position merely according to the name or field of the course; e.g., to say the teacher of courses in religion is a servant of the Word, while the teacher of biology or business is not. On the level of the grades, this may result in a teacher's fancying himself to be a servant of the Word as he conducts a period in religion, but not when he is teaching arithmetic or supervising play. Rather must a teacher, from parish day school or Sunday school up through the seminary level, be helped to find himself at work in the constructing and maintaining of the Church's fellowship in which all Christians speak the edifying Word to one another, and in "overseeing" as well as sharing the mutual ministry of the Word among Christians.

Exactly the same thinking must control the functioning of the Christian parent. He may easily withdraw from the radical ministry of the Word into paying others to minister for his children. Yet the picture of the parental relation, in both Old and New Testaments, is one of direct responsibility for spiritual nurture in which the ministering of the Word is essential; it becomes a central responsibility of the Christian Church, congregation and pastorate, to keep this ministering under way (Deut. 11:18-21; Eph. 6:1-4). Likewise the activities of trained workers in the Church or its institutions, such as deaconesses, for example, must be consciously directed toward the implementing of that task for which they are particularly trained and employed, the edification of the body of Christ through the Word of Christ.

These reflections are not to document support for either a "high" or "low" view of the ministerial office or the pastorate, the one accentuating order and authority, the other the priesthood of the laity. Nor are they to support "full-time service in the Church" as contrasted with "part-time service." Least of all are they to plead for a repristination of the exact structure of ministries in the Apostolic Age, for those were evidently fluid and pragmatic in every instance.[19] In every age the Church of Christ is grateful for his gifts to it, and the Holy Spirit is giving special graces for the edification of the Church. Hence the Church in every age should be alert to the presence of these gifts in its midst, resourceful in using them in as effective and pliant a structure as possible. It appears to this writer, however, that the handicap and lag unique to our time is that the Church, right in the midst of its busy deploying of people and agencies, tends to shape and use "ministries" which forget to be "ministries of the Word." It is like a light and power company which sets up and services a network of electric lines, but forgets to furnish the supply of power at the source and to recommend the use of the power at the terminal points.

Let the ruling principle in your hearts be Christ's peace, for in becoming members of one body you have been called under its sway. And you must be thankful. Let the message of Christ live in your hearts in all its wealth of wisdom. Teach it to one another and train one another in it with thankfulness, with psalms, hymns, and sacred songs, and sing to God with all your hearts. And whatever you have

[19] Cf. Davis, *op. cit.*, pp. 19, 22, 23.

to say or do, do it all as followers of the Lord Jesus, and offer your thanksgiving to God the Father through him.[20]

SUGGESTIONS FOR FURTHER READING

BRILIOTH, YNGVE (ed.). *World Lutheranism of Today: Essays in Tribute to Anders Nygren.* Stockholm: Svenska Kyrkans Diakonistyrelses Bokförlag, 1950. (Note particularly the essays by WALTER KÜNNETH, KARL HEINRICH RENGSTORF, and VILMOS VAJTA.)

CAEMMERER, RICHARD R. "The Office of Overseer in the Church," *The Lutheran Quarterly,* VIII, No. 1 (February, 1956), 3 ff.

FLEW, R. NEWTON (ed.). *The Nature of the Church.* New York: Harper, 1952.

MCNEILL, JOHN T. *A History of the Cure of Souls.* New York: Harper, 1951.

NIEBUHR, H. RICHARD, and DANIEL D. WILLIAMS. *The Ministry in Historical Perspectives.* New York: Harper, 1956.

[20] J. M. Powis Smith and Edgar J. Goodspeed (eds. and trans.), *The Bible, An American Translation* (Chicago: Univ. of Chicago Press, 1948), Col. 3:15-17. Copyright 1948 by the University of Chicago.

Chapter 13

THE CHURCH AND ITS POLITY

By Martin E. Marty

> If you would see disorder, go to hell.
> Surely disordered places and companies
> are rather hells than anything else, nay,
> in some respects worse; for there is a
> kind of order even among the devils
> themselves.
>
> RICHARD SIBBES, Puritan divine

> But our commonwealth (*politeuma*) is
> in heaven . . .
>
> ST. PAUL, Phil. 3:20

THE IMPORTANCE OF POLITY

The churches of the Augsburg Confession do not define themselves in the language of polity or church government. They find themselves somewhat uncomfortable in the presence of those who do. When the phrase "Faith and Order" appears in ecumenical talk, their spokesmen see Faith more than Order to be constitutive of the Church and its unity of expression. This unwillingness to make a particular order part of the essence of the Church in turn makes others uncomfortable. God is a God of order and not of confusion. What guarantee has one that the life of the Church will be faithfully regulated without a specific custodianship through a specific order?

The American humorist Will Rogers used to say, "I am not

a member of any organized political party. I am a Democrat." Could such confusion be the same for a member of the Lutheran Church which, stereotypically, is at home with episcopal polities in the Old World; with congregational, presbyterial, or synodical polities in the New World; and with variants of each of these in the younger churches which derive from Old and New World missions? Even more perplexing, while Lutheran theologians are noted for lively debate on every aspect of theology when the faith is concerned, they seem to coexist with little controversy despite their variant orders. Yet they are not so naive as to fail to see an organic connection between the roots and nature of the Church and her government. In this, few would argue with the Reformed theologian Karl Barth:

> The government of the Church needs to conform with the foundation of the Church. The Church was not founded by men, by a few persons who, being on the right side of the fence, were gathered together to cultivate their spiritual needs. The Church was founded by the Christ who called his disciples. The initiative was not taken by the apostles, but by their master who created for them the commission of the apostolate and entrusted them with it.

Contrary to those who see a specific polity to be of the *esse* and not merely the *bene esse* of the Church, Lutherans would therefore continue with Barth:

> Nor is the government of the Church, consequently, the business of a human initiative. It is an act of obedience unto the Lord of the Church. The Lord of the Church is Jesus Christ alone, such as he exists in time, that is, in the Scripture. Thus, no government, either monarchical or aristocratic or democratic, of the Church shall be able, as such, to pretend to authority. Rather it shall possess authority only to the extent in which it serves Jesus Christ . . . The essential of Church government is not its outward form but its submission to the Scripture.[1]

[1] Karl Barth, *The Faith of the Church*, trans. Gabriel Vahanian (New York: Meridian, 1958), pp. 145-146.

Such an attitude toward church polity is the exception to the rule in the Christian Church. The Eastern Orthodox bodies refuse to see the primacy of one bishop over the others but contend that the apostolic succession is of the essence (*Conf. of Dositheus, Decretum X, XII*). The very names of most Christian bodies imply a certain polity. So it is with Roman Catholicism, whose name is in abstract translation somewhat contradictory; it is particularly universal. It subsumes its universality and catholicity under the particular authority of the *Roman* bishop—in that geographic reference a whole polity is implied: an episcopal hierarchic pyramid with penultimate authority in the Vicar of Christ at Rome is of the essence of the Church. The Roman Catholic inheritance of ancient Rome's regard for order and authority is classically expressed by Bellarmine (*De ecclesia militante*, c. 2):

Our doctrine of the Church is distinguished from the others in this, that while all others require inward qualities in everyone who is to be admitted to the Church, we believe that all the virtues, faith, hope, charity and the others, are found in the Church . . . all that is necessary is an outward confession of faith and participation in the sacraments (*sed tantum externam professionem fidei et sacramentorum communionem*).

Even more dramatic is the encyclical of Pope Pius X (*Vehementer*, 1906):

The Church is the mystical Body of Christ, a Body ruled by Pastors and Teachers, a society of men headed by rulers having full and perfect powers of governing, instructing and judging. . . . In the pastoral body alone reside the necessary right and authority to guide and direct all the members towards the goal of the society. As for the multitude, it has no other right than that of allowing itself to be led and, as a docile flock, to follow its shepherds.

The extent to which this view of polity dominates Roman Catholic thought suggests the importance of a discussion of church government. In the renascence of interest in Roman Catholic-Evangelical theological dialog the first item on the agenda from the Roman point of view is Roman pontifical authority. Perhaps the most conciliatory of noted Catholics in our time is Karl Adam, who has participated in many efforts toward reunion of the churches. Despite all the concessions he can make he sets down an initial hurdle which is insurmountable to the non-Roman Catholic. He insists with the new Code of Canon Law (canon 218, par. 1,2) on "a truly monumental power of papal plenipotency" which is "independent of every human authority" and which embraces all churches, pastors, and faithful. The Roman Catholic conciliator, then, begins with polity: Christians find each other in Christ through Peter.

No less exasperating to the Lutheran churches and all others who do not insist on a particular polity is the stand of the Anglican or "Episcopal" communion which also implies its government in its name. From Richard Hooker, William Sherlock, and Jeremy Taylor in the sixteenth and seventeenth centuries to the participants in contemporary ecumenical discussion, Anglicans have insisted on the apostolic succession as constitutive of the Church. Thus the appeal for reunion from the Lambeth Conference of 1920 reaffirmed the position of the Conference of 1884. One of the four elements of the whole Church must be "a ministry acknowledged by every part of the Church as possessing not only the inward call of the Spirit but also the commission of Christ and the authority of the whole body. May we not reasonably claim that the Episcopate is the one means of providing such a ministry?" This insistence is matched with a gracious attitude toward the "spiritual reality of the ministries of those Communions who do not possess the Episcopate" but the approach has limited

Episcopalianism in its efforts to fill its self-created image as a "bridge" church.

If Anglicanism finds bishops to be of the *esse* of the Church, Methodism (whose name may also contain an obscure reference to the externals of church life) contends for an episcopacy only as a beneficial element, and in so doing is more open to concession. Another great Christian body which is named according to its polity is the Congregational connection. The spirited controversy over the possible surrender of any congregational "autonomy" in the merger known as the United Church of Christ suggests an interest in polity which the churches of the Augsburg Confession find bewildering. Finally, Presbyterianism is also named after its form of government. Lutheranism is clearly in the minority in this question.

In its relation to these groups, Lutheranism is somewhat divided because of its varying polities. The Lambeth Conference, in acknowledging ties to the "ancient episcopal Communions in East and West to whom ours is bound by many ties of common faith and tradition" includes the Lutheran Church of Sweden. The regard is reciprocal. The Church of Sweden has contented itself that in the Reformation of the sixteenth century it found preserved the apostolic succession. The German Lutheran bishop is less interested in such a claim. American Lutheranism feels at home alternately with American Congregationalism or Presbyterianism in matters of polity, though there may be terminological differences. It insists on agreement in matters of faith, not order.

NEITHER AUTHORITARIANISM NOR ANARCHY

We shall have to ask, then: What is essential to the foundation of the Lutheran Church as it expresses itself in various orders? The question will have historic and contemporary references; its documentary resources inhere in the Scriptures, the Lutheran confessions (particularly the *Augustana*), the writings of Martin Luther, and the tradition and practice of Lutheran bodies in history. Viewed in this light, the question prompts a minimal set of inclusive observations. About all one can say, negatively, is that all Lutheran polity seeks to resist authoritarianism on the one hand and anarchy on the other. This seems perfectly obvious until we consider the examples in Christian history, on the one hand, of groups more than content to be described in authoritarian terms or, at the opposite pole, among the Continental "enthusiasts" and left-wing Puritans, groups anarchic in spiritual inclination. The second and positive set of generalizations is this: resisting anarchy, the Lutheran Church has preserved Luther's concrete and empirical view of the working of the Holy Spirit (*konkreter Geistgedanke*), in visible and living and tangible matters (*leiblichen Dingen*)—among them the externals of church life. Resisting authoritarianism, the Lutheran Church has preserved a Pauline emphasis on the servanthood of Christ and his Church, with authority necessarily taking on the character of servanthood. If Anglicanism sees the Church as the extension of the Incarnation, Lutheranism (we might say) sees it as an extension of the Atonement: "Now I rejoice in my sufferings for your sake, and in my flesh I complete what is lacking in Christ's afflictions for the sake of his body, that is, the church" (Col. 1:24). Church polity *in its intention* must conform to this vicarious and self-sacrificial picture, though Lutherans would never dare arrogate to themselves the claim of achievement in this respect.

Practically considered, Lutheran abhorrence of authoritarianism finds expression in the Lutheran denial of an essential episcopal hierarchy with an ultimate personal authority on earth—as in Roman Catholicism—and a mistrust of monarchical forms of church government where authoritarianism is a possibility. The Scandinavian churches with episcopal orders are particularly sensitive on this issue and are doubly concerned to show the openness and freedom within their polities. Conversely, Lutheran rejection of anarchism finds expression in the Lutheran denial of a particularistic and isolationist congregationalism, with its insistence on democracy. Here American churches are particularly sensitive; here they have the greater measure of homework. Unwittingly, they have often picked up from a milieu shaped by Reformed churches and democratic impulses from the Enlightenment's afterglow an insistence on autonomy which is not consistent with the Word of God. While this may introduce an element of terminological confusion, we might observe that the vast majority of the world's Lutherans practically work through orders which appropriate the values and carry the liabilities of presbyterian and synodical orders.

Before we examine these generalizations in detail, two questions remain. First, if polity belongs in so many senses to the externals of church life, and if the Christian's commonwealth (*politeuma*) is to be found beyond history, should the Christian take time to bother with the issues of government and order in history? The answer should be obvious. It is impossible to speak of the Church without dealing with the two poles of which H. Richard Niebuhr has spoken: the Church is both an institution among institutions and the community of the Spirit. The two are related as are language to thought and thought to language. The people who make up the Church would be lost in an unorganized fellowship, particularly in an age when the axiom of organization has come to dominate. To deny the worldly (in the good sense of the term) side of church affairs is to participate in the Platonic heresy, which is as old as the first and second centuries and which is explicitly refuted by the Lutheran confessions. They deny that the Church is invisible, that it is a *civitas platonica*. The borders and boundaries of the Church are invisible indeed, but the confessions describe the Church as a flock, a gathering, a communion of people. These are never invisible; nor is their organization. In our own time, the profound relation of Christianity to *this* world is made clear in the writings of Dietrich Bonhoeffer, who places polity near the center of discussion:

> The questions needing answers would surely be: What is the significance of a Church (church, parish, preaching, Christian life) in a religionless world? . . . In what way are we the *Ekklesia*, "those who are called forth," not conceiving of ourselves as specially favoured but as wholly belonging to the world? [2]

It is precisely the questions of the Church *in* this world which concern our own generation. This does not mean that contemporary Lutherans believe that God's purposes are exhausted by history, but they take very seriously this world, which God created and in which he was incarnate, died, and rose again in the man Christ Jesus. Concern for this world involves concern for the shape of the Church in it. Polity, therefore, cannot be pushed to the edges of discussion, even though a particular polity does not preoccupy Lutherans.

A second persistent question is this: the reader will note in this chapter very little interest in discussing specific polities in the light of their New Testament warrant. This is an exception to most writing on church government whether of

---

[2] *Prisoner for God*, ed. Eberhard Bethge and trans. Reginald H. Fuller (New York: Macmillan, 1957), p. 123.

Lutheran or non-Lutheran orientation. The omission seems doubly dangerous in the church which makes so much of the *sola scriptura* principle. But the omission is deliberate as an attempt to seek redress for the frequent misuse of the Scriptures by apologists of varying and even opposing polities. The tendency is to gloss over the welter and richness of New Testament church life and to see in it a consistent prototype for episcopal, presbyterian, or congregational polity. Which does the New Testament favor? I would answer: all. A relatively impartial student of the history of church government can hardly be blamed if he verges toward cynicism in the comment that church bodies tend to proceed posterior-first into the New Testament for models. They—and Lutherans certainly are among them—often come to find a certain order meaningful. Sometimes the model is a contemporary political pattern which is congenial (monarchical, oligarchical, democratic, etc.), or a historic form of church life which is attractive. Sometimes practical considerations impose revisions upon a church. The tendency then is to scramble or back up to the Scriptures and to find there pictures or prescriptions which would warrant exclusive claims for the emergent polity. Thus American immigrants from Europe, where they would have justified episcopal order on biblical lines, found it advantageous to adopt quasi-congregational order. It then became necessary to prove that this was what the Bible intended all along.

In place of this tendency, the better Lutheran scholarship today has chosen not to seek substantiation for a particular order so much as to point out the richness and variety of texture in biblical patterns. No longer will the most overworked rubric on polity serve to justify each competing claim: "Let everything be done decently and in order." Now we must content ourselves to observe the many ways in which things have been done decently and in order. Among Lutherans, Rudolf Bultmann has served best to describe emergent orders.[3]

At the first the order of the Church was in the hands of "the twelve," though this was not seen as an office because of the expectation of the End. Peter, first of all, and with him John and James the brother of the Lord were the "pillars." The "elders" seem to have constituted an original and real office in the Eschatological Congregation (Acts 11:30; 21:18). (Presbyterians may applaud at this point!) But the office which characterizes the direction of such a congregation can be one founded only upon the proclamation of the words of reconciliation (II Cor. 5:18 ff.; Acts 1:21 ff., etc.). Succession is necessary for the continuity of this tradition, but it is not institutionally regulated (I Cor. 12:28; Eph. 4:11 ff.). As an institution, the apostolic succession or the custom of ordination with laying on of hands comes to light first in the Pastoral Epistles (whose date depends upon one's decision concerning Pauline or later authorship).

Later pictures, as in Matthew's Gospel, suggest a developing and regulated congregational polity. It is with the fading of the eschatological vision that orders tended to become more regulated and almost hardened into offices. *Presbyteroi* or elders are congregational leaders in Acts, James, Hermas, and both letters of Clement. *Episkopoi* appear first in Phil. 1:1. Bultmann notes the change in Paul from the less formal

---

[3] For Bultmann's summaries, on which our next three paragraphs are based, see *Theology of the New Testament*, trans. Kendrick Grobel (New York: Scribner's, 1951–1955), I, 58, 60 ff.; II, 104 ff. Within modern Lutheranism, the classic debate has been between Rudolf Sohm, who sees the developments toward order and form as evidences of the reintroduction of a legalistic ethos against which Jesus did battle, and Adolf Harnack, who sees order as a necessary part of the Church's life in history.

"those who labor among you," "fellow workers," "leaders,"
to the more formal "elders," *"episkopoi,"* *"diakonoi,"* etc.
The Pastoral Epistles provide the most formal canonical picture of developed polity. At first, while the activity of the
proclamation of the Word dominates as constitutive of the
Church, the Church knows "no office or law by which it is
constituted as the Church," and the charismatic offices serve
as constant safeguards against over-regularization. As early
as Acts 14:23, however, the appointment of elders and
episkopoi is traced back to the apostles. By the time of
Clement's First Letter, the office is regarded as constitutive
of the Church. The Didache reveals how the proclamation
of the Word became the business of the congregational officials. The trend is toward a conception in which, particularly
in the sacramental cultus, "the order which regulates the
culture is now regarded as that which guarantees its efficacy."
So great a terrain is covered from Paul's early journeys to the
time of Clement!

What is clear from this sketchy portrait is that decisions
about Early Church polity depend upon complex critical
questions (Pauline authorship of the pastorals, canonicity of
certain books, the weight that is to be given to noncanonical
but subapostolic writings), upon theological questions (is the
Eschatological Congregation more important for the life of
the Church today or shall our model be the Church as it settles
for compromises with the world for the "long pull"?), or upon
our interest in determining one clear picture as against relish-
ing the obvious variety within the New Testament. In any
case, it is too complex for anyone, Lutheran or not, to suggest
that matters of church government will be solved if we
"simply go back to the Bible."

We have tried to establish the importance of questions

concerning polity and to suggest the limitations of settling them on the basis of a simplistic biblicism. It is now in place to explore our major generalizations in the light of the Lutheran confessions and tradition.

THE CONFESSIONS ON AUTHORITARIANISM

Lutheran interest in polity by its very nature resists authoritarian tendencies. No one was better able to state the problem than Luther. His entire career saw him doing battle against the medieval sacramental-hierarchical system because of the violence it did to the Christian's free access to God through Christ. Yet he was never able on biblical grounds to move with the left wing of the Reformation away from an ecclesiastical-sacramental position which forced on him concerns for polity. "If thou wilt be saved thou must begin with the faith of the Sacraments (*A fide sacramentorum tibi incipiendum est, si salvus fieri voles*)." [4] The importance of Church and ministry is clear from characteristic sayings: "There would be no Bible and no Sacraments without the Church and the *ministerium ecclesiasticum.*"

But neither Luther's works nor the documents which are the matrix of Lutheran expression bind the consciences of the churchmen of the Augsburg Confession to a specific form of this ecclesiastical ministry. Rather the issue is resolved by throwing the weight in a different direction. Instead of being preoccupied with the "earthen vessels," the men and their offices, Lutheran expression is preoccupied with the "treasure" in the vessels and with the assembly of believers who constitute the Body of which Christ is the head. This shifting of the burden deliberately and pointedly forces those who accept

---

[4] *D. Martin Luthers Werke,* Kritische Gesamtausgabe (Weimar, 1883–   ), VI, 530.

the *Augustana* to be open about forms, ceremonies, externals, and organization of the churches.

Article VII of the *Augustana* is here, as so often, decisive in its weight: the one holy Christian Church which will be and remain forever is not the clergy; it is not a supra-historical entity; and it is not a cluster of autonomous democratic parliamentary bodies. It is

the assembly of all believers among whom the Gospel is preached in its purity and the holy sacraments are administered according to the Gospel. (*Book of Concord*, p. 32).[5]

Then the article shrugs its shoulders in the direction of the Rome of its day, the Lambeths to come, and the synods and town meetings of every day by whisking the issue away from their doorsteps and placing before them a different and overwhelming concern:

It is sufficient for the true unity of the Christian church that the Gospel be preached in conformity with a pure understanding of it and that the sacraments be administered in accordance with the divine Word. It is not necessary for the true unity of the Christian church that ceremonies, instituted by men, should be observed uniformly in all places. (*Ibid.*)

"It is enough, *satis esse*." With one magnificent gesture, the princes and theologians of the incipient Lutheran Church thus replied to their detractors that peripheral matters, human traditions, and even glimpses of actual church life in the New Testament if they were not clearly of divine command were beside the point. The Church was constituted through the Gospel and sacraments. Order and ministry were ancillary; they were but handmaidens. The assumption was this: if the Gospel is foremost, human tradition and human authority can never tyrannize or dominate the assembly of believers.

[5] References to the *Book of Concord* are to the new translation by Theodore G. Tappert (Philadelphia: Muhlenberg, 1959).

Of course, to write *satis esse* into the documents of the Church is not in itself a guarantee against authoritarianism. The history of the Lutheran Church has also illustrated a constant vigilance against misuse of authority; a constant attempt to recover the evangel in the face of arrogant organizational claims; a constant threat that authority be wielded arbitrarily. But the same history suggests that the power of the evangel has again and again broken through and that the Church on earth can hardly hope for better safeguards than the clause just quoted and the courage in the hearts of her sons. For these reasons (namely that Gospel and sacraments, and not a form of polity, are constitutive of churchly authority), matters of polity have seldom been central in Lutheran schisms or reunions. The big artillery is and must be saved for the times when the Gospel itself is threatened. In this, the churches of the Augsburg Confession tend toward a practice described by Emil Brunner when he speaks of apologetics:

Apologetics, as a wrestling with the enemy outside the camp, corresponds to the conflict with heresy within. It is a necessity only where the foundations (and not merely particular doctrines) of the Christian Message are attacked; that is, where in the spiritual conflict the whole is at stake, and not merely certain parts.[6]

Thus, in discussions with church bodies which insist on episcopal orders, most Lutherans can be fairly casual about the place and value of these orders because so many Lutherans have lived with them and because they regard them as ceremonies on which there need not be agreement (the *bene esse* of the Church). Ordinarily they would resist any attempts to impose episcopacy or apostolic succession as an essential of the Church, because to do so would bind consciences which

---

[6] *The Christian Doctrine of God*, trans. Olive Wyon (Philadelphia: Westminster, 1950), p. 99. Used by permission.

the Gospel has loosed and might introduce authorities which would detract from Christ's own because of the nature of their claim. Needless to say, Lutherans must also reaffirm Article VII of the *Augustana* against the bureaucratic and organizational tendencies of ostensibly congregational groups which do not have an episcopal order. Authoritarianism wears many faces.

THE CONFESSIONS ON ANARCHY

Lutheran interest in polity by its very nature resists anarchic tendencies. Luther urged this in his constant battles against friends from whom he would be saved, against the "enthusiasts" who were so confident of their charismatic ministries that they might be described as having "swallowed the Holy Ghost, feathers and all." The Gospel and the sacraments would not exist "without the Church and the *ministerium ecclesiasticum.*" While faith dominated order, order followed faith: there were to be regularly constituted means for the means of grace. Typical of these Lutheran concerns is the decisive Article V of the Augsburg Confession:

> To obtain such faith God instituted the office of the ministry, that is, provided the Gospel and the sacraments. Through these, as through means, he gives the Holy Spirit, who works faith, when and where he pleases, in those who hear the Gospel. . . . Condemned are the Anabaptists and others who teach that the Holy Spirit comes to us through our own preparations, thoughts, and works without the external word of the Gospel. (*Book of Concord*, p. 31).

A footnote in the new edition cited finds it necessary to add that the title of Article V, "The Office of the Ministry," would be misleading if it were not observed that the Reformers thought of the office of the ministry in other than clerical terms. That is exactly the point! It is interesting to observe that every reference to the clergy in the index of the new translation of the *Book of Concord* is derogatory. This may be in part a terminological accident due to translation, but it is no accident that the Lutheran confessions can detail the office of the ministry in nonclerical terms as being simply the provision of the Gospel and the sacraments.

This provision in itself could lead to the feared anarchy if left to itself, however, for the Gospel and the sacraments are still somehow in the hands of humans. A complicating factor is thus introduced in Article XIV:

It is taught among us that nobody should publicly teach or preach or administer the sacraments in the church without a regular call (*nisi rite vocatus*). (*Book of Concord*, p. 36.)

This article, "Order in the Church," is the shortest and appears the least complicated of any in the *Augustana*. Yet it leaves a host of problems.

Some in our day, among them Hendrik Kraemer, have criticized this form of solution to the office of the ministry when placed in the hands of men. Kraemer, arguing for a renewed recovery of interest in the laity as it was known in the New Testament, believes with some warrant that this attitude in the Lutheran and other classical Protestant confessions frustrated the potential of the laity at the edge of its finest hour. It was deemed necessary, he argues (again with excellent substantiation), because many feared that *die reine Predigt,* intellectually "pure" teaching, would be polluted if laymen preached and administered the Sacrament. Yet the instincts of the Confession are correct. The absence of all order is a condition which Richard Sibbes reminds us is below that of hell. Someone must be preoccupied with the doctrine, with the proper administration of the sacraments. Someone must see to the recording and the caretaking and the minutiae of administration. What is everyone's business is no one's business. So one must be *rite vocatus,* properly called.

What Kraemer and many other sons of the Reformation fail to accent is that this call is nowhere clearly defined. It does not necessarily introduce a new clericalism or authoritarianism in its abhorrence of anarchy. One is to be properly called, but happily propriety is not spelled out. He may be properly called by a bishop who has satisfied himself that a candidate possesses theological acumen and spiritual qualities. He may be properly called by a congregation which is following synodical procedures it has chosen to follow by affiliating with a synod and by acting through parliamentary procedures there. The Confession does not introduce a charismatic or sacramental ordination or priesthood. It does not spell out what is acceptable preparation for the ministry of Word and Sacrament. It leaves the major responsibility with the churches in later times and in other places. It insists only that the call be regular and proper: this safeguards against anarchy without necessarily stifling lay expression and without going beyond the evangelical center in establishing routines of clerical procedure. Let us now take another look at these two concerns as we see them in today's church life.

AUTHORITARIANISM AND EPISCOPACY

An excellent instance of the discussion of episcopacy in modern Lutheranism appeared in a memorandum prepared by Dr. Fridtjov Birkeli of the Lutheran World Federation for leaders of the African Lutheran churches in 1955. Madagascar-born Birkeli was trained and ordained in Scandinavia; thus he brings together the concerns of the younger churches and of Lutheran churches which retain the episcopacy.[7]

Birkeli faces with the Africans the problem of polity.

[7] See "Lutheran Episcopacy," *Lutheran World Review*, IV, No. 2 (August, 1957), pp. 169 ff.

Should they use models from their tribal organization or from Western democracy or from dictators? Does Christian or Lutheran church history have a specific answer? Does the Bible? "We must state very emphatically that no matter how much we study the Bible there is in it no one recommendation for a complete church organization, ready for us to use." The apostolic witness was passed on to the apostles and to the Church but its safeguard has never been the continuity but the Scriptures. For the most part, we might say that the succession continues in the congregation where the Gospel is proclaimed, even though elders and bishops very early were seen to be responsible in the congregations. Birkeli is a partisan of the episcopal view of the New Testament complex but is typically Lutheran in his mistrust of the historical argument:

> We have no indisputable historical proof of an unbroken episcopal succession with ordination through laying on of hands from the first apostles and onwards from bishop to bishop up to today. What is constitutive of good church order? The clergy are the successors of the apostles if the clergy are faithful to the faith of the apostles: faith is constitutive! Christ is *the* minister and the continuity; Lutheran theologians refused to follow Melanchthon in elevating the ministry as the third mark of the true church.

Birkeli observes that in Finland and Sweden, where the "historic episcopate" remains, the bishops do not argue that episcopal continuation is what makes a church a Christian church. He also notes that American church presidents often have more power than any bishop! Without deciding for African churches, Birkeli points out many advantages of episcopacy so long as it is not regarded as of the *esse* of the Church. His view would be acceptable to most of world Lutheranism.

ANARCHY AND CONGREGATIONALISM

If the record of episcopacy in Lutheranism shows that a quasi-monarchical form can exist without exerting authoritarian tendencies and without making unscriptural claims for its value, so too a modified congregationalism does not necessarily lead to anarchy. As a matter of fact, few if any Lutheran churches really have a purely congregational form. True congregationalism as seen in the denomination of that name or among Baptists usually implies that no other congregation or cluster of congregations is involved in the local church's responsibility for its doctrinal expression. Lutherans who profess a congregational polity willingly unite in doctrinal expression and ordinarily allow some measure of custodianship of doctrinal purity by synodical gatherings, proclamations, or officials. In this sense, as in so many others, the term congregational is misleading. Many contemporary Lutherans are suggesting that pure congregationalism is obsolescent in an era of change and mobility when the destinies of all local units are closely bound up with those of each other. As one instance, the financial resources of wealthy parishes could be put to better use on strategic front lines or in rear-guard operations. It is usually the wealthy, the secure, and the proud parish which makes the most insistent claims for absolute autonomy.

Others have come to criticize the very conception of autonomy in a church where the Word of God is to be decisive. Autonomy carries with it an assumption about man and his possibilities which is more consistent with the Enlightenment and social Darwinism than with the Word of God. The concept existed only for a moment of Christian history, but it made its way into the American church tradition, where it finds partisans to this day. Any conception of self-sufficiency, of complete competence, is—in the view of some—an expression of *hybris,* an overly optimistic view of the potential of man, and quite possibly a denial of the *Una Sancta's* interest in participation, in bearing one another's burdens.

What is emerging in both episcopal and congregational Lutheranism is an order which might more fairly be described on presbyterial-synodical lines. Birkeli's observation is a commonplace: few European bishops have possessed the authority which their nineteenth-century counterparts in all branches of American Lutheranism knew or which twentieth-century synodical bureaucracies know. Few congregations possess or are willing to exercise the autonomy they claim: witness the fact that almost every such expression leads to schism and to further fissiparation of Lutheranism's divided witness. On the world-wide level, there appears to be emerging a pyramidal system of delegated or representative authority in matters of faith and doctrine. The concern in such an instance should be that the pyramid not become overpoweringly large; that it not exercise impersonal and arbitrary authority; that it too be judged by the Word of God. Whether Lutheranism should begin to refer to itself normatively in presbyterial-synodical terminology or whether it should seek new terms consistent with its most widespread practices (always allowing for some episcopal and congregational exceptions as part of Christian freedom and Lutheran catholicity) is an issue we have no interest in deciding here.

THE "IT" IS IN ORDER TO THE "I"

It remains, then, to make a distinction which I have found fruitful in modern terms and faithful to the Lutheran confessions. Martin Buber, the contemporary Jewish philosopher, has said that the "I" can never be organized; only the "It" can be. Lutheran *order* must concern itself with the "I," that is, with the direction of persons who compose the assembly of believers responsive to Word and Sacrament. Lutheran *organization* is a much less important question, for it deals with the purely routine and administrative matters that have to do with the "It," with the rites and ceremonies which the *Augustana* leaves to Christian conscience.

The Lutheran confessions, without operating with this terminology, are consistently concerned with the issue. They reveal a certain edginess whenever organization becomes transcendent and when the persons with whom the Gospel deals are made objects or things in the Church's hierarchical structure. Councils, popes, bishops, and clergy are heavily faulted for this. Church order when conceived as part of a system of merit (in ceremonies, canons, exercises, holy days, etc.) causes concern.

Thus, according to the confessions, *popes* desire to be earthly gods, setting themselves over Christ to tyrannize hearts. Their pretensions to earthly authority result in their using men as objects to gain their goals. *Bishops* are tempted to develop rites or laws; they pervert their powers whenever they exercise secular rule. *Councils,* when they desert spiritual concerns and become involved in earthly estates, deny the nature of the Gospel. As we have noted, all references to the *clergy* are negative. Christ's kingdom does not consist in *church orders* which, when seen as meritorious, are contrary to the Gospel and burdensome to consciences. The person is more important than the order, and the strong must often give in to the weak in matters of order. *Ceremonies* can become the work of children and fools, and they do not serve man's justification. Christ may be obscured by them; he did not command establishment of ceremonies; he gave himself for persons. *Canons* usually represent the imposed authority of the pope; *exercises* are too recognized as the mere externals which in themselves they are, not meritorious. Consistently all of these evidences of church organization when seen as part of a system of merit or when not instituted by Christ or when bloated beyond significance are dangerous externals which violate God's relation to the persons for whom he gave Christ.

We come to what the confessions see to be safer ground with a parallel and occasionally overlapping set of terms which represent not order diminished to organization but order elevated to personal representation of the Gospel. Here, then, is the direction of persons represented by terms like bishop (in a different usage), preacher, pastor, parent, laity, church servants, and even on occasion princes! The *bishop* retains a proper place in evangelical order when he is not concerned with "bodily things" but with the Gospel, when he asks allegiance only in spiritual matters, and when he is in turn judged by Scripture. All pastors are bishops.[8] They are chosen by the congregation for the ministry of the Word. *Preachers* best carry out the office of the ministry in Luther's terms, because in Christ's stead and by God's appointment they bring the Word to bear on the human situation. *Pastors* are well regarded: the very term implies personal relations. So with *parents,* whose authority is personal and related to the Word of God. All of the *church servants* are equal and even the unworthy ones stand in the fellowship of believers in Christ's stead.

Church polity, then, is arbitrary in the sense that no specific polity is prescribed by Scripture or by the Lutheran confes-

[8] See "Treatise on the Power and Primacy of the Pope," *Book of Concord,* pp. 330 ff., where Jerome, Paul, Peter, and John are testimonies.

sions and traditions. When an exclusive claim is made for a polity, it is ordinarily accompanied by exalted views of its merit and by arbitrary authority exercised over Christian persons who are thus "thingified." Church polity is not arbitrary, but organic, in the sense that its many forms can all be rendered consistent with Scripture and with the Lutheran confessions and tradition when they are all seen to be servants of Christ and of the persons for whom he gave himself.

This is why we noted at the beginning that the Christian doctrine of the Holy Spirit remains as a safeguard against anarchy. With Luther, the churches of the Augsburg Confession believe that the Spirit "calls, gathers, enlightens, and sanctifies the whole Christian church on earth and preserves it in union with Jesus Christ in the one true faith." He is not only *Spiritus Creator* but *Spiritus Rector.* We also noted that if the Church is seen as an extension of the Atonement, Christ's servanthood will always be the mark of ecclesiastical order *and* organization. This does not mean that the Christian Church or the Lutheran Church is a pneumatocracy or, to use Eduard Schweitzer's unfortunate term, a Christocracy. It is what the *Augustana* calls it, the assembly of believers (*congregatio sanctorum, die Versammlung aller Gläubigen*), a fellowship of people responsive to God through his Holy Spirit in the Church and through his Son who calls them to service. For this task, in all Lutheran orders, all Christians are *rite vocatus,* properly called. Their *politeuma* is in heaven, but they care about their *politeia* now. Order is a means of the means of grace, another handmaiden to the Word. Whether it is organized with bishops, presbyters, synods, or congregations as the characteristic element, none of them is essential: none of them constitutes the Church. The preaching of the Gospel and the administration of the holy sacraments alone do that and they are the best guarantees, if "the Word of God is not bound," against the twin terrors of authoritarianism and anarchy in church government.

SUGGESTIONS FOR FURTHER READING

AULÈN, GUSTAF. *Reformation and Catholicity,* trans. ERIC H. WAHL-STROM. Philadelphia: Muhlenberg, 1961. (See especially the chapter on "Ordo.")

ENGELDER, THEODORE. *Walther and the Church.* St. Louis: Concordia, 1938.

EVJEN, J. C. "Luther's Ideas Concerning Church Polity," *Lutheran Church Review,* XLV (1925).

HANSON, ANTHONY TYRRELL. *The Pioneer Ministry.* Philadelphia: Westminster, 1961.

LUND-QUIST, CARL E. *Lutheran Churches of the World.* Minneapolis: Augsburg, 1958.

RICHARDSON, CYRIL C. *The Church Through the Centuries.* New York: Scribner's, 1938.

SCHLINK, EDMUND. *Theology of the Lutheran Confessions,* trans. PAUL F. KOEHNEKE and HERBERT J. A. BOUMAN. Philadelphia: Muhlenberg, 1961. (See especially the chapter on "Civil and Ecclesiastical Government." The original German edition, *Theologie der lutherischen Bekenntnisschriften* [3d ed.; Munich: Kaiser Verlag, 1948], has an extensive German bibliography on church government, pp. 338-339.)

SOHM, RUDOLF. *Kirchenrecht.* 2 vols. Leipzig: 1892–1923.

SPITZ, L. W. "Luther's Ecclesiology and His Concept of the Prince as *Notbischof,*" *Church History,* XXII (1953).

VAJTA, VILMOS. *Luther on Worship,* trans. U. S. LEUPOLD. Philadelphia: Muhlenberg, 1958. (See especially the chapter on "Ministry.")

Chapter 14

THE CHURCH AND THE CHURCHES

By Karl E. Mattson

DEFINING THE TERMS

The historical particularities with which the authors of this volume are in the first instance concerned when they confront today the question of "the church and the churches" are American Lutheranism on the one hand and the modern ecumenical movement on the other. Before we deal concretely with the relationship between the two, it would be well for us to define our terms.

American Lutheranism, our first term, appears on the scene as three large, supra-synodical groups: the American Lutheran Church, the Synodical Conference, and the Lutheran Church in America. For the purposes of this essay these groupings, rather than their constituent individual bodies, will stand in the foreground of our interest. Thus we simplify our task and make it possible to see our problem in broad perspective—too broad, perhaps, for those who protest that, by our concentrating on the three major groups, we obscure the differences among the member bodies which constitute these groups. Our only reply to this objection is that, from a long and somewhat broad acquaintance with Lutheran ecclesiastical leaders and theologians in America, we have concluded that the theological divergence between particular synodical bodies is often not as great as the divergence within an individual synod itself.

This conclusion has special relevance as we relate our thinking to the ecumenical problem. In referring to American Lutheranism, therefore, we are speaking of the American Lutheran Church, the Lutheran Church in America, and the Synodical Conference.

Our second term, ecumenical, has gained popular favor and increased usage in Lutheranism in America during the past thirty years. Strangely enough, the word did not appear in the title of any of the essays in the volume *What Lutherans Are Thinking* published by the Conference of Lutheran Professors of Theology in 1947, though it is stated in the Preface that the authors were asked "to write in the spirit of ecumenical Lutheranism." [1]

THE INTERNATIONAL ECUMENICAL MOVEMENT

W. A. Visser 't Hooft points out that there are at least seven different meanings of the word.[2] It may pertain to or represent the whole (inhabited) earth. It may pertain to or represent the whole Roman Empire. It may pertain to or represent the whole of the Church. It may refer to that which has universal ecclesiastical validity. It may pertain to the world-wide missionary outreach of the Church. It may pertain to the relations between the unity of two or more churches. It may express a quality or an attitude which expresses the consciousness of and desire for Christian unity.

It is this last meaning of ecumenical which is most often in the minds of those who use the word today. Moreover, as it is used in American Lutheranism, it also refers to a distinct historical development, the modern ecumenical movement.

[1] Edward C. Fendt (ed.), *What Lutherans Are Thinking* (Columbus: Wartburg, 1947), p. 5.
[2] Ruth Rouse and Stephen C. Neill (eds.), *A History of the Ecumenical Movement: 1517–1948* (Philadelphia: Westminster, 1954), pp. 735-744.

Historians most generally relate the beginnings of this movement to the Edinburgh Missionary Conference of 1910. Several independent movements had begun to express the concern for Christian unity. The earliest historical point of departure was the concern for the mission of the Church in the world.[3] The perpetuation of denominational differences was difficult to justify on the foreign field. Moreover, the weaknesses of the denominational pattern were most evident as the Church was planted in foreign lands and new cultures. Missionaries also discovered that alone and separated they were weak. Out of the Edinburgh Conference of 1910 came a continuation committee, and, in 1923, a more permanent organization under the name International Missionary Council. This Council consisted of representatives of missionary societies and boards of the sending churches and of representatives of councils from the younger churches and missions. Since Edinburgh, two large world gatherings have been held, one in Jerusalem in 1928 and the other in Madras, India, in 1938. The missionary enterprise brought with it a conviction, as a simultaneous reflex, that unity was necessary.

A second movement issued in a heightened sense of the need for further unity. The outbreak of World War I pressed the concern for world peace on the Christian conscience. This concern found a corporate structure in the World Alliance for International Friendship, organized in 1914. The interest in social questions broadened and it soon became evident that no Christian group could face these questions alone. Largely through the influence of Archbishop Nathan Söderblom of Sweden, a movement gained momentum to consider the life and work of the churches in relation to society. The

[3] Robert S. Bilheimer (ed.), *The Quest for Christian Unity* (New York: Association, 1952), pp. 95-98.

first world gathering was held in Stockholm, in 1925. A continuation committee was formed which in 1930 became the Universal Christian Council for Life and Work. A second world conference was held at Oxford, England, in 1937 at which the problem of the relation of church, community, and state was discussed. The aftermath of World War I, the rise of the Nazi menace, and a world-wide depression were driving Christians to consider their responsibility to society with a new seriousness. Coupled with this sense of responsibility was a demand that Christians must face these problems together.

Simultaneously with these two developments came a concern that the churches face their theological oneness and divergence. Co-operation in missions and in social issues inevitably raised living theological issues. Already in 1910, Bishop Charles Brent of the Protestant Episcopal Church was convinced that questions of theology must be faced along with the questions of missions and the responsibility to society. Bishop Brent persuaded his own church to take the initiative in calling a world conference on faith and order in Lausanne, Switzerland, in 1927. A continuation committee again came into being charged with the responsibility of continuing consultations on faith and order and of calling another world conference. The objective was to discover both the unity and the differences. A second meeting was held in Edinburgh in 1937. The theological concern had led to the same point as the concern for missions and social responsibility. The doctrinal structure of the Christian message demanded a serious concern for the unity of the body of Christ.

Any analysis of the modern ecumenical movement must also mention the laymen's and laywomen's movements as expressed in the world committees of the YMCA and YWCA. Here young men and women worked together irrespective of church affiliation. A great many of the pioneering ecumenical leaders, with John R. Mott as a notable example, found their training in this fellowship. The World Student Christian Federation, organized in 1895, gave students an opportunity to meet on a world-wide basis. It is from the ranks of the students trained in such a fellowship that leaders have largely been drawn to spearhead the modern ecumenical movement. Again the interest expressed itself and was maintained in world conferences, notably those held at Amsterdam in 1939 and at Oslo in 1947.

From the perspective of history, it seems inevitable that these concerns should have drawn together. The conviction was slowly growing that the next advance in ecumenical action ought to be the formation of a council world wide in scope and truly representative of the churches. The first steps were taken in the summer of 1937 when the conferences on faith and order and on life and work almost unanimously adopted a resolution that a body representative of both groups should be formed. A committee of fourteen was appointed by both groups to be responsible for calling a world assembly. War broke out in 1939, and it was not until 1948 that a world assembly of the churches could meet. The conference was held in Amsterdam, and the World Council of Churches became a reality. "Henceforth the churches themselves were in close and permanent association, an association carrying implications for the life of the churches which are only beginning to be explored." [4]

THE NATIONAL ECUMENICAL MOVEMENT
Simultaneously with the growth of corporate structures to express the world-wide unity of the Church, there arose a corresponding corporate structure on the national level. In

[4] *Ibid.,* p. 98.

1950, the list of national agencies operating in the United States and Canada numbered eight.[5] Foremost among these agencies stood the Federal Council of Churches of Christ in America, a federation of twenty-three Protestant and four Eastern Orthodox national bodies. The Federal Council was founded in 1908 for co-operative work in evangelism, in social service, and in advancing Christian influence in all human relations.

The Foreign Missions Conference of North America, dedicated to co-operation in world missions, consisted of fifty-four denominations with ninety-nine mission boards in the United States and Canada. The Home Missions Council of North America served thirty-seven home mission boards of twenty-two major denominations. Its primary purposes included exchange of information, co-operative work and planning, and ministries to special groups and in special situations.

The International Council of Religious Education was the instrument for co-operation among forty denominational boards of Christian education and thirty-three state councils of churches. The organization was an outgrowth of the first National Sunday School Convention in 1832. Primary interests were leadership education, educational evangelism, and Sunday, weekday, and vacation school programs for children, young people, and adults. The Missionary Education Movement of the United States and Canada, organized in 1902, represented the boards of home and foreign missions, departments of missionary education, and boards of Christian education in twenty-nine denominations. It was intended largely to provide the best possible materials and teaching aids on the mission of the Church at home and abroad. The National

---

[5] *Christian Faith in Action* and the Founding of the NCCCUSA (New York: NCCCUSA, 1951), pp. 41-44.

Protestant Council on Higher Education was dedicated to maintaining and spreading the influence of the Gospel on college and university campuses. Organized in 1911, it represented Protestant church-related colleges and boards of Christian education.

The United Stewardship Council, an association of twenty-eight communions in the United States and Canada organized in 1920, sought to supplement the work of the individual churches in enlisting systematic financial support and personal dedication to service. Its most noteworthy achievement on the American scene was the promotion of the United Church Canvass by which the claims of stewardship were presented to the American public through the media of mass communication. The United Council of Church Women represented sixteen hundred state and local councils of churches and twelve thousand World Day of Prayer groups. These are the eight original agencies which united to form the National Council of Churches in 1950.

Four more agencies, in addition to the original eight, integrated their work with the National Council of Churches. The first was Church World Service, the agency of twenty-three Protestant and Greek Orthodox denominations, charged with the responsibility for the program of relief, reconstruction, and interchurch aid. Organized in 1946 as a result of World War II, it also assumed the responsibility for the selection, clearance, and reception of displaced persons. The Interseminary Movement was an organization of students and faculty members of theological seminaries dating back to 1880 and dedicated to furthering an ecumenical outlook in the Christian Church. The Protestant Film Commission produced films for nontheatrical release and maintained liaison with the motion picture industry on behalf of sixteen major Protestant denominations and nineteen interdenominational agencies. The Protestant Radio Commission founded in 1949 was a service agency to make religion a vital force in American life through broadcasting. In 1949, it produced 601 network programs, and the over-all total of broadcasts was 2,128. It also held institutes for training Protestant leaders in radio and television techniques.

National development assumed the same pattern as the formation of the World Council of Churches. A fragmentary approach to the many problems of unity and co-operation was replaced by a single organization. Overtures looking toward further co-operation had been made as early as 1933. Specific preparations covered a period of ten years and in 1950 the National Council of the Churches of Christ in the United States of America became a reality when representatives of twenty-nine churches signed the newly adopted constitution.[6]

LUTHERAN PARTICIPATION

As a result of our awareness of these extensive and imposing attempts at further co-operation and unity both on the national and the international scene, we may ask the central question with which this essay concerns itself: What has been the participation in and the attitude toward these ecumenical endeavors by American Lutheran churches?

The pattern of official relationships is very confused if we look at American Lutheranism as a confessional unit. Churches of the Synodical Conference have no official relationship to either the World Council of Churches or the National Council of Churches. The American Lutheran Church included in its merger agreements a paragraph stating

[6] Samuel McCrea Cavert, "The Decade of Preparation," in *ibid.,* pp. 25-29.

its intention to become a member of the World Council.[7] It has since that time effected such a relationship. Nothing was said concerning any similar relationship to the National Council, and there seemed to be no intention to seek such a relationship. The Lutheran Church in America will have membership in both the World and National Councils. The disparity in the pattern poses a significant and interesting theological problem. Since all these Lutheran churches subscribe to the classic Lutheran confessions, the only conclusion to be drawn is that they assess the situation they face in the field of co-operation and unity with varying and contrary judgments.

If we move beyond the pattern of official relationships, the situation becomes even more bewildering. It is often true that a church with no official relationship to a given total organization co-operates with one or more of the agencies in the organization with no twinges of conscience. On the other hand, a church with an official relationship to the total organization may fail to participate in one or more of the organization's agencies, seemingly with no sense of inconsistency. Lutheran bodies may participate in state councils of churches in one section of the country and not in another. The pattern of American Lutheran participation in the modern ecumenical movement shows no consistent pattern. Nor is there any evi-

---

[7] "Inasmuch as The American Lutheran Church will face the responsibility of bearing common witness with other Christian Churches in the universal Christian Church, it is agreed that The American Lutheran Church shall at its constituting convention adopt resolutions applying for membership in the World Council of Churches, which resolutions shall be immediately effective without referral to districts. This membership shall, however, be subject to review at the first General Convention following the constituting convention of The American Lutheran Church, such action to be decided by a majority vote of the convention without subsequent referral to the districts. Procedures for review shall provide opportunity for presentation of the issues on both sides of the question, such presentation to be under the supervision of the Church Council," *Report of the Joint Union Committee to the Convention of the Negotiating Bodies,* 1958, p. 146.

dence, if we view American Lutheranism as a total entity, that the policies of participation, nonparticipation, or a selective participation are based upon reasoned and consistent theological insights.

Several general conclusions may, however, be stated. The highest degree of Lutheran participation and co-operation, with the least amount of reservation, has been found in relations with the World Council of Churches and its immediate predecessors on the international scene. The reasons seem rather self-evident. In its structure, the World Council has exhibited a strong doctrinal interest, largely derived from the Faith and Order Movement. This doctrinal interest has engendered confidence in the program of the World Council, since American Lutherans are preponderantly of the opinion that questions of doctrine must be faced before any large degree of co-operation or mutual recognition is possible. On the international front, Lutherans from America meet their brethren in the faith from other parts of the world, notably Europe, as the dominant and numerically largest group. The presence and enthusiastic participation of these Lutherans from other parts of the world has tended to heighten the sense of confidence and brotherhood. The World Council defined itself as a council of *churches,* thus abandoning an earlier principle that ecumenical endeavors were to be left to a group of individual experts co-opted for this specific task or a group of men and women who seemed to make the cause of unity their personal crusade. The principles of a council of churches as such—church representation, church responsibility, and the implied guarantee that the council had no pretensions to become a super-church—have added to the sense of confidence and joyous participation. These are principles easily understood and consonant with the pattern of thinking dominant in American Lutheranism.

Moreover, the need for co-operation and joint action was most readily apparent on the international front in the aftermath of two world wars and a world-wide depression. The menaces of Communism, Nazism, and Fascism, the desperate need of Christian brethren for material and spiritual aid, especially following World War II, the problem of the refugee, and an uneasy conscience as a result of pattern bombing and the use of the atomic bomb tended to dramatize the need for a united front on the international scene. A program of Christian action could be delineated more clearly in this area, with less confusion, than an equivalent program of co-operation oriented to the national and community level. The ecclesiastical leaders of Lutheranism in America were also more ready to assume such tasks than the rank and file in the churches, and they were better prepared for the task. The result has been a larger degree of participation in the World Council, and a more hearty response, than in any other area of ecumenical co-operation.

In contrast to participation in the World Council by two-thirds of American Lutheranism we find that only one-third has established official relationships on the national level to the National Council of Churches. The Synodical Conference and The American Lutheran Church are not members. The Lutheran Church in America, because of previous actions by three of its four constituent bodies, will continue such a membership. The United Lutheran Church was the only Lutheran body in America holding a membership in the Federal Council, the predecessor of the National Council, and this membership was only consultative.

The story of the process by which the United Lutheran

Church, The American Evangelical Lutheran Church, and the Augustana Lutheran Church joined the National Council at the constituting convention in Cleveland in 1950 is indicative of the attitudes and reservations of American Lutheranism. Representatives of these churches insisted on some fifty amendments to the constitution as the price of their participation. These amendments incorporated the following principles. The doctrinal statement must be the same as that of the World Council. Membership must be limited to Christian churches, and Christian churches are to be defined as those who accept Jesus Christ as Divine Lord and Saviour.[8] Representatives of state and local councils must qualify as members of churches in affiliation with the council and must be certified by their communions.[9] The council must be, in fact as well as in name, a council of churches. Delegates to the general assembly must be authorized by and responsible to the participating communions. It was largely on the basis of Lutheran insistence that these principles and procedures were written into the constitution at the constituting convention.

It is already apparent that Lutherans in America have been more reserved in their attitude toward the National Council than toward the World Council. Why this strange disparity of attitude, since both councils are dedicated to the same high purposes? Criticism in American Protestantism against the National Council has been especially severe on the political front. Largely through the influence of the social gospel, the

[8] Cf. Preamble of Constitution of the National Council, *Christian Faith in Action, op. cit.,* p. 265.

[9] "Each such representative shall be a member in good and regular standing of a communion included in the membership of the Council, and shall serve only when approved by action of his communion. Whenever voting in the General Assembly is by communions, these representatives shall vote with the communions of which they are members." Constitution, Article IV, Section 2C, in *ibid..* p. 267.

National Council and its predecessor, the Federal Council, have made a serious attempt to apply Christian principles to the crucial questions of national policy. The result very often has been that conservative and reactionary political groups have accused the National Council of radicalism. Criticism has at times gone so far as to accuse the Council's pronouncements of being subversive and communistic. Lutherans especially have been sensitive to these criticisms, since a large share of the Lutheran membership is traditionally affiliated with conservative political opinion, though this attitude is rapidly changing as a result of industrialization and membership in labor organizations. The National Council and its forebears have been more practically than doctrinally oriented, with the result that the churches who place a high evaluation on confession have felt less at home in this fellowship. Proportionately, Lutherans are very much in the minority on the national scene as compared to the world scene. Theologically, the National Council is more liberal and optimistic than the Lutheran doctrinal structure would seem to allow.

We may now ask an even more specific question: Why have the Lutherans in America shown a spirit of hesitancy and reservation toward the modern ecumenical endeavors, more hesitancy even than that which appears among Lutherans elsewhere in the world? The answers are to be found in the specific historical problems of American Lutheranism as it has taken root in American soil. The first great cause for the hesitancy of Lutherans in these ecumenical endeavors was the divided character of Lutheranism itself. Language barriers, varying ethnic heritages, successive waves of immigration, and varying religious emphases had sundered Lutheranism in America into many small synods. As a result, many of the leaders felt that the various Lutheran bodies must first settle the problem of unity among themselves before they could begin to deal with their relationship to other Protestants. Divergent arguments are still to be heard on this question. Some will insist that Lutheran unity must be treated as the prior question. Others insist that the relationship to the whole of Protestantism must not wait until some future date. The evangelical witness of Lutheranism as well as the necessity of finding a place in the total family of churches in America must be faced immediately. The historical development indicates that both questions must be faced simultaneously.

The fact that the pioneer and immigrant mentality cast a long shadow over American Lutheranism must also not be minimized. The Lutheran Church in America expanded rather late as compared to many of the other denominations. The fact that Lutheranism followed a pattern of ministering to immigrants in their native tongues had a tendency to isolate the church. Still more important is the manner in which the fundamental task of the church is conceived. The sense of calling among the early pioneer pastors was primarily the conservation of the religious heritage from Europe and the gathering of those people who shared a like religious, cultural, and ethnic heritage. As long as the Lutheran Church lived by these presuppositions it never quite belonged to the American scene in the way that other churches belonged. It was thought of as a European importation. This judgment was often enunciated by those who lived within the fellowship of American Lutheranism itself, as well as by others who viewed it from without.

In the meantime, the American melting pot was at work. In due time the third and fourth generation descendants of the immigrant had but a dim remembrance of a European heritage. The total religious or semi-religious heritage of

America was conveyed to these Lutherans through the public schools, the media of mass communication, and other institutions in the corporate life. Intermarriage brought many Lutherans into contact with other religious traditions. The mobility of the population at times made it necessary for the Christian family nurtured in a particular Lutheran background to affiliate with another Lutheran synod or another denomination. It was impossible to live in isolation. Lutheran congregations could no longer be established or maintained if they must depend entirely upon people who had previously belonged to the Lutheran tradition.

It was characteristic of the Lutheran churches in America, therefore, that in the late 1930's and early 1940's they adopted a new home mission policy. Almost uniformly the presuppositions show a radical change. Churches were no longer organized on the pattern of a selective fellowship of those who shared a like cultural, ethnic, or religious heritage. The new mission dedicated itself to serve the people in a geographical area, regardless of their previous religious affiliation. Simultaneously, the church developed a new sense of universality. The Gospel which had been oriented to a special group of people was found to have the power to speak to men of varying backgrounds and cultures. This discovery is perhaps the most important and far-reaching insight of American Lutheranism in the present generation. The implications are so great and so far-reaching that even now they are but dimly understood.

We may, however, suggest some of the possible developments. With this change in orientation came a new sense that the Lutheran Church is indigenous in American life. The question is then inevitably raised as to the mission and responsibility of the church. Either it must take the total religious responsibility for ministering to American life in the name of Christ or else it must come to terms with the fact that it must share that responsibility with others. The ecumenical issue is therefore inevitably raised in the pattern of Lutheran development in American life today. The issue is set in sharper focus in America than in Europe, since the multiplicity of religious traditions is greater.

THE TASK AHEAD

What specific practical tasks and theological problems does American Lutheranism face as it increasingly participates in ecumenical endeavors on the international, national, and local levels? If more conversation with and more sympathetic understanding of other church traditions is an inevitable concomitant of the American melting pot, what is to be the program for the future? American Lutheranism must surely face some issues which are integrally related to the questions of unity and co-operation.

First among these issues is a question about the Lutheran confessions: What is their place if we are obliged to articulate, in the historic expressions of the Church, that the Church is indeed one and universal? Ecumenicity and official relationship to ecumenical organizations has generally been approached on the level of expediency or as a result of the convictions of a few individuals. In the early stages, such co-operation was motivated among Lutherans by their desire to present a Lutheran witness to other denominations. The implication most often was that these other groups cannot fully understand the Gospel to the extent that we can who stand in the Lutheran orientation. While this motive has some validity, it is not exhaustive. Most often it contains two errors. First, the Lutheran theological structure and proclamation are credited with an absolute character, while the proclamation of other communions is assigned a relative character. Theological reflection inevitably brings the conclusion that any theological structure or religious proclamation, be it Lutheran or something else, has both a relative and an absolute character. This duplex character of all religious speech and thought roots in the fact that the Gospel must address a relative, sinful, and broken world and must use the words given to it by the secular world. The second error is the failure to recognize that a larger unity in Christ and co-operation with other Christians is as holy an obligation as is faithfulness to the confession which has been given.

Two extreme positions are immediately apparent in the structure of American Lutheranism today. The first extreme so emphasizes confessional loyalty that it becomes blind to the Christian obligation to be interested in the confession of every man who calls himself Christian and the obligation to be willing to enter serious and honest conversation with him. The judgment is expressed that fidelity to confession can be maintained only as we isolate ourselves from the other historic Christian traditions. The Lutheran confessions are a living testimony to the fact that the most fruitful eras theologically are those in which serious conversations have been carried on with those who show some measure of dissent. The historic confessions of Lutheranism and the self-consciousness expressed therein can only be understood as the result of serious conversation with both the Roman and Anabaptist traditions and a well-defined consciousness of a heritage which could do nothing but differentiate itself from either position. To construe confession as a responsibility to isolate ourselves in order to keep the Gospel pure is to violate the nature of the Gospel and misinterpret our human situation.

The second extreme position within American Lutheranism so emphasizes the obligation of unity and co-operation that it either ignores or forgets the obligation of faithfulness to the confession we have received. To be sure, this extreme is not expressed as an explicit conviction. It arises most often as a result of shoddy theological thinking, intellectual inertia, or a preoccupation with the externals of the Christian Church to the exclusion of emphasis on the faith by which the Church lives. The whole attitude may express itself in different contexts. It may appear as indifference to the significance of doctrine and confession, and the judgment may be enunciated that these elements in the life of the Church are not determinative. Or an attempt may be made to take refuge in some universalized expression of Christianity, thus denying the fact that the Christian proclamation by its very nature becomes involved in man's specific and concrete historical circumstances. The proliferation of a whole library of books bearing the title "The Essence of Christianity," written during a past generation, is a notable example of such an attempt. The Church universal never exists as an entity by itself any more than perfect justice exists by itself. Just as we know a more perfect justice which continues to haunt our thinking, a justice which stands above every empirical expression of it we have ever known, so the vision of the church universal exists in every local congregation or group of believers and is never apart from them.

American Lutheranism has suffered on this point from its dependence on a scholastic theological tradition. The implication has been that the Christian obligations must cohere in a logical whole. The choice has seemed to be one between a vision of a church universal and confessional loyalty. It would be much better if American Lutherans would reflect on the nature of their own tradition and proclamation. The kerygma rests on putting together those things which are seemingly irreconcilable. The holy God has traffic with sinners. The Christian is righteous and simultaneously a sinner. The God who dwells in light unapproachable comes in a state of humiliation.

On the one hand, the further expression and historical articulation of the unity in Christ and on the other hand, the loyalty to the faith once delivered to the saints are both legitimate Christian obligations. From our human point of view, these obligations very often seem to exist in tension with each other. The existence of such tension and seeming contradiction does not vitiate either theological insight. The responsibility of the Church and its members is to find a proper balance, giving due weight to each obligation, with a confident faith and ultimate hope that, under the guidance of God and through the inspiration of his Spirit, the difficulties can and will be overcome. To surrender or turn away from either responsibility is a violation of the faith we profess. The difficulties are no greater than discharging our responsibility to love and justice or to humility and conviction. The Lutheran genius recognizes the claims of both universality and particularity, can surrender neither without doing violence to its understanding of the Gospel, and lives with the confident faith that the human difficulties encountered in such an obligation have already been overcome and are being continually overcome by the Christ who came and who will come again.

THREE THEOLOGICAL PROBLEMS

As the Lutheran churches in America enter more fully the arena of ecumenical discussion several specific theological problems will appear and reappear. First among these is the need for further clarification of the word fellowship. At times strong tendencies have been found to give the word a logical content without regard for its specific context. American Lutherans must face the fact that fellowship with other Christians exists on different levels. The history of the modern ecumenical movement bears testimony to the fact that expressions of unity, co-operation, and fellowship do exist in varying historical contexts. The recognition of other traditions as expressions of the life in Christ, pulpit and altar fellowship, organic unity, shared social tasks, mutual conversation which frankly recognizes a common tradition as well as divergences, the possibility of finding some basis of co-operation in the midst of areas of agreement and disagreement—each gives the word fellowship a specific content. The task remains for American Lutheranism to explore these specific orientations in the light of its own confessional insights and to arrive at a consensus which exhibits theological validity.

Secondly, American Lutherans must so state the doctrine of the Word that representatives of other traditions can understand the connotations which the term thus assumes.

Lutheranism acknowledges as its theological basis, the standard by which all teaching is to be judged, the Word of God, supremely manifested in Jesus Christ and incomparably testified to in the Holy Scriptures. The theological structure of Lutheranism is Christological; every theological theme is explicated from the summit of revelation which is Jesus Christ. The doctrines of God, Man, Sin, Church, the Sacraments, are inwardly formed and illumined by the light received in Christ. Man, it is asserted, knows who he is only in the light of God's revelation to him and action for him in Christ.[10]

Theological lucidity can be achieved only if American Lutherans are willing to explore the specific meaning and con-

---

[10] Joseph Sittler, "The Lutheran Churches," in *The Quest for Christian Unity, op. cit.,* pp. 154-155.

tent of the doctrine of the Word as it relates itself to the true unity of the Church.

The third area requiring further analysis and conversation with other traditions in the interest of clarity and concreteness is the Lutheran insistence on *sola gratia*. The Edinburgh Conference of 1910 adopted the following statement on grace:

> When we speak of God's grace, we think of God Himself as revealed in His Son Jesus Christ. The meaning of divine grace is truly known only to those who know that God is love, and that all He does is done in love in fulfillment of his righteous purposes. His grace is manifest in our creation, preservation and all the blessings of this life, but above all in our redemption through the life and death and resurrection of Jesus Christ, in the sending of the holy and life-giving Spirit, in the fellowship of the Church and in the gift of the Word and sacraments.[11]

To this statement Lutherans would give a hearty approval. The final question is, however, one of emphasis and not of logical statements. The peculiar Lutheran genius sees man's alienation from God in sharp relief and makes man's need for reconciliation and forgiveness central and determinative. The central question of Luther's theology, "How shall I find peace with God?" is still the vantage point from which the Lutheran views the whole theological enterprise. The theological climate today is much more hospitable to such an estimate of the human situation than it was fifteen or twenty years ago. It remains for American Lutherans to make reconciliation and forgiveness intelligible and relevant to those who are nurtured in traditions where the tensions are not seen in such bold relief. Further ecumenical discussion will most likely create a new interest in theology, give the opportunity of seeing the Lutheran insights in bolder relief since they will appear in

---

[11] Leonard Hodgson (ed.), *The Second World Conference on Faith and Order* (London: SCM, 1938), p. 224.

new contexts, and issue in a deepened awareness of both the universality and historical particularity of Christ's Church on earth.

SUGGESTIONS FOR FURTHER READING

FERM, VERGILIUS. *The Crisis in American Lutheran Theology.* New York: 1927.

HAUGE, OSBORNE. *Lutherans Working Together: A History of the National Lutheran Council, 1918–1943.* New York: National Lutheran Council, 1945.

MACFARLAND, C. STEDMAN. *Christian Unity in the Making.* New York Federal Council, 1948.

Man's Disorder and God's Design. 5 vols. New York: Harper, 1949. (See especially Vol. 5, the official report of the First Assembly of the World Council of Churches, Amsterdam, 1948.)

WENTZ, A. R. *A Basic History of Lutheranism in America,* Part VI, chaps. 27-37. Philadelphia: Muhlenberg, 1955.

NOTES ON THE CONTRIBUTORS

WILLARD D. ALLBECK, Wittenberg Synod Professor of Historical Theology at Hamma Divinity School, Wittenberg University, is the author of *Theology at Wittenberg* (1945) and *Studies in the Lutheran Confessions* (1952), and co-author of *History of the Lutheran Church in America* (1934).

ROBERT W. BERTRAM is Head of the Department of Religion and Associate Dean of the Chapel, Valparaiso University.

RICHARD R. CAEMMERER, Chairman of the Department of Practical Theology and Dean of the Chapel at Concordia Seminary in St. Louis, is the author of *The Atoning Christ* (1947), *The Church in the World* (1949 and 1961), *Preaching for the Church* (1959), and *God's Great Plan for You* (1961), and the translator of *Luther's Lectures on Deuteronomy* (1960).

EDGAR M. CARLSON, President of Gustavus Adolphus College, is the author of *The Reinterpretation of Luther* (1947), *The Church and the Public Conscience* (1956), and *The Classic Christian Faith* (1959).

H. GRADY DAVIS, Guest Professor of Functional Theology at Chicago Lutheran Theological Seminary, is the author of *Design for Preaching* (1958) and *Why We Worship* (1961).

EDWARD C. FENDT, President and Professor of Systematic Theology at the Evangelical Lutheran Theological Seminary, is the editor of *What Lutherans Are Thinking* (1947).

KARL H. HERTZ, Chairman of the Department of Sociology at Wittenberg University, is a contributor to *Christian Social Responsibility* (1957) and the author of *Everyman a Priest* (1961).

WILLIAM E. HULME, Professor of Pastoral Theology and Pastoral Counseling at Wartburg Theological Seminary, is the author of *Face Your Life with Confidence* (1953), *How to Start Counseling* (1955), *Counseling and Theology* (1956), *God, Sex and Youth* (1958), and *The Pastoral Care of Families: Its Theology and Practice* (1962).

MARTIN E. MARTY, Pastor of The Church of the Holy Spirit in Elk Grove, Illinois, and Associate Editor of *The Christian Century,* is the author of *A Short History of Christianity* (1959), *The New Shape of American Religion* (1959), *The Improper Opinion* (1961), *The Infidel* (1961), the editor of *New Directions in Biblical Thought* (1960), and a contributor to *American Catholics: A Protestant-Jewish View* (1959) and *Religion in American Society* (1960).

KARL E. MATTSON, President of Augustana Theological Seminary, is the author of *The Glory of the Common Task* (1952).

JAROSLAV J. PELIKAN, Titus Street Professor of Ecclesiastical History at The Divinity School, Yale University, is the author of *From Luther to Kierkegaard* (1950), *Fools for Christ* (1955), *The Riddle of Roman Catholicism* (1959), *Luther the Expositor* (1959), *The Shape of Death* (1961), *The Light of the World* (1962), and the co-editor of the American edition of *Luther's Works.*

WARREN A. QUANBECK, Professor of Systematic Theology at Luther Theological Seminary, is the author of *Introduction to the New Testament* (1952), a contributor to *Luther Today* (1957), and the editor of *God and Caesar* (1958).

CARL F. REUSS, Director of Research and Social Action, The American Lutheran Church, is the editor of *The Christian in His Social Living* (1960), and a contributor to *Preaching the Nativity* (1961) and to *Contemporary Thoughts on Christian Higher Education* (1961).

FREDRIK A. SCHIOTZ, President of The American Lutheran Church, is the author of *Release* (1935).

GILBERT A. THIELE is Chairman of the Department of Historical Theology at Concordia Seminary, St. Louis.

GENERAL INDEX

INDEX OF SCRIPTURAL PASSAGES